Journey into Newness

The Soul-Making Power of a Wilderness

PATRICK C. HESTON

Foreword by John Featherston

WIPF & STOCK · Eugene, Oregon

JOURNEY INTO NEWNESS
The Soul-Making Power of a Wilderness

Copyright © 2022 Patrick C. Heston. All rights reserved. Except for brief quotations in critical publications or reviews, no part of this book may be reproduced in any manner without prior written permission from the publisher. Write: Permissions, Wipf and Stock Publishers, 199 W. 8th Ave., Suite 3, Eugene, OR 97401.

Wipf & Stock
An Imprint of Wipf and Stock Publishers
199 W. 8th Ave., Suite 3
Eugene, OR 97401

www.wipfandstock.com

PAPERBACK ISBN: 978-1-6667-3473-7
HARDCOVER ISBN: 978-1-6667-9078-8
EBOOK ISBN: 978-1-6667-9079-5

09/12/22

Dedicated with deepest love and gratitude
to
Edison Clinton Heston, Jr. and **Dorothy Loreen Ledbetter Heston,**
parents extraordinaire
who exemplified love and trust through tough times.

Your absence remains a wilderness to me,
your presence will mark the Promised Land.

"Even so, come Lord Jesus."

"Friends, when life gets really difficult, don't jump to the conclusion that God isn't on the job. Instead, be glad that you are in the very thick of what Christ experienced. This is a spiritual refining process, with glory just around the corner."

1 Peter 4:12–13, *The Message*

CONTENTS

Foreword by John Featherston   xi
Preface   xiii
Acknowledgments   xvii

PART I | WILDERNESS WONDERINGS

God of the Wilderness   3
Postcards from the Edge   9

PART II | WILDERNESS PATTERNS

Discontentment   17
Humility   25
Obedience   31
Trust   37
Discipline   43
Desire   49

PART III | WILDERNESS TYPES

The Sovereign Wilderness   59
The Sin Wilderness   69
The Systemic Wilderness   79
Wilderness as Call and Choice   90
Can an Oasis be a Wilderness?   98
Sojourners or Wanderers?   112

PART IV | MORE THAN MEETS THE EYES

For Our Good	121
For Others' Good	129
For God's Glory	136
A Touch of Grace	147
A Word of Love	158

PART V | TRUSTING GOD IN A WILDERNESS

Trusting God's Character	171
Trusting God's Presence	180
Trusting God's Provision	189
Trusting God's Wisdom	198

PART VI | WILDERNESS WORDS

Community	211
Wait	220
Praise	229
Obey	235
Hope	241

Epilogue	251
Bibliography	255
Subject Index	259
Scripture Index	281

FOREWORD

I first met Pat Heston when we were two young "preacher boys" in our twenties. I was pastoring a church in Joliet, Illinois, taking seminary classes at night. I read in the local paper that a neighboring church had hired a new pastor who was starting his ministry with them that week. On my way to the office the next day, I dropped by to welcome the "new guy" to town.

A friendship began that day that for over forty years has been one of the most important of my lifetime. Within a couple of years, I moved my little family back home to Texas, where we have been ever since. The Hestons and the Featherstons have not lived on the same side of the Mississippi River since 1981. That hasn't made the slightest difference. Pat and Connie have been the sweetest kind of family to us. We have walked with each other on mountaintops, into deep valleys, and through the many deserts and wilderness times of our lives.

When Pat speaks and writes about life in the wilderness, he knows what he is talking about. He has had long slogs through those lonely, dry, frightening places in his own life. What he has taken from those chapters is a fierce compassion for the other wilderness pilgrims around him. Pat is not only a wilderness veteran but is the most Spirit-gifted "Wilderness Chaplain" I know. He has a deep passion for reaching back into those dark places where he has been, grabbing the hand of the one who is stranded there, and leading them into the light and the hope he has found.

I will not keep you much longer from sitting at the feet of my good buddy. He is about to take you on a spiritual journey you absolutely do not want to miss. I ask that you indulge me one quick story which may help you understand the heart of this man.

Nearly thirty-five years ago, I was pastoring a large church in the Dallas/Fort Worth area. I was also in a spiritual death spiral that had led me into deep depression. That, in turn, led me into alcoholism and drug addiction. I sought help in the recovery fellowships. God used those amazing people to save my life. But after several months of sobriety, I was still deeply, spiritually sick.

I made the decision to go away for several weeks of in-patient treatment at a wonderful facility that helped people like me find God's solution to what was killing us. To do that meant that I needed to go public with my struggle. My church, my community, had no idea of the darkness I had been walking through. I stood up one Sunday, confessed it all to my church, and was driven that afternoon two hours out into the country from where I lived to get the help I so desperately needed.

Those first days were the darkest wilderness of my life. My secrets were no longer secret. People knew now what a fraud I was. Could God ever use me again? Would anyone ever want to hear me speak for him again? Those were the questions haunting my days and nights.

Several days later, one of my counselors pulled me aside and told me that I had a visitor. They explained to him that we were only allowed visitors on Saturday. He said that the man was really insistent and said that he had traveled a long way to get there. He wasn't going to leave until he saw me, even for just a few minutes. The counselor walked me to the little reception room at the front of the clinic. I walked through the door and directly into a bear hug from Pat Heston.

He had called my office for a phone visit. My secretary, who knew how much I loved and trusted Pat, updated him on what had happened. Pat promptly dropped everything he was doing, went straight to the St. Louis airport, and bought a ticket for the first available flight to Dallas. When he landed, he rented a car, drove to my house to check on my wife and children, and then drove two hours out into the country to that little clinic.

He was told he could only have a few minutes. He held me, he cried with me, he prayed with me. He looked at me with the love of Christ and assured me that not only was God not through with me, but that his best work in me and through me had not yet begun. Then he stood up, hugged me again, drove the two hours back to the airport, and flew back home to St. Louis.

That is the heart of this man who is about to take you, through the pages just ahead, on this amazing journey to spiritual newness. Please listen to him. He knows. He has been in those dark and lonely wilderness places. God showed him the way out and on. He wants very much to show you, too.

JOHN FEATHERSTON
Founder, Lead Pastor
Serenity Churches
The Colony, Texas

PREFACE

Sometimes, I think, the worst thing we can do with the Bible is put it in the hands of theologians. There is an old story about a theologian before whom stood two doors. One, when opened, led to the kingdom of God. The other, when opened, led to a discussion of the kingdom of God. The theologian chose the latter.

As a theologian—someone whose passion and even livelihood is the word of God—I understand how real is the danger of discussing the word without living the word; of mastering the word (in truth, no more possible than mastering the Amazon or Himalayas) without being mastered by the word, both written and living; and of assuming that, in the words of A. W. Tozer, "If we have the doctrine, we have the experience,"[1] that if we have studied the map, we have somehow magically traveled the territory.

Many theologians in Jesus' day lived by such assumptions. King Herod, after catching wind that the so-called "king of the Jews" had been born right under his now-out-of-joint nose,[2] called an emergency gathering of Scripture scholars—*"all the people's chief priests and teachers of the law"*[3]— demanding from them the location of the birthplace, precise latitude and longitude, of the new-born threat to his throne.[4] And, as Herod knew they would, the theologians nailed it. "In Bethlehem in Judea," they replied, even citing the Scripture verse.[5] Meticulous caretakers of Israel's holy road maps, they knew the lay of the land, the best routes, and directions to essentially anywhere and everywhere. They were the ancient world's Google Maps. Herod wanted to know "Where?" and they pointed and replied, "Here!"

---

1. Tozer, *Keys to the Deeper Life*, 15.
2. Matt 2:1–3.
3. Matt 2:4a.
4. Matt 2:4b.
5. Matt 2:5–6.

Meanwhile, Magi—religious minded scholars in their own right—had traveled all the way from Persia, or somewhere in that vicinity, in a lengthy, pilgrimage-like search for the infant king whose star they had seen and which had launched their quest.[6] If, as certain modern-day scholars suggest, Magi were an elite class of scribes, it is one of only a couple of times that Christian Scripture has anything good to say about scribes, those scriptural Rand McNally know-it-alls. One of those praiseworthy scribes was Ezra, who "devoted himself to the study and observance of the Law of the Lord, and to teaching its decrees and laws in Israel."[7] Note the mention of, not just *study*, but also *observance*. It is one thing to know the map, but another to travel the territory.

There is sharp contrast in Matthew 2 between the Jewish theologians who were able to locate Jesus on a map but never made the journey to him in any kind of meaningful, worshipful, salvific way, and the nameless Magi who actually traveled the territory and made their life-changing journey to Jesus. Theologians always have and always will face the very real and fundamental danger of being so familiar with the map—dare I say, so in love with the map?—that we equate mastering the map (as if that is even possible) with traveling the territory. The two, however, are not synonymous.

Theology done properly moves us beyond being merely students of the map to also being travelers of the territory. In turn, we transition from the ink of studying, discussing and writing to the blood of living. In the words of Barbara Brown Taylor,

> I know that the Bible is a special kind of book, but I find it as seductive as any other. If I am not careful, I can begin to mistake the words on the page for the realities they describe. I can begin to love the dried ink marks on the page more than I love the encounters that gave rise to them. If I am not careful, I can decide that I am really much happier reading my Bible than I am entering into what God is doing in my own time and place, since shutting the book to go outside will involve the very great risk of taking part in stories that are still taking shape. Neither I nor anyone else knows how these stories will turn out, since at this point they involve more blood than ink. The whole purpose of the Bible, it seems to me, is to convince people to set the written word down in order to become living words in the world for God's sake. For me, this willing conversion of ink back to blood is the full substance of faith.[8]

6. Matt 2:2.
7. Ezra 7:10.
8. Taylor, *Leaving Church*, 107.

My personal pilgrimage through a series of drawn-out wildernesses—dry and desperate seasons where life hurt, the way grew hard, faith faltered, and hope wore thin—began and ended in blood, with numerous transitions to ink and back. In other words, my personal wilderness drove me to the Bible's many wilderness narratives which, then, drove me back to my wilderness with new eyes and mind and heart, new faith and hope and life.

I learned from both ink and blood that a wilderness is no respecter of persons. Rich or poor, wise or foolish, mature or immature, committed disciple or fringe follower, believer or unbeliever, none of us are strangers to desert days, none of us escapes wilderness terrain. To each, there come occasions when life turns on us, when it appears even God turns on us. Having once seemed close and personal, loving and powerful, he now—in a wilderness season—can seem lightyears away, infinitely aloof, and either indifferent to our sufferings or impotent to help us through them. But I also learned that if we remain faithful through even the worst deserts imaginable, then, like Job, we will "come forth as gold,"[9] like Jesus, we will find new power and new life on the other side.[10]

If we are looking for easy answers to frantic, right-now, real-life questions, or the promise of an easy, happy life where hopes are realized and dreams fulfilled, we will not find them in the Bible's wilderness narratives. Deserts will cause us to despair of ever finding such things. Deserts will disillusion us. But when we finally turn loose of our personal hopes and dreams; when we are, at long last, free of illusions, then and only then can the desert begin to do its saving and sanctifying work within us. A wilderness is that place where, that process by which the God of the Wilderness sees to it that we become everything and possess everything he desires. It is seldom a pleasant experience but can be, instead, extremely painful. The end, however, is always joyful, always a new beginning, always a new us. Like Jesus, we endure—and endure faithfully—because of the joy that awaits:

> Keep your eyes on Jesus, who both began and finished this race we're in. Study how he did it. Because he never lost sight of where he was headed—that exhilarating finish in and with God—he could put up with anything along the way: cross, shame, whatever. And now he's there, in the place of honor, right alongside God. When you find yourselves flagging in your faith, go over that story again, item by item, that long litany of hostility he plowed through. That will shoot adrenaline into your souls![11]

9. Job 23:10.
10. Luke 4:1–14; Heb 12:2.
11. Heb 12:2–3 (The Message).

In a Bible full of real-life exhibits, Jesus is Scripture's Exhibit A that a wilderness, if approached properly and lived faithfully, is a journey into newness with soul-making power. That is decidedly the theme of Jesus' desert days, as it is all the Bible's wilderness narratives. It is also clearly the theme of this book.

I am more pastor than theologian, student than scholar, approaching my subject practically rather than academically, seeking the meaning of the Bible's many wilderness stories for my life and for our lives today. What follows is not an academic experiment so much as an exercise in living. There is a lot of blood on the ink that follows.

Decades ago, desert days drove me to Scripture's wilderness narratives, where I sought clearer understanding of my own desperate times. I am a student of, but also a sojourner and survivor of wilderness terrain. The words which follow are gleanings from my personal wilderness walks and from many companions I have known on those walks—many from scripture; others closer to my time; some in my time, even in my place.

Like Mary, the mother of Jesus, I treasure all these things and ponder them in my heart.

In the pages that follow, the reader is invited to ponder with me.

I pray that this ink, born in blood, will meet you in the blood of your wilderness and become the gift of God's grace to you as it has been to me.

Patrick C. Heston
Alton, Illinois
2021

ACKNOWLEDGMENTS

As an author writing in the realm of wilderness theology, I am indebted to those who have shaped my life, my character, my theology and my writing; those who have been my greatest guides and encouragers, my unfailing prayer partners, my closest companions across inhospitable wilderness terrain; and, in the end, those who believed in an unknown writer with a story worth telling.

My father, Edison Heston, was a lover of people, a teacher of Scripture, and a spiritual gyroscope through his own storms as well as mine. My mother, Loreen Heston, was a toucher of hearts, a molder of souls, and had a way with words that cut to both heart and soul. From them, I learned how to live faithfully, love fiercely, and to put my mind and my heart into words.

My brothers Mike and John are pastors, and my sister Sandi might as well have been. All three are exceptional communicators of scriptural truth and bring God to bear upon lives listening to or reading their words. They were and remain formative influences in my life for good and for God, as well as for speaking and writing.

My wife Connie is not only the love of my life and my bride of fifty years, but also a front-lines prayer warrior who goes to battle daily for me, her kids, her grandkids, her friends, and a long list of others she intercedes for daily. She has been my greatest encourager and is the major reason I get up each day and am able to shape thoughts and feelings into words. There would be no book without her.

I count my sons Ryan (wife Vicki) and Shannon (wife Sarah), as well as my daughter Lindsay (husband Benjamin) as among God's greatest gifts to me. I was once, at a malleable time in my children's lives, the dispenser of spiritual wisdom to them, but the role now seems somewhat reversed as they have become dispensers of spiritual wisdom to me. All of them are spiritual confidants from whom I draw wisdom and strength for my journey. I would not be who I am without them. They fill me out. They complete my life. To a person, they have always encouraged me to write.

As to my grandchildren—Taylor, Caden, Carter, Ember, Elias, Amalia, and Eleanor—suffice it to say that being their papa has taught me more about God than any book I have read or theology class I have taken. The seven of them stretch across the spectrum from public school teacher to talkative toddler, and they are each the delight of my life. There would be no *Journey Into Newness*, either in terms of my book or my life, without them.

Beyond family, there are friends who have shaped both who and what I am, both what I do and why I do it. Their fingerprints are not only all over my heart, mind, and soul; they are all over this book as well—from cover to cover. There would not be my story without theirs.

I begin with those who have unexpectedly slipped ahead of me into heaven. Dr. James A. Reinhard: my dear friend, my gentle mentor, my closer-than-a-brother prayer-and-accountability partner of twenty-plus years, who believed in me and in the vision of this book. Jeff Higginson: my life-long friend and spiritual confidant, who knew this book like he knew my heart—inside and out—and who loved to call me Yoda, his spiritual Jedi Master, when in truth, it was the other way around. And Andy Baker: as what-you-see-is-what-you-get as anyone I have ever dared to call "friend," whose humble wisdom, utter sincerity, and cut-to-the-chase faith helped guide this book page-by-page every step of the way and helped guide my life as well. Your names belong alongside mine on the title page of this book in much the same way as they are engraved on my heart.

My deepest thanks as well to long-time friends and prayer partners Phil Warren, David Runyan, and John Tennyson, who were unfailingly there with me and for me in many a wilderness. I would not have come forth as gold were it not for your loving and intentional iron-sharpening-iron influence in my life. David was with me almost from the beginning of this book, and remained an unflagging encourager to get it published, even when I flat-out wanted to call it quits.

A special thanks to my college chums and dear friends for over half-a-century—Steve Collins, Ted Shirley, Bob Szoke, Leroy Thompson, Rod Harmon, Dave Schultz and Dave Butts, as well as those a bit ahead of me in school, especially Lynn Laughlin and Don Green. The nine of you took me as I was and welcomed me into your heart as friends. I will always be grateful. You have always been the behind-the-scenes motivation to get this book finished and in print.

Among my most consistent and passionate encourages were, from my youth, Paula McElwee, who saw a diamond in a rough and thought it worth polishing, and from later years, Reda and Tammy Iskarous of River Bend

Family Ministries, and a pair of arm-twisters par excellent, Kent Paris of Nehemiah Ministries and my alter-ego John Featherston of the Serenity family of churches, who wrote the foreword for this book. My deepest thanks to each of you for not quitting on me, even when I wanted to quit on myself.

In later years, I have grown deeply and forever indebted to a pair of incredible pastors, laboring and leading in a place cracking down hard on Christians: Dinesh KC and Rajendra Rai, who are God's kingdom workers in that spiritual wilderness known as the nation of Nepal. You challenge my presumptions and my faith constantly, as you help me by teaching and example to walk more in sync with the words I have written on these pages. You, and the many faithful Jesus-followers in that tiny land with big mountains, have taught me more than any preacher, teacher, classroom, or book about how to live with and for God in the toughest of times and places.

My thanks as well to Bethalto (IL) First Christian Church, where this project first began as a weekly Wednesday night Bible study, to Bond Christian Service Camp where it morphed into the heart of a high school week of summer camp, and to Emmanuel Free Methodist Church in Alton, Illinois, where it culminated and took on its final form.

A special shout-out to Caryn Collins of Fort Worth, Texas, and to Dr. Kenneth Dobson of Payap University in Chiang Mai, Thailand, who were invaluable help in editing and critiquing the original manuscript. It is tighter, stronger, better because of you. To my brother John Heston, as well as to my friends John Tennyson and Dr. Kenneth Dobson, thank you for your no-holds-barred but loving critique of my theology, and for saturating all your suggestions in grace. I am ever grateful.

My deepest thanks to Wipf & Stock Publishers, who judged a book by its content and not by its unknown author. To my editors, Caleb Kormann and Savanah N. Landerholm, thank you for your belief in me, for your patience with me, and for the wonderful things you did with my words. Thank you for making me look significantly better and smarter than I actually am.

Finally, to you, the reader. Thank you for purchasing and reading this book. The years of living it and writing it have been one of the richest blessings of my life. I pray that you also are blessed as you take the time to journey with me.

PART I

WILDERNESS WONDERINGS

"For anyone who is . . . trying to find an easy moral here, this is the place to despair."

Frederick Buechner

GOD OF THE WILDERNESS

Deuteronomy 1:2 may be one of the saddest commentaries in Scripture. There, in a sparse parenthetical statement, we are told matter-of-factly that it takes eleven days to travel from Mount Horeb to the first city in the Promised Land. The deep sadness of the statement, however, does not register until we remember that it took the nation of Israel forty years to complete that trek—an entire generation. Along the way, they lost an entire generation of real people: mothers and fathers, brothers and sisters, aunts and uncles, cousins and nieces and nephews.

What turns a trip of eleven days into a death march of forty years?

The people of Israel began their wilderness journey following emancipation from Egypt. That journey in and ultimately through a wilderness was due to the sovereignty of God, who "did not lead them on the road through the Philistine country, though that was shorter. For God said, 'If they face war, they might change their minds and return to Egypt.' So God led the people around by the desert road toward the Red Sea."[1]

God, it turned out, was in no hurry. He led his chosen to the foot of a mountain, where they camped as he consolidated them into a nation and provided them a moral code and compass. Eventually, perhaps eighteen months later, Israel was standing on the banks of the Jordan River, eyeing the Land of Promise, ready to enter. At that point, the nation rebelled, snubbing Joshua and Caleb's optimism-born-of-faith and siding with the majority of scouts who had spied out the land only to return with a defeatist description. The result was a command from God to reverse course. The people "turned back and set out toward the desert along the route to the Red Sea."[2] What followed were decades spent enduring a wilderness as a consequence of their rebellion at the riverbank.

---

1. Exod 13:17–18.
2. Deut 2:1.

I have spent the larger portion of five decades in ministry either in my own wilderness or walking alongside others in theirs. In the process, I have learned that being a follower of Jesus does not mean we will skirt wilderness terrain or that God will shield us from pain, providing a divine detour around problems. God's people are not immune to abuse, Alzheimer's, heart attacks, or cancer. Such things as bankruptcy, failed marriages, fractured relationships, miscarriages, unemployment, foreclosures, and Lou Gehrig's disease do not visit pagan homes while they "pass over" the homes of those safely tucked under the blood of the lamb.

In John Bunyan's masterpiece *The Pilgrim's Progress*, Faithful reminds Christian that those who follow God's call and walk his way should expect trials that "come, and come, and come again afresh."[3] Bunyan understood from Scripture, as well as from life experience, that trials are no exception to the Christian life, but are the rule of all life.

Christians have friends who suffer, loved ones who die, parents who divorce, and children who rebel. When those following Jesus make bad decisions, violate God's principles, or cozy up to sin, they suffer consequences just like those who do not follow Jesus. Scripture does not avoid that issue or attempt to hide the truth. Eugene Peterson candidly pointed out,

> No literature is more realistic and honest in facing the harsh facts of life than is the Bible. At no time is there the faintest suggestion that the life of faith exempts us from difficulties. . . . On every page of the Bible there is recognition that faith encounters troubles.[4]

Sometimes, because of our sin, we enter a wilderness, a seemingly God-forsaken season in our lives that is beset with heartache and even heartbreak.[5] I know such deserts, such dry and desperate times brought on by rebellion or refusal to listen, far better than I care to admit.

Other times, we walk a wilderness due to sins of others.

---

3. Bunyan, *Pilgrim's Progress*, 121.
4. Peterson, *Long Obedience*, 42.
5. In Scripture, a wilderness is—like that which was part of Israel's history—a literal, physical place with specific longitude and latitude and able to be identified on a map. But it is in no way limited to something material and tangible. As James Luther Mays pointed out, "Wilderness is more than a place; it is a time and situation . . ." (Mays, *Hosea*, 44). Beyond simply a place, a wilderness is any period of our lives where God seems silent and passive, perhaps even absent, and our way grows difficult and demanding as suffering intensifies. Hence, David's adultery with Bathsheba, his conspiracy to have her husband killed, as well as the guilt, cover-up, and judgment that followed represented a severe wilderness period for Judah's king.

A friend, a hospital chaplain, contracted the HIV virus when an emergency room patient with AIDS pulled the IV from his own arm and stabbed him. My friend eventually died, leaving behind a wife and young children. Their wilderness is burdensome and seems to stretch on forever, without boundary, without end. For the rest of their lives, they must endure a desert that was someone else's doing, not their own.

Occasionally, we find ourselves in a wilderness that can only be described as one of God's sovereignty. We are there not so much because of what we or someone else has done as we are because of what God is doing.[6] Of all deserts, that may be the most difficult to understand and accept, as well as the most challenging for faith to negotiate, because we are often blind to any explanation for it. The debilitating aspect of any prolonged wilderness, but especially one of God's sovereignty, is simply that it is hard for most of us to conjure up long-term trust just knowing that God is up to something, without knowing what that something is.

A wilderness can be a disorienting place. It does not take too many days of hoofing it on hot sand, staring at repetitious landscape, and sagging under the scorching sun to become tired, thirsty, weary, and, sometimes, very confused. Even confused about God. Face it: there are times when God just does not make sense.[7] Judges 1:19 highlights the puzzling and often paradoxical ways of this God of the wilderness: "The Lord was with the men of Judah. They took possession of the hill country, but they were unable to drive the people from the plains, because they had iron chariots." I do not understand that. It does not make sense to me.

---

6. Either God is sovereign or he is not. Our sins do not undo God's sovereignty. Because God is always sovereign, however, he allows consequences of sin to be part of the amended scenario and unfolding scheme—a thought developed in more detail later. In that sense, all wilderness experiences can be grouped under the heading of God's sovereignty. In a more practical sense, however, and in an attempt to help us understand the way in which various wildernesses function in our lives, I choose to look at them in terms of those resulting from our own sins, the sins of others, and the sovereignty of God.

7. In a fanciful entry from his fictional diary of God, Colin Morris imagines God writing, "My relationship to my children is inevitably full of paradox; in the game of life I am not the solution but the riddle. Men and women can neither fully know me nor ever escape me. I can neither be found nor evaded. They seek me vainly, but I find them: when they try to evade me I haunt them. The theologians who can always find a word for most things call me 'ineluctable'. It is a quality that adds tang to my dealings with my children. If I were completely undiscoverable they would lose interest and abandon the search; if I were simply inescapable, they would eventually through familiarity begin to ignore me. As it is, there is no certainty in the relationship, no possession beyond any shadow of doubt—otherwise faith would be an irrelevance and unbelief sheer madness." Morris, *Week in the Life of God*, 66.

Finite eyes see incongruity in the ways of an infinite God, especially when those eyes are squinting in the glare of a desert sun. Then again, God's ways are often incongruous, whether or not we are stranded in a wilderness. Israel is a good case in point. The same God who brought Egypt to its knees, burying Pharaoh's war chariots at the bottom of the sea, seemed short on muscle when his people reached the plains of the Promised Land. Why was that? According to Judg 1:19, it was because the people of the plains, unlike the inhabitants of the hill country, had iron chariots. Again, I do not understand that. I am not sure I ever will.

In the face of that simple statement, offered almost as an aside, I am left with a string of unanswered questions. Why should that stop God? Why should that frustrate his people? After wearing down Pharaoh and breaking free of a legitimate world power, why the sudden trouble after crossing the Jordan River? Egypt had iron chariots too, vast and superior in numbers to any the Hebrew children would face elsewhere. I simply do not understand why God would spend forty years driving a team of ex-Egyptian slaves all the way down a desert field only to watch them fumble the ball in the end zone because the other team had better equipment.

I have asked myself why. I have been asked why . . . repeatedly. If you want my answer, I will give it to you. I do not know. I wish I did, but I do not. I simply, honestly do not know. That is the same answer I give when modern wilderness trekkers ask me, "Why won't God, who created the world and raised Jesus to life, cure my husband's cancer?" Or "If God can stop the sun dead in its tracks, why won't he stop my pain?" Or "How could God deliver Daniel from a den of lions and not deliver my daughter from her rapist?"

I have heard those questions, and many others like them. My answer is always the same. I do not know. "Well, I don't understand it," people tell me. Neither do I. They want to know why. I do not know why. I am consistently unable to answer that question in any way that satisfies them. I used to attempt an answer anyway. I do not anymore.

Rabbi Harold Kushner was wise enough to know that the issue is never *why* bad things happen to good people, but rather *when* they happen. I am at least smart enough to know that to play with divine incongruity as if it were a puzzle that, given enough time, can be solved to our satisfaction is a futile past time. When we who are finite share space with him who is infinite, incongruity is a given, not a game. We must live with it, not play with it.

The Christian life is not as simple as having God on our side, because the God on our side has a mind, will, and purpose all his own. His ways and thoughts are not like ours—not even remotely.[8] For that reason, at

---

8. Isa 55:8–9.

times—and certainly when we are slogging through a wilderness—God can even appear to be our enemy.⁹ I do not understand that either. I do not even try to grasp it anymore. I long ago gave up trying to close chasms which human wisdom cannot explain. I make no attempt to do so in these pages. All I can do, all I *will* do, is testify to the truth of Scripture—Scripture which, by the way, provides far more statements of fact about the wilderness than it does answers to questions for those who find themselves in one. As Nicholas Wolterstorff learned through the death of his son, "To the 'why' of suffering we get no firm answer,"¹⁰ that "instead of explaining our suffering God shares it."¹¹ Frederick Buechner wrote somewhere that God gives himself, not answers.

In an over-simplified sentence, knowing the *who* of a wilderness—the God of the wilderness, who gives himself to us in the wilderness—is of greater value than knowing the *why* of a wilderness. As Anne Lamott wisely pointed out, "'Why?' is not a helpful question."¹² Still, the absence of an answer to our questions of *why?* can make for a long and difficult journey.

A wilderness is a hard place. There is no getting around that reality. The more wildernesses I walk, alone or as a spiritual companion with others, the less judgmental of Israel I am. I am uncertain how I would handle a wilderness of forty years, but I am confident that I would face doubts and

---

9. Whether it was Job who felt that God had turned on him (Job 6:4), or Jacob who experienced God (perhaps in the form of a surrogate) picking a fight with him and eventually wounding him (Gen 32:22–25), or others whose stories are recounted in Scripture, God appears in such troubling narratives as one who confronts and stands against. Many modern wilderness pilgrims, I among them, have expressed similar emotions, feeling that God has in some way betrayed them and has, in effect, become their enemy. Speaking personally, my occasional wilderness feelings that God has become my enemy have found their source in the hurt of harsh circumstances and represent a skewed perspective of reality. It is true that "anyone who chooses to be a friend of the world becomes an enemy of God" (Jas 4:4b), but the door remains open, through humility and submission, for that enmity to be removed and fellowship with God to be restored (Jas 4:5–10). It seems—speaking from my experience alone—that when I have cozied up too close to the world, finding its friendship a greater draw than God's, Yahweh has wisely used a wilderness as an exacting but loving means of wooing me back into friendship with him, where my true life lies. On such occasions, I have sometimes felt as if God had made me his enemy when, in fact, I had made an enemy of him through friendship with the world. As the God of the Wilderness works to break the hold friendship with the world has on me (a hold which can only harm me), my feelings often misconstrue his motives, making me think that God is working against me rather than for me (See Gen 3:5), and that he is no longer my friend—much like a child might misconstrue a parent's "tough love."

10. Wolterstorff, *Lament for a Son*, 74.

11. Wolterstorff, *Lament for a Son*, 81.

12. Lamott, *Grace (Eventually)*, 112.

snags and hitches and false starts and frustration and anger and venting and rebellion much as that entire nation did. In many ways, their stories are mine. Personally, I am glad those wilderness stories are in Scripture.

Of Israel's desert days, the apostle Paul wrote, "these things happened as examples,"[13] later expanding, "*these things happened to them as examples and were written down as warnings to us.*"[14] In the wilderness narratives of God's chosen people—and in other such stories from Scripture—we are given a map to guide us across our own desert terrain. That is how the Bible's many wilderness stories, not just those of Israel, speak to and assist our lives. They provide the detailed map, the essential equipment, and the survival skills for a wilderness trek of any length, in any place, at any time. They furnish priceless, first-hand journals of those having gone before, who know the lay of the land, the safest routes, the secrets of survival, and the way to the promise.

"The Bible . . . reveals God's story," wrote Richard J. Foster, "that we might hear from the living God that this story is not only for a nomadic tribe thousands of years ago. It is not only for bands of persecuted followers of the Jesus way under threat from the Roman Empire. God's story is for all of us."[15] The information in those stories is invaluable, representing a true gift from God, providing mercy and grace "to help us in our time of need."[16]

What follows is my own journal of sorts. I write as a wilderness trekker to other such travelers. I have been in the wilderness. I have spent much time there. I met God there. I found his grace and mercy there. He taught me some things. I wrote them down. Here they are.

---

13. 1 Cor 10:6

14. 1 Cor 10:11.

15. Foster, *Life With God*, 185. There is a marvelous mystery to Scripture that ties ancient stories to our own stories in ways that make a real and fundamental difference in our living. In *Messengers of God*, Elie Wiesel wrote concerning the Job narrative that "whenever we attempt to tell our own story, we transmit his" (Wiesel, *Messengers of God*, 211–12). Dietrich Bonhoeffer wrote that by encountering biblical stories "we are torn out of our own existence and set down in the midst of the holy history of God on earth. There God dealt with us, and there He still deals with us, our needs and our sins, in judgment and in grace. It is not that God is the spectator and sharer of our present life, howsoever important that is; but rather that we are the reverent listeners and participants in God's action in the sacred story, the history of Christ on earth. And only in so far as we are there, is God with us today also" (*Life Together*, 53.)

16. Heb 4:16.

POSTCARDS FROM THE EDGE

I skirted the edge of civilization—at least, as I knew it—in October of 1988 when I rode the luxurious Indian Pacific across Australia from west to east. That train ride was, perhaps, the most aesthetically pleasurable experience I have ever had, an unforgettable journey of nearly two thousand five hundred miles.

More than a day of that trip lay across the longest straight stretch of railroad track in the world, an isolated iron road traversing the stark and arid Nullarbor Plain. The Nullarbor begins as brick-red earth dabbed with splotches of blue-green bushes and clusters of eucalyptus trees which look like giant clumps of broccoli with their stems painted white. But with each click of wheel-and-rail, flora diminishes and eventually disappears, replaced by flat, rocky expanse that stretches in every direction to touch the horizon.

The first few towns out of Perth, like Kalgoorlie, are old yet full of energy and spirit. But they peter out into remote villages as desolate as the outback in which they reside. Towns like Zanthus, Naretha, and Rawlinna are single rows of three or four clapboard houses, a train station, a signpost, and a telegraph pole or radio tower. Away from the towns, dirt roads wind into red emptiness. Clouds of dust, kicked up from an occasional all-terrain vehicle, are the only signs of life.

Some seventeen hours into the journey, small bushes punctuate the flat landscape. Two more hours and the brush befriends every so often a lonely, dwarf-like gum tree, standing in stubborn protest against the drought and desolation of the region.

Roughly half a day into the state of South Australia heavy brush congregates, along with eucalyptus trees, small mounds and sloping hills, giving the welcome feel of rhythm to the now-rolling earth. It is nearly thirty hours into the trip before a paved road appears, cutting across red terrain. Mesas, mountains, and lakes seize the landscape. Shortly, a rust-dyed gulch carves its way through fertile farmland. Strong crops spring from lush, well-watered meadows while grazing sheep spread over rolling green hills.

Vicariously, at least, I had crossed the wilderness and arrived safely in the Promised Land. That is one way to experience a wilderness. In fact, there is nothing like viewing a wilderness through the picture window of an air-conditioned compartment as you are whisked from point to point on a train boasting a five-star restaurant and porters bringing cookies and tea at twilight.

Israel did not have that luxury as the nation crossed its wilderness. They were on the other side of the picture window—the side where conditions were harsh and elements were conspiring to kill them. There are always two sides to life. Sometimes we are on the train; other times we are in the outback. Sometimes life is an oasis;[1] other times life is a wilderness.

An oasis is a place of welcome shade, where we are shielded from sun and heat; a place of replenishment, where fruit is supplied to satisfy our hunger and water is prevalent to quench our thirst. An oasis is a place of safety and satisfaction, rest and refreshment, peace and provision. In an oasis, our prayers are answered, our burdens lifted, our strength replenished, our sufferings relieved, our faithfulness rewarded, and our deliverance arrives. In the oases of our lives, God is an ever-present companion and helper,[2] and it is a somewhat simple thing to trust him.

Things are radically different in a wilderness. A wilderness is a place of scorching sun, debilitating heat, blistering sand, severe and desperate lack. There is little shade, food, or water in a wilderness. It is a place of emptiness, barrenness, and disorientation; a place characterized by adversity and affliction, want and weariness, trial and trouble. In a wilderness, our prayers go unanswered, our burdens increase, our dreams are deferred or even denied, our strength is progressively sapped, our sufferings steadily intensify, our faithfulness goes unrewarded, and our deliverance is once more delayed. In the deserts of our lives, God seems very silent and passive, perhaps even uncaring or impotent, and it is an extremely difficult thing to trust him.

---

1. In the ancient world, the city stood in contrast to the wilderness. It was a place of rest and refuge to weary travelers and frightened fugitives. Hence, Beersheba, with its plentiful wells and protective walls, meant recuperation to Abraham (Gen 21:22–34), promise and provision to Isaac (Gen 26:23–33), a square meal and sound sleep to travelers, as well as sanctuary to the pursued. Whether one was exiled or exhausted, a city like Beersheba meant provision and replenishment. But during Israel's forty years of wandering, there is a stark contrast between the wilderness itself and the oases Israel encountered within that wilderness. Hence, my choice to use oasis as the opposite of wilderness.

2. "God is our refuge and strength, an ever-present help in trouble" (Ps 46:1).

The difficulty is compounded by the fact that deserts we wander rarely, if ever, have definable boundaries. Desert days can drag on, seeming interminable, much as Israel's must have. Scripture allows us to read about other people's experiences without actually sharing those experiences. That puts an inevitable distance between us and them. It allows us, for example, to measure Israel's march through the wilderness in terms of books and chapters, whereas those wandering people of God endured every one of those nearly fifteen thousand days in one sixty-second interval after another.[3] Scripture allows the reader to jump ahead a few chapters and see how the story ends. The printed page gives us a decided advantage over wilderness-bound Israel which could not see the end with the naked eye[4] and lacked the faith-fueling confidence that comes from knowing the rest of the story.[5]

Abraham and Moses were both called to a wilderness. For the former, the wilderness was figurative; for the latter it was literal. Abraham endured that tortuous, heart-wrenching trek into the mountains of Moriah with his only son, Isaac, in tow—the boy ready to be sacrificed, though only God and Abraham knew it. Moses seemingly wasted his best years leading fickle, often faithless Israel across desert terrain. Moses at least had a definite time frame to work with—forty years of wandering, one year for each of the forty days the spies had explored the land[6]—but it is easy to lose track of passing time after the first few thousand sunrises and sunsets. Abraham, on the other hand, had no specific time frame, only an estimate of how long the physical journey to Moriah would take. But how long was that? On this side of the wilderness, just how long is a three-day journey when the end of it means a knife across your child's throat; and on that side of the wilderness, just how long does it take to recover from a child's death? The only thing Abraham knew with certainty was that God had led him into a wilderness

---

3. As Carolyn Custis James wrote concerning the barren women of Scripture, "Their stories are captured in a few terse sentences which can disguise the fact that these wrenching ordeals dragged on for years" (James, *Gospel of Ruth*, 80).

4. The people understood that their wilderness trek would take forty years but measuring a stretch of forty years and envisioning it are two entirely different things. Realistically, Israel could not possibly envision the end of their journey or what that end might look like.

5. Israel knew the story to the extent that it would culminate in forty years. They would exit the wilderness and enter the Promised Land. Precisely, who they would be, where they would be, what they would find there, and what their life would be like at the end of their desert days—the rest of the story, as it were—they did not know and could not know at the time.

6. Num 14:34: "For forty years—one year for each of the forty days you explored the land—you will suffer for your sins and know what it is like to have me against you."

that would demand everything of him. The rest of the story was unknown, the future open-ended.

To Abraham, God said, "Take your son . . . and go to the region of Moriah. Sacrifice him there on one of the mountains I will tell you about,"[7] having earlier said to him, "Leave your country, your people and your father's household and go to the land I will show you."[8] Abraham had no way of knowing how long it would take God to *tell* him on the one hand or *show* him on the other. He certainly had no idea how long it would be until God filled in the details of his promise regarding Isaac. Would it be a few days or the passing of an entire generation?

In the case of Moses, God was as specific as he had been ambiguous with Abraham. He told Moses up front that the trek would take forty years. But was knowing that a blessing or a curse? In Abraham's case, the destination might be reached around the next bend. In Moses' case, the next bend was four decades away. I am not sure which, if either scenario was the easier one with which to live. Either way, by peering into the unimaginable or looking ahead forty years, it was hard to see the destination.

God's wildernesses seem routinely to be of the no-end-in-sight variety, requiring that we trust God to be God, trust him to lead us in and through the wilderness, whatever its duration and wherever its end. The not-knowing aspect of a wilderness can be comfortably skimmed over by the reader of Scripture but must be uncomfortably endured by the one actually in a wilderness. The contrast is akin to that between my parents living through the harrowing days of World War II and my hearing, long years later, their stories of those days. When my father, then a young man, headed for the European Theater, his wife waited anxiously at home, with their first-born child. How long would the war last? How would it end? Would my father make it home? If so, when? I know the answers to those questions. I am a product of his coming back. In addition, I have heard my parents' stories. I have read the history books. That is a luxury my parents never had in the early 1940s as they lived one uncertain day after another.

Wars and wildernesses are alike in that way. There is no graspable time frame, no seeable boundary, and no rest-of-the-story able to be read in advance. A no-end-in-sight wilderness can do things to a person. Some of us have been deeply scarred by our wilderness experiences. A few of us, aware of how the desert has cruelly twisted our souls and psyches, live defined by that misshapen mess that passes for our person. One point of view, however, is never enough to encompass or comprehend reality. Our lives

---

7. Gen 22:2.
8. Gen 12:1.

are stereoscopic. We live at the focal point of two divergent lines of sight. It takes two images, not one, to truly define us.

As a child, one of my favorite ways to spend rainy days was with shoeboxes full of double postcards and my great-grandmother's stereoscope. A stereoscope had a handle on which sat a rack—a pair of eye pieces or lenses through which to view a double postcard. Each rectangular postcard contained two separate images of the same scene, depicting left eye and right eye views of that scene. When placed into position and viewed through the stereoscope, the photos merged into a single three-dimensional scene.

Essentially, a stereoscope worked like the human eyes in concert with the brain. Our eyes see with binocular vision, in which both eyes are used to produce a single image. It is received by the retina as a flat two-dimensional image of the same thing at slightly different angles. Our brain then merges the two images into one three-dimensional presentation of the image so that it is no longer flat and partial, but rounded and full.

For those of us who have been damaged by deserts we have traveled, it is imperative that we not view our lives through our personal perspective alone, which is much like our eyes minus the merging mechanism of the brain: inadequate, flat and partial; instead, we must view our lives in tandem with God's perspective, which provides the holistic, full and rounded image that is the truth about us.

In that sense, our lives can be compared to double postcards. One snapshot contains all the painful parts of our lives, including long wilderness stretches of suffering, regret, failure, loneliness, burden, betrayal, and the like; all those things that life has done to us or we have done to ourselves. The other snapshot is comprised of all the things God is doing as he "works for the good of those who love him."[9] I believe that to consider only one of those images—life from our perspective alone—is to view our lives as one-sided or one-dimensional. It is to interpret the story of our lives as a series of fragmented and contradictory pieces that make no sense and hold no meaning. It is to formulate a completely misshapen and inaccurate picture of who we truly are.

Without God's perspective, without allowing him to merge his perspective into our perspective, we arrive at an interpretation of life—certainly of our own lives—that is incomplete and incorrect. It is God's side of the postcard that clarifies both the purpose of a wilderness and the meaning of our lives, making sense of all the disconnected and discordant elements of our existence. It is God's side of the postcard, when joined to our side, that

---

9. Rom 8:28.

provides one holy and holistic view of our true selves, revealing harmony and beauty which we thought could never be.

Part of what it means to trust the God of the Wilderness is to believe that his picture of things, when viewed alongside the senselessly tangled and tragic scenes of our lives, produces an image of wholeness and newness, full of hope and a future. That is certainly what I *want* to believe. More than that, it is what I *do* believe . . . when I come to terms with the God of the wilderness.

PART II

WILDERNESS PATTERNS

"It is the place where I so much want to be, but am so fearful of being. It is the place where I will receive all I desire, all that I ever hoped for, all that I will ever need, but it is also the place where I have to let go of all I most want to hold on to. It is the place that confronts me with the fact that truly accepting love, forgiveness, and healing is often harder than giving it. It is the place beyond earning, deserving, and rewarding. It is the place of surrender and complete trust."[10]

HENRI J. M. NOUWEN

---

10 Nouwen, *Return of the Prodigal Son*, 11.

DISCONTENTMENT

"A wilderness is that place of discontent . . ."

When it comes to enduring a wilderness, few can speak with the authority of Moses. He spent forty years driving his father-in-law's sheep through the desert of Midian, a consequence of his own rash act in Egypt. Then he spent an additional forty years herding stubborn Israel through the wilderness of Sin (Sinai), an aptly named desert for readers of English, as God's people experienced the consequences of their doubt and failure to obey at the Jordan.

Those combined eighty years—two-thirds of Moses' life—stood in stark contrast to his early days in Egypt's most opulent oasis, the palace of Pharaoh, where he grew up pampered and privileged. Deciding one day to turn his back on that royal status and bet the remainder of his life on the promise of a God he could not see, Moses spent the rest of his days chasing a promise that stayed always beyond his reach.[1]

In the end, Moses came up short of the Land of Promise, dying in the same wilderness he and Israel had endured for the previous four decades. From a human vantage point, it seems unfair that such a godly man would spend his last eighty years tramping across inhospitable deserts, the last half of those years through no fault of his own, and never crossing into Canaan. That fact alone gives Moses considerable credibility when he speaks about God's purpose for a wilderness. A man like that, who understands better than anyone in Scripture the ways of the wild and the anguish of prolonged journeying, deserves our serious attention.

This is what Moses said to the people of God as they emerged from the wilderness and stood yet a second time on the threshold of the Promised Land:

> Remember how the Lord your God led you all the way in the
> desert these forty years, to humble you and to test you in order

---

1. Heb 11:24–27.

to know what was in your heart, whether or not you would keep his commands. He humbled you, causing you to hunger and then feeding you with manna, which neither you nor your fathers had known, to teach you that man does not live on bread alone but on every word that comes from the mouth of the Lord. Your clothes did not wear out and your feet did not swell during these forty years. Know then in your heart that as a man disciplines his son, so the Lord disciplines you.

Observe the commands of the Lord your God, walking in his ways and revering him. For the Lord your God is bringing you into a good land—a land with streams and pools of water, with springs flowing in the valleys and hills; a land with wheat and barley, vines and fig trees, pomegranates, olive oil and honey; a land where bread will not be scarce and you will lack nothing.[2]

That is the closest thing we have in the Bible to a definition of a wilderness. It was certainly Moses' understanding of a wilderness. To summarize his words: A wilderness is that place of discontent where a person is humbled by God, tested in obedience, taught to trust, and trained through discipline in order to become everything and possess everything God desires.

A wilderness is one of those experiences that can be successfully endured only because of the joy that awaits, much after the manner of Jesus, who "for the joy set before him, endured the cross, scorning its shame, and sat down at the right hand of the throne of God"[3] or much after the fashion of Job, who declared confidently that if he ever emerged from those desert days alive, he would "come forth as gold."[4]

Like many wilderness travelers, the apostle Peter knew that life "gets really difficult" but there is "glory just around the corner."[5] "Just around the corner"—that can be scant comfort when we are in the throes of a debilitating wilderness and dealing with a God to whom "a day is like a thousand years, and a thousand years are like a day."[6] What does a God like that consider "just around the corner?" Is he thinking a few more steps or thousands of miles? Meanwhile, we're stuck in the . . . meanwhile. Until we get around that corner, what is a wilderness trekker to do?

The wilderness was the *meanwhile* that lay between Israel's bondage in Egypt and its promised blessing in a new land. *Meanwhile* can be a long, hard

2. Deut 8:2–9.
3. Heb 12:2.
4. Job 23:10.
5. 1 Pet 4:12–13, *Message*.
6. 2 Pet 3:8.

stretch of time. The images used by Moses when speaking to the Hebrew people about their just-completed desert days are harsh. Those survivors still felt the sting of such words as humility, testing, hunger, and discipline. Yet, all those desperate decades and meandering routes eventually emptied into a good land with no scarcity, no lack. God saw to that.

Israel's wilderness was a stern and pitiless place, but not meaningless. Moses identified a divine pattern and purpose to it all. A wilderness truly is a place of discontent, but its purposeful pattern brings us, if we remain faithful, to the place where we become everything and possess everything God desires for us. It is the *meanwhile* that is the hard part. After all, who knows how long *meanwhile* is going to be?

Years ago, my oldest grandson fanatically followed the exploits of Thomas the Tank Engine. At the time, I spent two days a week with him. On stuck-inside days, we watched a tiny bit of television. Our routine was to watch either a pair of episodes of Thomas or to watch the DVD "Thomas and the Magic Railroad." I can still see nearly every scene and quote nearly every line of dialogue from that film, though I have not seen it for years.

At one point, in response to a question posed by a concerned young girl, the character Mr. Conductor said, "Well, my family is usually pretty good at getting themselves out of trouble . . . eventually," to which Thomas replied, more to himself than to others, "I don't know what 'eventually' means, but it sounds very, very long." It can be.

It is in the *eventually*, the *meanwhile*, the *just around the corner* of a wilderness that we must trust God. Trusting *ourselves* in a wilderness—depending on *our* instincts and sense of direction—invites disaster. Still, it is hard to trust God in such a place of discontent, especially when God, on occasion, seems almost senile and his actions appear senseless. Yet, the very discontent of a wilderness is intentional, purposeful and essential.

In Jesus' story of the prodigal son,[7] it was not in the oasis—the boy's high times with his high roller friends—that the young man finally *"came to his senses,"*[8] but in the destitute wilderness of a pigpen. As Scott Hahn observed, "Only such a catastrophe could have brought about the prodigal son's conversion. It wasn't a warm wave of nostalgia that set him on the road to his father's house. It was hunger, shame, and the fear of death."[9] Put simply, it took the discontent of a wilderness to get the prodigal back home where he belonged.

---

7. Luke 15:11–32.
8. Luke 15:17.
9. Hahn, *Lord, Have Mercy*, 111.

By contrast, an oasis is a place of contentment. Date palm trees providing shade and satisfying hunger, welcome springs supplying physical refreshment and quenching thirst represent a sure-fire recipe for contentment. That is the problem. Seriously, it is. It is too easy to become content in an oasis. And when we are content, we are not sufficiently attuned to God. Contentment subtly draws us away from God.

Early in their journey from Egypt, God's people camped at Elim, an oasis that boasted *"twelve springs and seventy palm trees."*[10] After resting there, they were quickly on the march once more, and just as quickly complaining.

> The whole community grumbled against Moses and Aaron. The Israelites said to them, "If only we had died by the Lord's hand in Egypt! There we sat around pots of meat and ate all the food we wanted, but you have brought us out into this desert to starve this entire assembly to death."[11]

Notice that they did not yearn for the twelve springs and seventy palms of a few days earlier, but for Egypt, months in the past, all its slavery and danger a fading memory compared to the main menu there. Dates are nice as a change of pace, or even as a side dish, but beef was on the menu back home. Egypt meant contentment to this discontented lot. The problem was, however, that Israel routinely found trouble when sitting around campfires and food pots and eating all they wanted. In the wilderness, nearly every time God's people reached an oasis, settled down, and became content, they grew restless for sin. It was all so very predictable. They kicked off their sandals, laid back their sun-tanned heads, slaked their thirst, ate their fill, forgot about God, and slipped into something more comfortable—sin. It happened in settlements[12] as well; the key part of that word being "settle." At Shittim, for example:

> The men began to indulge in sexual immorality with Moabite women, who invited them to the sacrifices to their gods. The people ate and bowed down before these gods. So Israel joined in worshiping the Baal of Peor. And the Lord's anger burned against them.[13]

10. Exod 15:27.

11. Exod 16:2b-4.

12. Just as Abraham experienced problems in settlements (cities), clashing with individuals from cultures foreign to his, the Hebrews after Abraham found trouble of a different sort in settlements. They would habitually "settle in" to such places, much as Lot settled into the life and lifestyle of Sodom. The result was that God's people, as they had done when settling into in an oasis, quickly found their way into sin.

13. Num 25:1b-3.

Such actions were the rule of Israel's desert days, not the exception. In fact, the Levites, when summarizing Israel's behavior in the wilderness, admitted a tendency to follow contentment into sin. *"As soon as they were at rest,"* they conceded to God, *"they again did what was evil in your sight."*[14] Did you catch that? *"As soon as they were at rest."*

Moses knew that kind of rest to be a legitimate danger as God's people stood ready to enter the oasis of their dreams, that long-awaited Promised Land. He clearly warned what contentment could do to them on the other side of the wilderness:

> When you have eaten and are satisfied, praise the Lord your God for the good land he has given you. Be careful that you do not forget the Lord your God, failing to observe his commands, his laws and his decrees that I am giving you this day. Otherwise, when you eat and are satisfied, when you build fine houses and settle down, and when your herds and flocks grow large and your silver and gold increase and all you have is multiplied, then your heart will become proud and you will forget the Lord your God, who brought you out of Egypt, out of the land of slavery. He led you through the vast and dreadful desert, that thirsty and waterless land, with its venomous snakes and scorpions. He brought you water out of hard rock. He gave you manna to eat in the desert, something your fathers had never known, to humble and to test you so that in the end it might go well with you. You may say to yourself, "My power and the strength of my hands have produced this wealth for me." But remember the Lord your God, for it is he who gives you the ability to produce wealth, and so confirms his covenant, which he swore to your forefathers, as it is today.
>
> If you ever forget the Lord your God and follow other gods and worship and bow down to them, I testify against you today that you will surely be destroyed. Like the nations the Lord destroyed before you, so you will be destroyed for not obeying the Lord your God.[15]

Moses grasped an elusive but vital truth: When we are content, we are not sufficiently attuned to God. Thus, a wilderness is a place of God's purposeful discontent, designed to help us find our only true contentment in him.

Carlo Caretto observed:

---

14. Neh 9:28.
15. Deut 8:10–20.

> If the Israelites had enjoyed freedom in Egypt, Moses could never have persuaded them to attempt the march of liberation. If the desert had been full of beguiling oases instead of snakes, hunger and thirst, they would never have reached the Promised Land.[16]

If liberation and promise are the goals, if finding true contentment in God alone is the destination, then a wilderness becomes an essential experience. Otherwise, contentment can easily descend like fog, blanket us, remain on us, and defy lifting. Once that happens, the seeking stops and the settling begins. Macrina Wiederkehr was correct in her assumption that "perhaps the opposite of a seeker is a settler."[17] The discontent of a wilderness keeps us from settling down where we are not meant to stay. It is designed to keep us seeking, to keep us moving toward the end God has in mind for us.

When understood in terms of God's purpose for a wilderness, discontent is a blessing—a well-disguised one, to be sure, but a true blessing nonetheless. A wilderness is sometimes necessary because there are stubborn parts of us that will not pay attention in an oasis or surrender in times of contentment. There are things we cling to and things that cling to us—dangerous things, sometimes even deadly things—with a grip that only a wilderness, with its powerful discontent, can pry loose. Once that grasp is relaxed, God is free to grasp us for his purposes and our true fulfillment; and, of course, our hands are now free to grasp God. That is why Meister Eckhart wrote somewhere, "It is when clinging to things ends, that God begins to be."[18] The blessing-in-disguise nature of discontent leaves us short of fulfillment here and now, while fueling our longing to ultimately become and possess all God desires for us. It is in the wilderness that we learn things about true contentment that cannot be learned elsewhere or by other means.

I join Macrina Wiederkehr in confessing that "I have an amazing ability, at times, to settle for shallow living,"[19] and that breeds contentment that makes me not unlike a drunk settling into a snow drift on a sub-freezing night, nestling into its pseudo-warmth as exposure slowly kills him. Thankfully, God has used a wilderness, more than once, to rouse me awake and bring me into true warmth: The embrace of his life-giving, life-sustaining contentment.

---

16. Caretto, *Why O Lord?*, 79.
17. Wiederkehr, *Tree Full of Angels*, 126.
18. Wiederkehr., *Tree Full of Angels*, 122–23.
19. Wiederkehr, *Tree Full of Angels*, 92.

The lesson of a wilderness is always that "man does not live on bread alone but on every word that comes from the mouth of the Lord."[20] A wilderness is where we learn that God, and God alone, is sufficient for all our wants and needs. A wilderness is where we learn that being loved by God is all the contentment we need. God uses our times and places of discontent to remind us that our only true contentment is in him. Our desert days teach us that to have God is enough, that in our quest for happiness, fulfillment and true life, God is all we need. I am not certain that lesson can be learned—I mean, *really* learned—anywhere but in a wilderness.

Perhaps, at this point, a little child should guide us.

Cheryl was a friend of mine who died of cancer at the age of nine. She was not a member of our church but came to our Wednesday night youth meetings because her church did not have a midweek program for kids her age. She had only one arm, the doctors having removed the other in a last-ditch effort to save her life. I met her shortly after that surgery. Seldom have I seen the simple but profound faith, hope, and love that I witnessed in her.

As Cheryl's times in the hospital grew more frequent and prolonged, I regularly visited her. Sometimes she was having a good day and if the mood struck her, might show me the sights of the cancer ward. She would smile and laugh, and I would say something like, "You really kind of like it here, don't you Cheryl?" "Yes," she once answered, "but you come here to die . . . and I'm going to die." Other times she would be sad, even depressed, and would fight back tears—occasionally unsuccessfully—as she spoke of leaving family and friends. I would say something like, "I know it must hurt terribly to say goodbye to people you love so much." "Yes," she once told me, "but I'll see Jesus soon."

I attended her funeral after she went to see Jesus. Near the end of the service, her pastor informed us that a few weeks before, he had asked Cheryl to write out her definition of life so he could share it on this occasion. "Tell us what life means to you," he requested. "Tell us what it's all about." He then announced, "I hold in my hand what she wrote," and held up in front of us a plain-looking piece of notebook paper. After an emotional pause, he added, "I would like to read it to you."

I sat back in anticipation of a profound discourse on the meaning of life from this precious nine-year-old who found such godly contentment, even though held in the clutches of such a cruel disease, for I had come to expect such life-wisdom from Cheryl. But this was even more than I expected. It was to this day, I think, the most profound thing I ever heard anyone say; yet it was so simple. It comprised only six words.

---

20. Deut 8:3.

I do not think I could sum up life in six words. Could you? That beautiful child did. "What's life all about, Cheryl?" the pastor wanted to know, and so did I. Honestly, I wanted to know her answer to that question, as well as to several others. "How did you find contentment in a place of such discontent?" "What did you learn in your wilderness, Cheryl?" "How did you endure the trial and come forth as gold?" "What got you through, and got you through joyfully, victoriously?" "Tell me your secret, Cheryl. I want to know. I need to know." "How were you so content in God through such a painful and prolonged ordeal?"

Cheryl answered all my questions and, in the process, summed up life itself, with remarkable brevity and wisdom. She wrote simply, "I love God. He loves me." That was it. And that *is* it. That is what life is all about. That is all I need. That is all any of us really need. It is one of those things we learn—*really* learn—in a wilderness . . . and *only* in a wilderness.

HUMILITY

"A wilderness is that place of discontent where a person is humbled by God . . ."

A wilderness has a way of humbling us. Its primary purpose is to reveal that we are no match for life without God. By its very nature—"it was not a safe or kindly place to be"[1]—a wilderness forces us to realize how desperately we need God so that we might depend utterly on him for survival, for sustenance, for life.

Three times in his final instructions to the nation of Israel, as they stood with forty years of wandering behind them and prepared to enter the Land of Promise, Moses said that God had led them into the wilderness precisely to humble them.[2] Humility was the recurring refrain of Israel's desert days and is, even now, as much a part of a wilderness as are jagged rocks and spiked thorn bushes. In the hands of God, that which humbles us, like that which makes us discontent, is purposeful and loving, designed to bring us "into a good land."

In humbling us, God is not forcing his boot against the backs of our necks, or rubbing our noses in our faults and failures, or raping our personhood and dignity. He is, rather, teaching lessons essential for survival, reminding us—in the words of Moses—"that man does not live on bread alone but on every word that comes from the mouth of the Lord."[3] It is impossible to understand a wilderness apart from that single truth.

Bread, in biblical thought, referred to something literal, but also had strong metaphorical meaning, as it did when Jesus taught his disciples to pray, "Give us today our daily bread."[4] Obviously, that was a literal request to

---

1. Korda, *Lawrence of Arabia*, 24.
2. Deut 8:2, 3, 16.
3. Deut 8:3.
4. Matt 6:11.

be taken at face value—"Give us enough food to get us through the day"—but, in Scripture, bread seems always broader than the grain from which it was made, giving a fuller character to the prayer: "Give us everything we need to sustain and fulfill our lives." Bread is a staple item, necessary for life and its enjoyment. Had Jesus spoken to Asians, rather than to Palestinians, he probably would have said, "Give us today our daily rice," or to others, "Give us today our daily potato." In other words, Jesus taught his disciples to pray, "Give us what we need to get us through the day." Always lurking beneath the surface of the Bible's statements about bread, however, is highly refined symbolism. Bread is not simply a baked loaf of grain. Bread, in its broader sense, refers to all those things in life that we look to for happiness and fulfillment.

Deuteronomy 8:3 calls us to see God—not bread, not the physical world—as our true source of life, our true enjoyment and fulfillment. That being true, bread is then anything and everything that masquerades as life's true source and our true fulfillment. We could put almost any word in place of "bread" and the truth of Deuteronomy 8:3 would remain intact. Pick a word—pleasure, sex, money, possessions, popularity, success, security, status, relationships—and *that* is the target of Moses' words. Take whatever word describes that which is, to us, life's staple item, that which we deem essential to our fulfillment, and *that* is what Deuteronomy 8:3 is saying: *"You shall not live by that alone."* For one very important reason: God alone is our true fulfillment.

Anything or anyone other than God has the potential of drawing us away from him. When we are drawn away, a wilderness becomes a gift of grace intended to draw us back. In a sentence, a wilderness humbles us away from dependency on all the wrong persons and things, and to dependency on God alone.

Humility is the posture of utter dependency on the love, mercy, and grace of God. It is the portrait of Jesus during his earthly life and ministry, from beginning to end—entering life as a helpless infant or making his way to Calvary's cross "with nothing and no one but God to depend on."[5] If God does not sustain wilderness people, they are not sustained. If God does not save wilderness people, they are not saved. Without God, we are "so many dried-up trees in the heart of a desert."[6]

That is, of course, equally true in an oasis, though not as apparent. Taking up squatter's rights in an oasis tends to incline our hearts more toward the gifts than toward the giver. It is easy, amid plenty, to forget that an oasis

---

5. Franzmann, *Follow Me*, 37.
6. Wiesel, *Night*, 35.

is a gift of God's grace, that even among refreshing springs and shade trees, we are completely dependent on God for all things, including the springs and trees themselves. It is not unusual in an oasis—and it was certainly the case with Israel—for the gifts to obscure the giver. What sets a wilderness apart is that it forces us to recognize God, the giver, above and apart from his gifts. A wilderness opens our hearts to the truth that God himself, not the gifts he gives, is our life. We can, if we must, survive without the gifts. We cannot, under any circumstances, survive without God.

A wilderness reminds us that there is no God but God. God alone satisfies our hungers and thirsts, our longings and cravings. When we become so attached to non-gods, looking to them as our true source of satisfaction, a wilderness becomes an essential experience to break that attachment so we might be attached wholeheartedly to the one true God.[7] "For most of us," wrote John Kirvan, "the spiritual journey will be cluttered with a pantheon of gods who are not God and clearing our soul of all the pretenders will be the work of a lifetime."[8] It is assuredly the work of a wilderness.

A wilderness is a ruthlessly revealing place, exposing the uncomfortable truth of our lives: How routinely we place the material world ahead of the spiritual; how we feed our physical hungers while starving the spiritual; how we pursue the world so passionately while pursuing God so timidly, sometimes nonchalantly; how we look to persons, things and trinket gods to fulfill us rather than finding our fulfillment in the one, true God alone.

A wilderness breeds humility, driving us into the arms of God to find our true dependency, our true fulfillment, our true life. Desert days are designed to loosen our grip on the persons and things of this world, and to loosen their grip on us.[9] As that grip is released, we are able to surrender our

---

7. See Hahn, *Lord, Have Mercy*: "We are driven by the appetites we have cultivated. We travel in the direction to which we've turned our bodies, our hearts, our minds, our eyes. But if we wish to reach our destination—if we wish one day to be home in heaven—we have to turn away from our earthly attachments and turn directly Godward. It won't do us any good to turn half way; that still points us the wrong way. Until we break off our attachments, our conversion will not be complete" (Hahn, *Lord Have Mercy*, 131). Until we break off our attachments, our wilderness will not be complete. Only when we let go of all that keeps us from God alone, grasping instead God alone and completely, will our wilderness have reached its purposeful intent.

8. Kirvan, *Raw Faith*, 100.

9. In Kingsolver, *Poisonwood Bible*, the little child Pascal points to a jar of cream, an aerosol spray can, and stacks of lidded containers, asking, "What's that Aunt Adah? And that?" Adah answers, "They're things a person doesn't really need," which, in turn, causes Pascal to question, "But, Aunt Adah, how can there be so many kinds of things a person doesn't really need?" A wilderness forces us to come to terms with the *"so many kinds of things"* we do not need (Kingsolver, *Poisonwood Bible*, 441). Not only are they unnecessary for our true fulfillment, but they often obscure our true fulfillment as

all to God. Sometimes, a lot of pressure must be applied to loosen that grip. When God uses a wilderness to pry open our clenched fists, we routinely resist. Our grip grows tighter and, as it does, God's prying becomes more intense. More often than not, that is an extremely humbling experience, as most of us probably know first-hand.

I was once convicted by God to release something that had become to me a passion—perhaps, even an addiction. Honestly, in retrospect, I think it was probably an idol. What did I do? I refused to release it. For years, I resisted the conviction and call of God. As a result, I found myself in a prolonged wilderness. I kept resisting; God kept prying; the wilderness experience kept growing more intense. It was a hurtful place.

As years passed, God kept telling me to release the thing, that nothing would change until I did, that I would not exit the wilderness until I turned away from my idol. I stubbornly and arrogantly refused. I did everything I could think of doing *except* obeying, even as I prayed to be released from the desert. "God," I would say, "the thing does not have that kind of hold on me. I do not have that kind of hold on it." I think I actually believed that. I know I wanted to. It went on like that for about a decade. Meanwhile, God was humbling me, bringing me low.

One day, God unexpectedly answered my argument, my insistence that the thing had no hold on me and that I had no tight hold on it. I heard him say—not audibly, but clearly—"If there is no hold, why won't you release it?" It was a question I could not evade. It was impossible to sidestep. I had no satisfactory answer, so I did the only thing I could: I released it. As I did, a new world of freedom and blessing opened before me. If I may revise the words of Walter Brueggemann, "the world I had wanted so much to cling to was taken away from me . . . by the grace of God."[10]

There are those things and persons in our lives that must be neglected, even forsaken, so as not to neglect or forsake God. Occasionally, we find ourselves in a wilderness because all other efforts have failed and we are still held by or holding to that which draws us from God and, therefore, draws us from our true fulfillment and our true life. In pride, we refuse to let go.

Helmut Thielicke wrote:

> I heard of a child who was raising a frightful cry because he had shoved his hand into the opening of a Chinese vase and

---

they occupy our minds and hearts, proving dangerous and, sometimes, deadly. Thus, a wilderness seeks to loosen either our grip on such things or their grip on us so that God alone may be seen and known as our true fulfillment.

10. Brueggemann's actual statement was "the world for which you have been so carefully prepared is being taken away from you . . . by the grace of God." Quoted by Taylor, *Leaving Church*, 53.

then couldn't pull it out again. Parents tugged on the child's arm, with the poor creature howling all the while. Finally there was nothing left to do but break the beautiful, expensive vase. As the mournful heap of shards lay there, it became clear why the child had been so helplessly stuck. His little fist grasped a paltry penny, which he had spied at the bottom of the vase and which he, in his childish ignorance, would not let go.

We human beings constantly deal with God exactly like that foolish child. For the sake of a wretched penny in our grasp that we want to keep, the valuable container of our sonship with God is smashed. If we wanted only this highest good, to be God's children, then we would also receive the penny, the healing, the protection, and everything else along with it.[11]

That to which we stubbornly cling in pride, that which we doggedly refuse to release at God's command, often results in the shattering of *ourselves*—a brokenness, a humbling that can only be termed a wilderness. Such a wilderness is often critical if we are ever to release our grip on the paltry pennies of this world and, instead, take hold of the one true God as if our lives depended on it. We are humbled in those areas where we will not surrender. Because we will not unclench our fists, or our hearts, and let God have what he calls us to release, he must pry. As a result, we end up stuck in a wilderness as surely as that small boy's arm was stuck in a vase. A wilderness humbles us so that "the valuable container of our sonship with God" might not be smashed.

If Moses, who was *"more humble than anyone else on the face of the earth,"*[12] needed some wilderness humbling—remember that he twice struck the rock with his staff, was dressed down by God in the presence of all Israel, and told that he would not enter the Promised Land[13]—then it is a sure bet that I need humbling. Moses forgot, or so it seems to me, that although he was first chair (as Aaron and Miriam were once sternly reminded),[14] he did not conduct the orchestra. God did. There is only one conductor. There is no God but God. A wilderness strips us of many things, but mostly of our stubborn refusal to admit that.

---

11. Krutza, ed., *Knee Exercises*, 35. In a similar vein, Thomas à Kempis wrote, "We become all absorbed in those things which profit us little or nothing at all, but our soul's salvation—the thing of vital importance—is negligently passed over. How easily man tends downward to outward; but unless he sharply recovers himself, he is content to dwell in material interests and pleasures." Thomas à Kempis, *Imitation of Christ*, 190.

12. Num 12:3.

13. Num 20:1–12.

14. Num 12:1–16.

A wilderness pries free our fists from many things, but mostly from our pride. That prying, that stripping, is intentionally humbling, leaving us standing before God with nothing except his crushing presence. In truth, that is enough.

Commenting on Teresa of Avila's words that "If you have God, you will want for nothing. God alone suffices," John Kirvan wrote:

> Teresa is saying that if at the end of the day we 'lose everything' and have nothing left but God, it will be enough.
> And God will be there, not as a replacement for what we have lost or surrendered, but as that for which there is no substitute and who alone is enough.[15]

After all, there is no God but God. He uses a wilderness to humble us into holiness, stripping us of all else we cling to so that we might cling to him for who he really is: the only thing worth clinging to in all of life. He brings nothing into our lives but what is necessary for our healing and wholeness, and he strips us of all that hinders our becoming everything and possessing everything he desires. That is the wonderful way of humility. It teaches us to live, not on bread alone, *"but on every word that comes from the mouth of the Lord."*

---

15. Kirvan, *Raw Faith*, 118.

OBEDIENCE

"A wilderness is that place of discontent where a person is humbled by God, tested in obedience . . ."

Perhaps the most famous—or infamous—test in Christian Scripture is God's test of Abraham, recorded in Genesis 22. "No story in Genesis is as terrible, as powerful, as mysterious, as elusive as this one."[1] It may represent as severe a wilderness as any person of God ever walked.

The story opens with the narrator giving the reader information that Abraham did not possess, that the unimaginable demand placed upon this lonely man of promise was a test: *"Some time later, God tested Abraham."*[2] The test begins with a divine reminder of the uniqueness of the son Isaac and his significance to his father Abraham. Each reference to Isaac pushes more deeply into the heart of Abraham. *"Take your son . . . your only son . . . Isaac . . . whom you love . . . ."*[3] What is about to be asked of Abraham is "the surrender (of) that which is most his own and that which he most loves."[4] The words that follow are truly horrific and there is no way to adequately gauge their impact on Abraham: *"Sacrifice him . . . as a burnt offering on one of the mountains I will tell you about."*[5]

In a monstrous story that defies comprehension and commentary, it may be a single Hebrew word—*'olah*—that provides our best hope of

1. Kass, *Beginning of Wisdom*, 333.
2. Gen 22:1.
3. Gen 22:2a.
4. Kass, *Beginning of Wisdom*, 136.
5. Gen 22:2b.

grasping the gut-wrenching terror and torture of such a wilderness. That word is most often translated *"burnt offering"* and means literally *"to ascend."* As an offering was totally consumed by fire, the smoke rose heavenward as affirmation of absolute surrender on the part of the worshiper, who lifted his own life to God along with the life sacrificed. Of course, that means one thing when a sheep is on the altar, another when it is your own son under the knife or going up in flames. The words *"offering"* and *"sacrifice"* may fit the former, but what word is there in the history of human language to describe the latter?

Holocaust?

That English word is built around the Hebrew *'olah* in the tale of the binding of Isaac and may afford us our best chance of comprehending at least a portion of what it means to enter a wilderness of testing like Abraham . . . or Job . . . or Israel . . . or Jesus. Holocaust—a great or total destruction of life, certainly of life as we know it.

Abraham binding Isaac to the wood; Job losing his wealth, his health, his family, his friends; Israel burying an entire generation in the desert; Jesus assaulted by Satan at the beginning of his ministry, hung like raw meat on a hook at the end—holocaust. Berkeley's translation even uses that word, as God tells Abraham to sacrifice Isaac *"as a holocaust."* Never underestimate the level of testing a wilderness may entail. It represents serious spiritual business on the part of God who, both for our sakes and the kingdom's, refuses to leave us as we are.[6]

A wilderness is not a simple grade school test where we answer seven questions right out of ten and earn a passing grade, but a test of heart, mind, strength, and soul; a test of will and worship, of longings and loves, of motives and obedience; a test proving how far God will go to possess us and how far we will go to be possessed; a test that at its most severe may strip us of all but God, leaving us bereft of the gifts but bound to the Giver. Life goes on after a wilderness, just never as it did before. Old things go up in smoke; a new thing is born.

Holocaust.

---

6. See Kingsolver, *Poisonwood Bible*, 493, where the fictional Ada Price remarks, "We would rather be just like us, and have that be all right." Kingsolver, *Poisonwood Bible*, 493. That mindset is indicative of many, if not most wilderness wanderers in Scripture—certainly of Israel which, while still fleeing Egypt, complained to Moses, *"Why didn't you just leave us as we were?"* (Personal translation of Exod 14:12). God, however, will have a people wholly his, and for most of us, most of the time, that involves significantly more than remaining *"just like us."* At times a wilderness is necessary because being left as we are is not *"all right"* with God, whose divine purposes exceed our fleshly satisfaction.

Make no mistake about it—a wilderness is an altar, involving everything Scripture crams into that image, and inscribed with the words, *"To obey is better than sacrifice."*[7] It was so in Abraham's case, as God stopped the father short of slicing the knife across his son's throat, having already cut into Abraham's chest to reveal a heart that beat in unquestioning obedience to him.

Moses' reminder to Israel at the edge of the Promised Land—*"Remember how the Lord your God led you all the way in the desert these forty years, to . . . test you in order to know what was in your heart, whether or not you would keep his commands"*[8]—sounds eerily similar to the words Abraham heard at the end of his excruciating test: *"Now I know that you fear God, because you have not withheld from me your son, your only son."*[9] In a wilderness, we are tested in obedience that our hearts might be revealed.

Our twenty-first century chop shop theology (that has stripped God's grace of all its biblical severity and left it as one-sided love stranded on concrete blocks) chafes at the idea of such rigorous testing and goes to great lengths to explain away such stern stories, even the God of those stories.[10] Still, the Bible, New Testament as well as Old, assumes periods of testing, seasons of wilderness walking, to be part and parcel of the lives of God's people.[11] The apostle Peter even advised, *"Do not be surprised at the painful trial you are suffering, as though something strange were happening to you."*[12]

7. 1 Sam 15:22.

8. Deut 8:2.

9. Gen 22:12.

10. Whereas there is value in reading biblical stories through the lens of our prevailing culture, we miss much of the truth and intent of those stories if we divorce ourselves from the culture in which they were written or related. We must be careful not to throw out the truth of the story in an effort to discern the author's alleged agenda. See Thomas C. Foster, *How to Read Literature*, 228–29: " . . . don't read with your eyes. What I really mean is, don't read only from your own fixed position in the Year of Our Lord two thousand and some. Instead try to find a reading perspective that allows for sympathy with the historical moment of the story, that understands the text as having been written against its own social, historical, cultural and personal background. There are dangers in this, and I'll return to them. I also need to acknowledge here that there is a different model of professional reading, deconstruction, that pushes skepticism and doubt to its extreme, questioning nearly everything in the story or poem at hand, to deconstruct the work and show how the author is not really in charge of his materials. The goal of these deconstructive readings is to demonstrate how the work is controlled and reduced by the values and prejudices of its own time." Foster, *How to Read Literature*, 228–29.

11. Some Old Testament references are 1 Chr 29:17; 2 Chr 32:31; Job 7:17–18; 23:10; Ps 66:10; Prov 17:3; Jer 9:7; 11:20; Zech 13:9. A sampling of New Testament references include 2 Cor 2:9; 1 Thess 2:4; Jas 1:3; 1 Pet 1:7; 4:12.

12. 1 Pet 4:12.

Peter went on to say, in *The Message* translation of that same text, *"This is a spiritual refining process."*[13]

A wilderness tests us the way a furnace tests gold.

I knew a man who assayed gold. To test its purity, he would weigh the clump, wrap it in lead foil, place it in a cupel—a small, shallow, porous cup—and stick it in the furnace until the metals melted. Then he removed the cupel from the furnace and allowed the metals to cool. The cupel absorbed the lead, as well as any other non-precious metals in the gold, and left behind what he called a *button*, a miniature mass of pure gold. He placed it in acid, rinsed it, dried it, and then weighed it to determine what percentage of the original clump was pure gold.

It was a test by fire, a refining process—the impurities and non-precious parts burning away, separating from the gold to leave something pure and priceless. In such a way, God tests his people. In such a way, a wilderness works. It is purposeful. It is a spiritual refining process. *"The crucible for silver and the furnace for gold,"* wrote Solomon, *"but the Lord tests the heart."*[14] That helps us to better understand our desert days. *"I the Lord search the heart"*[15] stands conspicuously over the entrance to every wilderness in Scripture, announcing the inevitable refining process that awaits those who travel its often-tortuous routes. A wilderness is a time of testing that both reveals and refines.

In a very real sense, a wilderness does not make or break a person; it reveals a person. It reveals what is in our hearts. It reveals whether or not it is within us to obey God, whether or not we will persist in attempting opposite things with our lives.[16] It reveals what percentage of our hearts belongs purely to God.

In Israel's wilderness wandering, even God's provision of manna for his people was intended as a test, designed to open hearts and reveal contents. Yahweh said to Moses, *"I will rain down bread from heaven for you. The people are to go out each day and gather enough for that day. In this way I will test them and see whether they will follow my instructions."*[17] Later, Moses would remind Israel that God's assaying of their hearts, though often painful, was necessary *"in order to know what was in your heart, whether or*

---

13. 1 Pet 4:13.
14. Prov 17:3.
15. Jer 17:10.
16. Stevenson, *God in My Unbelief*, 16: "He was still wanting to do opposite things with his life. The same impulse from God was obeyed or driven out of reckoning."
17. Exod 16:4.

not you would obey his commands,"[18] and *"to find out whether you love him with all your heart."*[19] Even Israel's faltering forty-year march of on-again-off-again faithfulness became, as Paul put it, an example *"to keep us from setting our hearts on evil things as they did."*[20]

The God of the Wilderness is concerned with the heart of the one in the wilderness. King David learned that truth, as both Moses and Abraham had, the hard way, the wilderness way. Abraham had a more severe test and Moses a more prolonged one, while David spent some difficult, even desperate days trapped in a wilderness during both Saul's persecution[21] and Absalom's conspiracy.[22] In addition, what about that episode of rooftop Peeping Tom where, before you could say "Your place or mine?" David had Bathsheba in bed and Uriah in the grave?[23] That resulted in as stern a wilderness as David ever knew. Though it was not an actual physical place, it was a lengthier and more oppressive period than any literal wilderness David ever walked. Could it be called a *spiritual* wilderness? There, God's intent was to get at the heart of things—specifically, at the heart of David. Judah's king was speaking from such wilderness experience when he prayed, *"I know, my God, that you test the heart and are pleased with integrity."*[24] In a wilderness, God's gaze never strays from the heart.

By contrast, our gaze, like Israel's of old, is all over the map when we find ourselves in a wilderness—staring in self-pity at ourselves or, other times, in fear and apprehension at the hostile, barren vastness of it all. God, of course, is far more focused. He is ever looking at the heart, beneath the surface and beyond appearance, past all facades and frantic attempts to fool even ourselves, to that unplumbed depth no human eye has ever seen, where only God's gaze goes.

Even Samuel, who among all God's prophets was the most spiritually perceptive, had to be reminded, when seeking a king among Jesse's sons, not to consider outward appearance but to peer more deeply into the person. *"The Lord does not look at the things a man looks at,"* God instructed him. *"Man looks at the outward appearance, but the Lord looks at the heart."*[25] Always at the heart. The God whose attention in a wilderness is on the heart

18. Deut 8:2.
19. Deut 13:3.
20. 1 Cor 10:6.
21. 1 Sam 23:7—27:3.
22. 2 Sam 15:1—19:8.
23. 2 Sam 11:1-27.
24. 1 Chr 29:17.
25. 1 Sam 16:7.

of the one there wants our attention there as well. For that reason, there is no way to bypass the exposing of our hearts as we walk, sometimes drag ourselves along that desert terrain. We will know, as God will know, whether it is in our hearts to obey him.

We will be tested in obedience. On the one hand, all impurities that impede or prevent that obedience, all that will not surrender to gentler words and ways, will know its day of reckoning in a wilderness. On the other hand, for those who respond to God's testing with obedience, for those who remain faithful, even in and through the horrors of a holocaust, all but the pure and priceless will burn away and they will be refined as gold. God will have a people wholly his. That is why a wilderness, for all its severity, is an experience in God's grace—". . . a terrible grace," wrote Macrina Wiederkehr, but "a terrible and beautiful grace."[26] "Terrible" and "beautiful" are twin descriptions of biblical grace, and of a biblical wilderness. "As a place," wrote James Luther Mays, "the wilderness is bare and threatening but as an epoch in the history of God and Israel it represents a point of new beginning."[27]

A wilderness always marks a new beginning for those whose hearts obey God. Like birth, it can be difficult, painful, and exhausting, but it is birth. A new thing emerges. A God thing.

---

26. Wiederkehr, *Tree Full of Angels*, 95. Concerning that grace, Thomas à Kempis wrote, "I gladly accept that grace which makes me more humble and prudent and more ready to deny myself. A man who has been taught by the gift of grace and chastened by the scourge of its withdrawal will not dare to think that any good comes by his own doing, and will openly confess that he is poor and naked." Later (223), he wrote, "Your grace is the teacher of truth, the master of discipline; it brings light to the heart and solace in affliction; it banishes sorrow, dispels fear, nourishes our devotion and moves us to tears of repentance. What am I without it but a withered tree, a bit of dry timber to be cast into the fire? Grant, therefore, O Lord, that Your grace always go before me, be ever at my back, keeping me ever intent upon good works to be done, through Jesus Christ, your Son and my Lord. Amen." Thomas à Kempis, *Imitation of Christ*, 87.

27. Mays, *Hosea*, 44.

TRUST

"A wilderness is that place of discontent where a person is humbled by God, tested in obedience, taught to trust . . . *"*

Part of the problem with being a slave-people in Egypt for a little more than four centuries, only to become suddenly free, is that even freedom has trouble trumping an ingrained slave mentality. In truth, *being* free does not necessarily translate into *living* free. Israel was proof of that reality. Having for so long trusted Egypt for their entire existence—waking, sleeping, eating, working, surviving—the people of God found freedom a risky, if not frightening venture. After all, it is hard to know whom to trust, even *how* to trust, when all you have known is nearly half-a-millennia of bondage and dependency. A slave mentality is hard to overcome. As Sally Kempton observed, "It's hard to fight an enemy who has outposts in your head."[1]

Historically, freed slaves in any culture at any time have three options: To remain with their masters, opting for security; to leave their masters but remain in the area, opting for familiarity; or to leave, not only their masters, but also the land of their bondage, opting for a complete break with their past and a subsequent new life. More often than not, security and familiarity are powerful enough draws to keep ex-slaves relatively close. Almost without exception, that means repeating the process of slavery and once more becoming economically dependent on the land and the landlords just left.

Pharaoh must have known that, would have counted on it. In fact, when Moses delivered God's ultimatum to set his people free, Pharaoh tried

---

1. Kempton, *Esquire*, July 1970, quoted in Lamott, *Grace*, 105. As South African freedom fighter Steven Biko was once quoted as saying, "The most potent weapon in the hands of the oppressor is the mind of the oppressed."

first to keep the slaves on the plantation: *"Go sacrifice to your God here in the land"*[2] then, as a second option, suggested they at least stay in the area: *"I will let you go to offer sacrifices to the Lord your God in the desert, but you must not go very far."*[3]

Pharaoh was not a political novice with no idea how the system worked. Instead, he was a shrewd politician who was willing to give the burgeoning Hebrew population what they thought they wanted—freedom—knowing that if he could do that while keeping them within eyesight of Egypt, dependency would most certainly kick in and they would once more turn their trusting eyes toward him. With a masterful stroke of genius, Pharaoh offered a pair of politically shrewd proposals. Best wishes, but why not make your new life here? Best wishes, but don't be strangers.

The proposals may not have seemed attractive to the Hebrew children in the early, heady days of emancipation, but they soon became attractive, if not irresistible, as Israel, once out of Egypt, struggled to trust God to do for them what Pharaoh always had.[4] Even with their backs to the land of slavery and their faces to the land of promise, even while putting significant distance between themselves and the Egyptians, *"in their hearts (they) turned back to Egypt."*[5] That easy-to-overlook phrase, uttered by Stephen centuries after Israel's wilderness wandering and only moments before he was martyred for Jesus, is radical—literally. Our English word *radical* comes from the Latin *radix* which means *root*. Stephen, indeed, got to the root of the whole issue with freshly freed Israel: *"In their hearts (they) turned back to Egypt."* As always, it is a heart issue with the people of God.

Stephen's words harken back to a moment some two years after those Hebrew slaves had last seen Egypt, had last felt the task masters' whips across their backs. At long last, they were ready to receive from the Lord the land they had been promised. Spies were sent *"through the Negev and on into the hill country,"*[6] then returned to report a land of almost unimaginable abundance yet strewn with obstacles. Confident that the Lord had given them the land, one of the spies, a man named Caleb, encouraged the people, *"We should go up and take possession of the land, for we can certainly do it."*[7] But the people refused.

2. Exod 8:25.
3. Exod 8:28.
4. Exod 4:10–12; 16:1–3; 17:1–3; Num 14:1–4.
5. Acts 7:39.
6. Num 13:17.
7. Num 13:30.

Why? Stephen explained that even though they were dipping their toes in the waters of the Promised Land, in their hearts the vacation was over, and they were headed home to Egypt. In their hearts, they could not bring themselves to trust God. While in Egypt, Israel knew they would have meat and bread aplenty; Pharaoh would see to that.[8] But away from their old Egyptian home, they wondered aloud:

> "Can God spread a table in the desert?
> . . . he struck the rock, water gushed
>   out,
> and streams flowed abundantly.
> But can he also give us food?
> Can he supply meat for his people?"[9]

In other words, can God be trusted . . . especially in a wilderness?

Pharaoh, for all the hardships he piled on the Hebrew slaves, could nonetheless be trusted to provide food, drink, and shelter for Israel's ever-increasing numbers. God, on the other hand . . . well, that was the question, the persistent question of Israel. Can God be trusted?

More certain of Pharaoh than they were of God, the people's hearts turned back to Egypt, even as they teetered on the edge of promise. From God's perspective, hearts turned back to Egypt meant only one thing: Lack of trust in him. I love the flow and feel of *The Message* translation as it relates the events to which Stephen later alludes:

> *The whole community was in an uproar, wailing all night long. All the people of Israel grumbled against Moses and Aaron. The entire community was in on it: "Why didn't we die in Egypt? Or in this wilderness? Why has God brought us to this country to kill us? Our wives and children are about to become plunder. Why don't we just head back to Egypt? And, right now!"*
>
> *Soon they were all saying to one another: "Let's pick a new leader; let's head back to Egypt." . . .*
>
> *God said to Moses, "How long will these people treat me like dirt? How long refuse to trust me?"*[10]

The wilderness that followed on the heels of that incident had as much to do with trust—learning who and how to trust—as it did anything else. If God is who he says he is, trust should not be a problem. Since we are who we are, however, trust *is* a problem. That was particularly true for once-enslaved

8. Exod 16:3a.
9. Ps 78:19b-20.
10. Num 14:1-3, 11.

Israel, reared as it was on trusting things and people rather than God, programmed to find dependency in Pharaoh, not in Yahweh. In a wilderness, especially, we default, we turn our eyes and hearts in trust to that on which we have learned to depend. A wilderness is about un-learning that and re-setting the default mechanism of our hearts to God. A wilderness is about learning to trust God . . . alone and completely.

Typically, neither the un-learning nor the learning happens without the severe assistance of a wilderness. When our old slave master is sin, it usually takes a wilderness for us to transition from freedom-in-fact to freedom-in-practice. The insidious thing about sin is that it not only makes us slaves, but also creates within us a slave mentality. Slave mentality—particularly that which has been ingrained over generations—does not simply disappear once we are handed our freedom. That is why a *set-free* person is not always a *live-free* person.

Sin also actively fights us and seeks to master us, determined to enslave us and to keep us enslaved. It will do everything it can to keep us from making a complete break—offering security and familiarity, suggesting compromise and rationalization, almost anything to keep us at least in its suburbs—knowing that should it succeed, dependency will most likely kick in and our eyes will once more look back in trust. If, by the grace-of-God-in-Jesus, we ever break free, sin will, like Pharaoh's army chasing Israel, pursue us to bring us back to the land and life we left. It is a life-long struggle, as we well know. As ex-slaves,[11] carrying at least the vestiges of slave mentality,[12] we are particularly vulnerable to becoming slaves all over again.[13] Just as some things are seldom overcome without prayer and fasting,[14] so sin and its subsequent slave mentality are rarely overcome without a wilderness.

A wilderness, for all its sternness, is a place or period where our hearts are re-created[15] and recalibrated so as to not turn back to Egypt. It is a place or period where our minds are renewed[16] and reprogrammed so as to no longer think like slaves. It is a place or period intentionally designed to teach us that trusting what we left behind perpetuates slavery, whereas trusting God alone and completely is the means of obtaining the promise—that of becoming free people, of becoming everything and possessing everything

---

11. Rom 6:1–23.
12. Rom 8:5–17; Gal 5:16–25.
13. Rom 6:15–23; Gal 5:1; Col 3:1–10.
14. Matt 17:21; Mark 9:29.
15. Ps 51:10.
16. Rom 12:1–2.

God desires. A wilderness is about learning to trust—how to trust, whom to trust and why to trust.

For four decades, God's freed-from-Egypt children walked the desert sands, "fallen, dragging their packs, dragging their lives"[17] and, I would add, struggling but learning, with varying degrees of success, to trust God. Almost from the beginning of their Exodus, when Israel was caught between the rock of the Red Sea and the hard place of Pharaoh's advancing chariots, they were forced to trust God or die. Such is the demanding nature of a wilderness.

As an entire generation of Hebrews followed a meandering, confusing course through the desert, they had to learn to trust God for all they needed to survive—for provision and protection, for wisdom and guidance. It was trust God or die. Often, in the insightful words of James Luther Mays, " . . . Israel thought their own satisfaction exhausted Yahweh's purpose,"[18] but God's purpose was of a higher order. It involved a people learning to trust him alone and completely, learning to trust God to be God, learning to trust God or die.

Taking a significant step further, we could say that a wilderness is about learning to trust God *and* die. Most times we enter a wilderness to die. What Dietrich Bonhoeffer wrote of discipleship seems equally true of a wilderness: "When Christ calls a man, he bids him come and die."[19]

As Jesus stood ready to enter the most frightening wilderness of his life, a wilderness that once embraced and entered would claim his life, he explained *"to his disciples that he must go to Jerusalem and suffer many things at the hands of the elders, chief priests and teachers of the law, and that he must be killed . . . ."*[20] Peter promptly took him aside and began rebuking him. "Never, Lord," he said, *"This shall never happen to you."*[21]

Peter, and doubtless the other disciples, recoiled at the very thought of Jesus entering such a wilderness. They failed to understand, as Jesus understood, that trusting God always demands dying, which is why Jesus, of his own free will,

> *"became obedient to death —*
> *even death on a cross!"*[22]

---

17. Wiesel, *Night*, 15.
18. Mays, *Hosea*, 175.
19. Bonhoeffer, *Cost of Discipleship*, 79.
20. Matt 16:21.
21. Matt 16:22.
22. Phil 2:8.

To drive home the truly shocking reality that to trust *is* to die, Jesus continued, saying not just to Peter but to all the disciples, *"If anyone would come after me, he must deny himself and take up his cross and follow me. For whoever wants to save his life will lose it, but whoever loses his life for me will find it."*[23]

Things are lost in a desert, from our bearings to our strength. It is the very nature of the wild, with its harsh conditions and demanding terrain, to take things from whoever enters. Things die in a desert—from scapegoats to stranded travelers. It is the very nature of the wild, with its stern difficulties and threatening dangers, to claim the life of whoever or whatever enters. That is equally true of what we might term *spiritual* deserts. A wilderness is all about dying—dying to our lives, dying to ourselves, dying to that to which we must die in order to live as God means us to live.

A wilderness is about learning to trust God to be God and dying to all else.

A wilderness is designed to teach us that, in the barren emptiness where there is neither food nor water, God can be trusted as the good shepherd who provides for his people green pastures and still waters.[24] A wilderness is designed to teach us that in the confusion and disorientation of whipping winds and stinging sand, God can be trusted as the guide and staff who leads his people in and to safety. A wilderness is designed to teach us that in the hurt and horrors of the wild, where fear and pain are both real and intense, God can be trusted as the balm of healing and peace for his people. A wilderness is designed to teach us that we find through losing and we live through dying.

In a wilderness, we are taught to trust God to be God, to trust God alone and completely, to trust God to the point that we are willing to lose our lives in order to find them and die to ourselves in order to live.

---

23. Matt 16:24–25.

24. Mays, *Hosea*, 175: "In the barren emptiness of the wilderness where there was neither water nor food, Yahweh was the good shepherd to his people."

DISCIPLINE

"A wilderness is that place of discontent where a person is humbled by God, tested in obedience, taught to trust, and trained through discipline . . . "

God often finds a wilderness profitable to prevent his people from returning to places from which they were delivered. Its terrain and conditions provide the discipline needed to move forward toward God's promise instead of backward toward enslavement. Like all discipline, a wilderness does not seem ". . . *pleasant at the time, but painful. Later on, however, it produces a harvest of righteousness and peace for those who have been trained by it.*"[1]

The discipline of a wilderness is a direct attack on our deep-seated desire to return to Egypt—a desire that can prove deadly, certainly for former slaves. That return was a danger God was cognizant of and addressing from the moment Israel packed up and headed for the Promised Land:

> *When Pharaoh let the people go, God did not lead them on the road through the Philistine country, though that was shorter. For God said, "If they face war, they might change their minds and return to Egypt."*[2]

When God sets his people free, retreat and return are not an option. At least, not to God. All his resources are poured into getting his people from where they were to where they need to be.

---

1. Heb 12:11.
2. Exod 13:17–18.

It is possible we are being told more in Exod 16:13 than may be evident on a first read. Perhaps Israel's comment about their days in Egypt—*"There we sat around pots of meat and ate all the food we wanted"*[3]—suggested a deficit of concern beyond much of anything but feeding their appetites after a long day's march over hardscrabble earth. Such daydreaming likely betrayed a fundamental lack of interest in moving God's direction.

Like a cardiologist trying to get an obese, at-risk patient off junk food and onto a healthy diet, off the couch and into an exercise regimen in an effort to help that person find health and long life, so God seeks to get his people off the deadly diet they knew in Egypt and onto a diet of feasting on his word,[4] off the path of their own passions and pursuits and onto the path of his promise in an effort to help them become everything and possess everything he desires. That often takes harsh measures. It often takes a wilderness.

In a wilderness, we are trained through discipline. Without such discipline, we all too easily become spiritually flabby and lazy, content to sit around pots of our own pleasure. Without a wilderness, chances are that every time God got us up and moving his way, we would soon find a reason to hightail it back to Rameses, where the steady diet of the day would tickle our taste buds while hardening our spiritual arteries.

A wilderness is essential if we are to stop the subtle but lethal practice of making occasional day trips into spiritual progress, only to return safely at night to our homey little shanties in the land of sin. From time to time, in the face of incessant U-turns that strand us at spiritual dead-ends, a wilderness is God's means of turning us around and setting us on the way to his promise.

In Scripture, a wilderness is both an individual and group experience.

A wilderness can be a corporate exercise in discipline, much as it was for Israel in its wandering; for God's people in the days of exile, the days of the Judges, the days of Roman occupation of their land; and for churches such as Ephesus, Smyrna, and Pergamum mentioned in Revelation 2. Most wilderness experiences in Scripture appear to be of the corporate nature.

A wilderness, however, can also be a personal exercise in discipline, an isolated "dark night of the soul," to use the familiar imagery of St. John of the Cross. This book arose from my personal wilderness and is intended to help others in their personal wilderness. Even then, however, no one is a solitary traveler, not the author nor the reader. In or out of a desert, lonely individualism is a myth of modern American Christianity. Our lives are

---

3. Exod 16:13.
4. Deut 8:3.

part of a corporate whole, part of the community of God's people. We hold a common faith and share a corporate experience. We journey together or we do not journey as God intended.

Still, the experience of a wilderness can be, at times, more personal than corporate. In those times, even a solitary pilgrim, struggling to survive a desert, can glean valuable insight from the shared wildernesses of Scripture—Israel's for example. The apostle Paul seems to have seen the applicable moral of that specific group-discipline as meant for all, other groups and individuals included.[5]

Regardless of whether a wilderness represents the dark night of a single soul or a long corporate journey, it can be, and often is, a stern discipline. As such, it is designed to either correct our course or forge our character—perhaps both.

There is formative discipline to a wilderness that is difficult to find in any other place or by any other means. There is a certain spiritual substance and strength that is hard to develop apart from wilderness stretches. As has often been pointed out by students of Scripture, none of the major prophetic voices emerged without a disciplining period in the wilderness. Moses may be the most obvious of that group, but there were others who, for example, spent prolonged stretches in prison (Jeremiah) or in exile (Ezekiel). John the Baptist *"lived in the desert until he appeared publicly to Israel,"*[6] conducted most of his ministry in a desert or on its fringe,[7] and spent the end of his life in prison where he was beheaded.[8] Meanwhile, Jesus faced severe and prolonged spiritual testing during his forty-day stretch in a wilderness.[9] Again, wilderness discipline is formative discipline.

There are, of course, two sides to wilderness discipline, as there are two sides to any discipline. On the one hand, discipline is treatment that corrects; on the other hand, discipline is training that develops character.

Elijah the prophet, following a phenomenal revival in which he played the key role, made a sudden and somewhat unexpected U-turn that took him from the cool heights of Mount Carmel to the dry heat of the desert, and left him sitting on his haunches while God asked, *"What are you doing here?"*[10] If the truth be known—and it soon was—what Elijah was doing there was hoping God would offer him early retirement. God, however, had

---

5. 1 Cor 10:6, 11.
6. Luke 1:80.
7. Matt 3:1–6; Luke 3:1–3.
8. Matt 14:1–10; Mark 6:14–27; Luke 3:20.
9. Matt 4:1–11; Mark 1:12–13; Luke 4:1–13.
10. 1 Kgs 19:9a.

no such plans for his prophet. Instead, he utilized a wilderness to get the stalemated man off dead-center, rouse him from his spiritual lethargy, lift him out of his depression and dreams of fireplaces and rocking chairs, and get him back to the task to which God had called him.[11]

In the case of Elijah, a wilderness represented discipline which corrected, somewhat like the course correction that brought America's Apollo 8 astronauts safely back to earth after they veered slightly off course on their return trip from the moon in December of 1968 (as if there is such a thing as *slightly* off course in space or, for that matter, in a wilderness). That course correction was essential if those space pioneers were to reach their intended destination rather than to ricochet off Earth's atmosphere and be lost forever to cold, steely vastness. A similar course correction was essential if God was to get Elijah from where he was to where he needed him to be.

Likewise, most of Israel's wilderness time was discipline that corrected. Initially, however, God led them into the desert, not to correct or to punish, but to develop within them true spiritual character, to fashion them into true spiritual community. There is one side to wilderness discipline that fashions godly character and develops within us precisely what God desires; a side that has nothing to do with misdirection or misbehavior. There is a wilderness that is less about our sin and more about God's sovereignty, a wilderness that accomplishes God's will in ways we seldom discern while walking its difficult terrain.

A friend and prayer partner of mine recently pointed out that in the gospel narratives of Jesus calming the storm at sea,[12] the disciples struggled mightily in their own wilderness of sorts, albeit a wet one. Matthew and Mark called the storm *"furious,"*[13] while Mark and Luke both added that the waves were swamping the boat.[14] That frightening wilderness of wind and waves was so terrifying that salty fisherman thought they were going to drown and cried out to Jesus for help.[15]

An oft missed but significant truth of that story is that Jesus is the one who gave instructions for them to launch out onto the sea.[16] The disciples had done nothing wrong, nothing deserving of punishment or correction. They were simply, obediently following Jesus' instructions, but just the same found themselves in a life-threatening wilderness. Through it all, however,

---

11. 1 Kgs 9b-21.
12. Matt 8:23–27; Mark 4:35–41; Luke 8:22–25.
13. Matt 8:24; Mark 4:37.
14. Mark 4:37; Luke 8:23.
15. Matt 8:25; Mark 4:38; Luke 8:24.
16. Matt 8:18–23; Mark 4:35–36a; Luke 8:22.

their faith was anchored more securely in this Jesus who held sway over sea and sky,[17] and their character developed a tenacious strength it would have otherwise lacked. More than that, the synoptic gospels[18] report that when Jesus and his disciples reached the other side of the lake, a violent demon possessed man met them.[19] Jesus healed the man, casting out the demons, then sent the man away, saying, *"Go home to your family and tell them how much the Lord has done for you, and how he has had mercy on you."*[20] The man promptly obeyed and, according to Luke, *"began to tell in the Decapolis how much Jesus had done for him. And all the people were amazed."*[21]

There is more to a wilderness—more to crossing a storm-tossed sea—than is understood at the surface. There is more at stake, more on the line in our cries of *"Lord, save us!"*[22] than our own salvation. The storm is simply God's vehicle to get us to the other side. We are so invested in fighting the raging storm that we seldom see the end, the destination God has in mind. We seldom see what lies on the far shore of the sea as we struggle at the oars in the storm. Always, however, our struggling serves kingdom ends; always, our struggling shapes us for kingdom purposes as we remain faithful to the one who called us to launch out.[23] Sometimes, the only way to where, or who, God wants us to be is through a storm on a sea he has called us to cross. There is a sovereign, soul-making side to a wilderness and its discipline.

Even Jesus was led by the Spirit to spend significant time being disciplined in a wilderness. As the sinless Son of God, he was not sentenced to forty days in a desert to be taught a good lesson for his misbehavior or to receive an essential course correction. In fact, during those desert days, it was Satan, not God, who was attempting to alter Jesus' course.[24] By contrast, God was using the desert, and the tests faced there, to forge from the metal of Jesus' life a strong-as-steel, unyielding spiritual character.

Admittedly, it may be difficult for some to think of Jesus in such terms, but the writer of Hebrews did. In a sentence that is unnerving to many, the author wrote concerning Jesus:

17. Matt 8:27; Mark 4:41; Luke 8:25.
18. Matthew, Mark and Luke.
19. Mark and Luke mention one man; Matthew a pair.
20. Luke 5:19.
21. Luke 5:20.
22. Matt 8:25.
23. As Carolyn Custis James wrote, "God harnesses the sufferings of his children and compels the bad things that happen to us to serve his good purposes for us and for our mission in this world." James, *Gospel of Ruth*, 132.
24. Matt 4:3–10.

> *Though he was God's Son, he learned trusting-obedience by what he suffered, just as we do. Then, having arrived at the full stature of his maturity . . . he became the source of eternal salvation to all who believingly obey him.*[25]

In the sense that we normally think of discipline, correction, or even punishment for misdeeds, Jesus certainly did not merit it. He was the one person in all of history who truly did not deserve such wilderness discipline. But that aspect of discipline is only part of the Bible's teaching on the subject and, arguably, not the most prominent part. The other part, that of developing spiritual character and fashioning what God is after in a life, was an aspect of wilderness experience that even Jesus needed. The discipline of the desert was a divine and sovereign forge used by God to shape his Son into the perfect savior of souls.

There are numerous men and women mentioned in Scripture who did not deserve a wilderness of discipline but found themselves stranded in one anyway. I do not think Joseph deserved to be sold into slavery by his brothers[26] or lied about by Potiphar's wife and summarily thrown into prison.[27] Neither do I think that Hagar's actions warranted Sarai's mistreatment[28] or eventual rejection.[29] But, then again, neither wilderness was about deserving something. Instead, each was about needing something: a forge from which could be formed spiritual character, and from which could be fashioned the finished product God was seeking. A wilderness is always about becoming. It is always about the other side of the lake, and what waits for us there.

God is engaged in serious business whenever we walk a wilderness. Whether his intent is course correction or character configuration, he is seeking what he so passionately and purposefully desires. We would do well, then, during our own wilderness times, not to *"make light of the Lord's discipline."*[30] For it is in a wilderness, in such seasons of training-through-discipline, that both our course and character are shaped by God.

---

25. Heb 5:8–9.
26. Gen 37:12–30.
27. Gen 39:1–23.
28. Gen 16:1–16.
29. Gen 21:8–21.
30. Prov 3:11; Heb 12:5.

DESIRE

"A wilderness is that place of discontent where a person is humbled by God, tested in obedience, taught to trust, and trained through discipline in order to become everything and possess everything God desires."

I was given sage advice years ago in the context of the board game chess. In the decades since, I have found it to be crucial advice, not simply for that game, but even more so for life. The advice is: always keep the endgame in view. Speaking personally, when I fail to follow that advice, each time I lose sight of the eternal and focus on the temporal, I suffer. The same was true for Israel.

For the most part, Israel's forty-year trek through the wilderness consisted of repeated bad moves on the people's part, followed by repeated reminders from God to keep the endgame in view. In fact, the whole purpose of that particular wilderness—for that matter, the purpose of any wilderness—can be understood as God, the true master of life, keeping the endgame in view and moving his people toward the end he desires for them.

Dr. Nicholas Perrin's vantage point is helpful:

> Think of it this way. An airline ticket agent who wants to ensure that your bags will be checked through to the appropriate final stop will sometimes ask, "What's your final destination?" The Israelites were not checking their bags into the desert or Sinai; the final stop—the "telos" of their travels—was the Promised Land. All this is bound up in the original call issued to Moses at Sinai, in particular, where Yahweh said: "I have seen the misery of my

people who are in Egypt. I have listened to their cry due to their taskmasters, for I know their sufferings. And I have come down to deliver them from the Egyptians and to bring them out of that land and into a good and broad land, a land flowing with milk and honey" (Exodus 3:7–8a). The focus on the final destination also emerges in Moses' song of victory, when Yahweh deals with Pharaoh and the Egyptians one last time, once and for all: "You stretched out your right hand; the earth swallowed them. In your unconditional love, you led the people whom you redeemed; you guided them to your holy dwelling place" (Exodus 15:12–13). Remarkably, Moses, the very morning after the Red Sea crossing, saw Yahweh as having already taken his people to the land of promise: "you guided them"—perfect tense. This can be explained only one way: Because God's purposes for Israel had been so clearly confirmed through the Exodus, the end goal—though still far off into the future—seemed all but a done deal.[1]

We may lose our focus in a wilderness, but God never does. The endgame is paramount to him. A wilderness is all about God getting what he is after at the end: People who become everything and possess everything he desires. A wilderness becomes the cauldron in which that end is accomplished through the burning away of our impurities and the forging of our character. There is no becoming who God wants us to be, there is no possessing what God wants us to have, without a wilderness. There is no easy path, no convenient correspondence course, and no short cut to Christlikeness. Christlikeness is, after all, the intent of a wilderness.[2]

In retrospect, looking at the definition of a wilderness through New Testament eyes, God seeks to craft the character of his son in our lives.[3] Christlikeness is to characterize us. We are meant to have a *Jesus Shape*

---

1. Perrin, *Exodus Revealed*, 194–95.

2. One could argue, without disagreement from me, that the true endgame in Christianity is seeking and saving the lost. The salvation of the lost is, of course, fundamentally tied to the sanctification of the saved. Sanctification makes effective witness possible. Without Christlikeness, the world quickly dismisses our disingenuous witness for what it really is. That is not to say that we must perfect sanctification before we can witness effectively, but only that the world must see the genuine process of sanctification at work within us for our witness to be truly powerful and effective. It is when people see beyond us to Jesus that salvation is most likely to occur. In other words, we are not sanctified for our own sake, our own selves alone (Jesus himself prayed of his disciples, *"For them I sanctify myself, that they too may be truly sanctified"*—John 17:19), but for the sake of the kingdom and for the sake of others, that the lost might be saved. Granting that, however, in this chapter, my focus is purely on the personal sanctifying purpose and power of the wilderness experience.

3. Rom 8:28–29; 2 Cor 3:18; Eph 4:11–16.

about us.[4] That is God's purposeful intent for our lives, both individually and corporately. As we become progressively more like Jesus, we enter into all that God has for us; we become everything and possess everything he desires.

There is both a refining and a strengthening aspect to a wilderness, just as there is to a cauldron. As smiths once refined liquid silver in a cauldron over intense fire, burning away impurities, so God, the ultimate craftsman, is known to refine his people by placing them in a refiner's pot over intense heat, burning away sin's foreign matter and the world's contaminants, that he might have the finished product he seeks.

An important fact to keep in mind is that it takes no ordinary pot and no ordinary fire to refine silver. Holding a lighted match under a kitchen skillet will not get the job done. The fire must be intense, and the pot must not give off contaminants. Beyond that, it takes special watchfulness on the part of the silversmith. Letting the fire burn too low, failing either to skim impurities from the top or to vaporize them with acid, results in an inferior product.

Similarly, it takes a special process to refine people. A weekend on a hammock strung between date palm trees in an oasis will not accomplish God's end, will not get at the fat and flab, the sin and selfishness around the heart and soul. There must be a wilderness, frequently fiery and intense, to melt down the stubborn sinful stuff that is so much a part of us. There must be God's resolute attention to detail, as well as his firm resolve to have the intended finished product.

In C. S. Lewis' *The Screwtape Letters,* Screwtape said to Wormwood concerning God:

> Sooner or later He withdraws, if not in fact, at least from the conscious experience, all those supports and incentives. He leaves the creature to stand up on its own legs—to carry out from the will alone duties which have lost all relish. It is during

---

4. I first encountered the concept of a *Jesus shape* through a sermon I heard preached by Dr. S. Scott Bartchy. The premise was that the Spirit who was poured out upon the church on the Day of Pentecost was the Spirit of Jesus, i.e., it was *his* Spirit which *he* poured out (Acts 2:33—*"Exalted to the right hand of God, (Jesus) has received from the Father the promised Holy Spirit and has poured out what you now see and hear"*). The result of that outpouring—beyond just the miraculous nature of the day itself—was that the church now lived with a *Jesus shape,* effectively continuing the life and ministry of Jesus in the world. What Jesus *"began to do and teach"* (Acts 1:1), the church continued to do and teach under the influence of the Spirit. Those things Jesus did in Luke's gospel were done by the church in Luke's book of Acts. The Spirit serves God's intended purpose of shaping us, as individual believers *and* as the people of God, into the likeness of his son Jesus.

such tough periods, much more than during the peak periods, that it is growing into the sort of creature He wants it to be.[5]

The *creature* of which Lewis wrote is a child of God. The *tough periods* are wilderness times. God's purpose in it all: growing us "into the sort of creature He wants (us) to be."

In much the same way that silver is finally free of impurities when the artisan sees her or his clear reflection in the molten mass, so God's wilderness will have served its purpose and reached its end when the impurities are gone from our lives, and we clearly reflect the image of his son. There is no refiner's reflection without the refiner's fire. When it comes to refining silver or refining lives, there are no shortcuts.

A nineteenth-century contraband slave, identified only as Brother Thornton, understood well the refining process of a wilderness. Speaking to refugees at Fortress Monroe, Virginia in 1862, he said:

> We have been in the furnace of affliction, and are still, but God only means to separate the dross, and get us so that like the pure metal we may reflect the image of our Purifier, who is sitting by to watch the process. I am assured that what God begins, he will bring to an end. We have need of faith, patience and perseverance, to realize the desired result. There must be no looking back to Egypt. Israel passed forty years in the wilderness, because of their unbelief. What if we cannot see right off the green fields of Canaan, Moses could not. He could not even see how to cross the Red Sea. If we would have greater freedom of body, we must free ourselves from the shackles of sin, and especially the sin of unbelief. We must snap the chain of Satan.[6]

Sometimes, however, the cauldron is not for removing impurities but for creating a stronger alloy. The cauldron of Jesus' wilderness testing, for example, was not intended to burn off impurities— he had none[7]—but to strengthen his character. In our lives, as well, the intense heat of testing or affliction, the cauldron of our various wildernesses, is often used by God to make the pliable metal of our lives better, stronger, more durable, and more useful in his service.

Wilderness suffering is never meaningless but always purposeful. The acute emptiness of a debilitating desert is never merely a *careless* emptiness—God randomly plopping us down on hot sand without any real

---

5. Lewis, *Screwtape Letters*, 47.
6. *American Missionary* 6.2 (February 1862), 33.
7. Isa 53:9; Heb 4:15; 1 Pet 1:18–19.

intent—but always, in the words of Annie Dillard, "the careful emptiness inside a cello or violin."[8] Intentional. Purposeful. Creative.

Wilderness time always serves a divine purpose. "Suffering may be among the sufferer's blessings," wrote Nicholas Wolterstorff in the painful aftermath of his son's tragic death. "In the valley of suffering, despair and bitterness are brewed. But there also character is made. The valley of suffering is the vale of soul-making."[9] Soul-making is the endgame of a wilderness. That endgame is all about what God wants, what God seeks.

Eugene Peterson wrote:

> We live in a time when everyone's goal is to be perpetually healthy and constantly happy. . . . If any one of us fails to live up to the standards that are advertised as normative, we are labeled as a problem to be solved, and a host of well-intentioned people rush to try out various cures on us. . . . The gospel offers a different view of suffering: in suffering we enter into the depths; we are at the heart of things; we are near to where Christ was on the cross.[10]

In light of such reality, Carolyn Custis James wondered:

> I have to ask myself how I can possibly expect to know Jesus as he would want to be known if my life remains unscathed by trouble and grief. How can I hope to grasp anything of God's heart for this broken planet if I never weep because its brokenness touches me and breaks my heart? How can I reflect his image if I never share in his sufferings? And how will any of us ever learn to treasure his 'hesed' and grace if we never experience phases where these blessings seem absent? I wish I could learn these lessons vicariously, but I'm afraid that isn't the norm for any of us. Without knowing suffering and confusion firsthand, we're stuck in the superficial and we cannot know, much less express, the heart of Christ to others.[11]

Soul-making is the endgame of a wilderness.

As God used a wilderness to forge the character of his own son, so he uses a wilderness to forge the character of his son within and among us. Though that is a glorious end, the process itself can be far from enjoyable. It takes a gift of grace for us to look beyond the wilderness to the Land of

---

8. Dillard, *Pilgrim at Tinker Creek*, 106.
9. Wolterstorff, *Lament for a Son*, 97.
10. Peterson, *Long Obedience*, 138.
11. James, *Gospel of Ruth*, 132.

Promise, beyond the cross to the resurrection, beyond the trial to the finished product. If we never look beyond the wilderness itself to the intended end God has in store for us, if we never see the coming-forth-as-gold part that Job saw or the joy-set-before-us part that Jesus saw, then we all too easily become whiners and complainers, after the example of Israel, and like those ancient wilderness wanderers, we find ourselves working against God rather than cooperating with him in his process.

Again quoting Lewis,

> Did you ever think, when you were a child, what fun it would be if your toys could come to life? Well suppose you really could have brought them to life. Imagine turning a tin soldier into a real little man. It would involve turning the tin into flesh. And suppose the tin soldier did not like it. He is not interested in flesh; all he sees is that the tin is being spoiled. He thinks you are killing him. He will do everything he can to prevent you. He will not be made into a man if he can help it. . . .
>
> The real Son of God is at your side. He is beginning to turn you into the same kind of thing as Himself. He is beginning, so to speak, to 'inject' His kind of life and thought, His 'Zoe,' into you; beginning to turn the tin soldier into a live man. The part of you that does not like it is the part that is still tin.[12]

Much of what we dislike about a wilderness, much of what hurts us, much of what we chafe at and fight against, is simply God doing what needs to be done—occasionally stoking the fire, regularly skimming scum from the surface—for us to become everything and possess everything he desires. Whether for banishing sin or building strength, a wilderness always serves God's endgame. With no exception of which I am aware, God's finished product always bears his imprint, which reads, "Made in a Wilderness."

That was God's message through the prophet Isaiah:

> "See, I have refined you, though not as
>   silver;
> I have tested you in the furnace of
>   affliction.
> For my own sake, for my own sake, I do
>   this."[13]

David's song of the wilderness endured by God's people sounded similar strains:

---

12. Lewis, *Mere Christianity*, 154–55, 162.
13. Isa 48:10–11a.

> "He trained us first,
>   passed us like silver through refining fires,
> Brought us into hardscrabble country,
>   pushed us to our very limit,
> Road-tested us inside and out,
>   took us to hell and back;
> Finally he brought us
>   to this well-watered place."[14]

There is always a *"well-watered place"* in God's endgame. Those who remain faithful to God through a wilderness become everything and possess everything he desires. Make no mistake about it: that *"well-watered place"* is awaiting us, but it lies always at the far end of a wilderness.

---

14. Ps 66:10–12, *Message*.

PART III

WILDERNESS TYPES

"This is His judgment, that we are allowed to live without Him in His very presence."

J. W. STEVENSON

THE SOVEREIGN WILDERNESS

Sin and sovereignty are the primary reasons we find ourselves in a wilderness.[1]

At times we wander, as Israel did, because of our own sin and rebellion—perhaps even because of our own stupidity. A friend of mine once got drunk, did some acrobatics from a highway overpass and fell to the pavement below. He spent weeks teetering between life and death, then months in a hospital recuperating, and an even longer stretch in therapy. The first time I visited him in the hospital, he asked, "Why did God do this to me?" Having flunked "Pampering 101" in seminary, I said, "God didn't do anything to you. You did it. You got drunk. You climbed up there. You did the circus act. Don't blame that on God."

Whether or not we are stupid, we *are* all sinners.[2] Face it—Israel had to—most messes we get in, many wildernesses we traverse are the result of our own sin, whether that sin is a wrong moral decision here, a violated biblical principle there, or a moment of rebellion somewhere else.

Other times, however, as when the Spirit directed Jesus from the Jordan after his baptism, we are sovereignly led into a wilderness. A sovereign wilderness is a season which God either purposes or permits and by which he refines our character or resets the direction of our lives—possibly both. When God *purposes* a wilderness, he charts a course intended to keep us as true to his ultimate will as a needle is to the pole. When God *permits* a wilderness, it is often to map a way through a detour and back onto the path of his ultimate will.

I am convinced that, for the most part, those dry and desperate seasons I call the deserts of our lives are not part of God's original plan for us. Saying it another way, a wilderness is rarely God's *Plan A* for his people. The world in which we live is not perfect but fallen—in the same way that we do

1. See footnote 11.
2. Rom 3:23.

not have it all together, but are broken—and that reality can produce its own stretch of wilderness time. Fallenness and brokenness sometime strand us at spiritual dead ends or in a wilderness we never expected—detours of sorts. On those occasions, God rerouts us to get us back on the path where we might become everything and possess everything he desires for us. Sometimes the reroute itself can be a wilderness, but an essential one if we are to reach our divinely purposed destination.

Most wildernesses, at least those in Scripture and in my own experience, are necessary because of deviations from God's *Plan A*. Those deviations most often emanate from points of fallenness and brokenness. They become detours on our spiritual journey, obstacles standing between us and God's ultimate will for us. One thing about this God of the Wilderness, though, he is in no way threatened or thwarted by obstacles and detours. Rather, he works in and through them to see his original purpose realized. For that reason, in his sovereignty, God permits detours.

The concept of God's sovereignty most currently in vogue has strong-arm tendencies to it. Because God is sovereign, it is assumed, he simply bulldozes every impediment in his path, plowing straight ahead and taking the most direct route possible to the realization of his will. In other words, being bigger and stronger than anyone or anything that can come against him, God simply forces his will on persons and events. After all, nothing can limit a sovereign God. It seems to me, though, that a sovereign God can and does limit himself—as with Bethlehem and the cramping restrictions of human flesh or as with Calvary and the inescapable human experience of death—and must be free to limit himself or he would not be sovereign. A God incapable of imposing limits on himself might be many things, but sovereign is not one of them. A God incapable of living within his own self-imposed limits might be many things, but sovereign is not one of them.

I think, in general, that people prefer strong-arm sovereignty because we are threatened by hitches and glitches, by surprises and monkey wrenches thrown into our machinery. God, on the other hand, seems almost to welcome them. At the very least, he is not threatened by them, and is certainly never sidetracked by them. Rather than flexing his celestial muscles and pulverizing the obstacle in his path, which we might expect or even prefer, God simply makes his way around it, almost with an attitude of "Okay . . . well, if that's the way it's going to be, then I'll just go this direction." And he does.

Sovereignty need not bulldoze to get where it is going. Sovereignty is in no way threatened by obstacles strewn in its way. Sovereignty has an infinite number of alternative routes that will still reach the end it has in mind. Sovereignty—certainly that visible in the Old Testament descriptions of God—does not mind delays and detours. Sovereignty is not about the strong-armed threatening of someone; it is about not being threatened by anyone. Sovereignty is not about the strong-armed thwarting of something; it is about not being thwarted by anything.

There is, I believe, a certain vulnerability to God's sovereignty, as odd as that concept might sound. Whether Moses becoming a hunted man and fleeing Egypt for the desert, or Joseph being effectively erased by his brothers, or a handful of disciples being devastated by a crucifixion, God takes the hand he is dealt, plays his card, trumps the opponent and wins the game. Always. Sovereignly. Therefore, when Plan A circles the drain and we suddenly find ourselves stuck with Plan B or Plan C or some plan further down in the alphabet of sovereignty, God is more than capable of reconfiguring the route and still getting us to the place his will intends for us. That is why terrible things that happen to us—even through no fault of our own, even due to the schemes or sins of others—cannot and will not thwart God's sovereign purpose. Our wilderness walking, with all the obstacles and roundabouts we may encounter along the way, does not mess with sovereignty. Nothing and no one messes with sovereignty. Because God is sovereign he will see us through, even though we may see no way through. That fact is true, no matter whose *fault* a wilderness is.

We seem better able to deal with crisis if we can assign blame. But in a sovereign wilderness, that is not always possible. Sometimes the only explanation for a wilderness we walk—a wilderness that is not our fault or directly the fault of another—is that we live in a broken world. Quite simply, "we are broken ourselves and can't escape the brokenness and loss of our fallen world."[3]

When it comes to assigning fault for a wilderness, it may prove helpful to think in terms of the New Madrid Fault, which has been known to occasionally impact my midwestern world. That fracture in the earth's crust renders the St. Louis area, where I live, vulnerable to earthquakes. If an earthquake were to occur along that line, devastating my house and its contents, it would not be my fault; rather, it would be due to a fault line running through the region.[4] Because of sin, there is a fault line running

---

3. James, *Gospel of Ruth*, 36

4. See Hahn's work *Lord Have Mercy*, where speaking of original sin, he wrote, "Even the word choice—fault—might lead you to believe that original sin is something that renders us guilty. But it isn't. Think of fault here in the sense of the San Andreas Fault, the fracture in the earth's crust that renders California vulnerable to devastating earthquakes. That's what the fault of original sin does in the soul. It isn't my fault, but it's like a fault line that runs through my soul and inclines me to be separated from God." Hahn, *Lord Have Mercy*, 73.

through humanity. Occasionally it rocks our world, impacting our lives. It is not our fault, but we suffer nonetheless. In a broken world, fault lines are inescapable. It is not unusual for God's people to suffer because of someone else's sin. Whether the holocaust of the Jews, the toppling of New York City's twin towers, or a drunk driver striking and killing someone, we know that innocent people, many good and godly people, suffer due to the sins of others. Like fish living in a pond, when the water turns stagnant, all suffer.

Facing the repercussions of our own sins is difficult enough, yet most of us understand cause-and-effect, what the apostle Paul called the law of sowing and reaping,[5] and accept the fact that we must pay, at least to some degree, for our own sinful choices, as well as for our neighbors' sinful choices to which we acquiesce. But understanding and accepting suffering when it is due to someone else's sinful choices, over which we have no control, is decidedly more difficult.

Israel suffered for a generation because, initially, ten men chose not to trust God.[6] That lack of trust, and the disobedience which followed, spread through the camp like wildfire on a parched prairie.[7] Moses, Joshua and other innocent people suffered because of the sins of others. Later, in the Land of Promise, all the people of God walked a desert of defeat and death because one of their number, a man named Achan, acted unfaithfully.[8]

In those cases, neither wilderness was God's original route for his children. On the East side of the Jordan, God had only one stop in mind—at the mountain to get the tablets inscribed with ten commandments—then it was onto the Promised Land. Once across the river, God had only victory in mind—Ai was to fall as Jericho had—then it was on to take possession of the country. In both instances, God's children forced detours. God's response was not to fatalistically throw up his hands and whine, "Well, these people have royally messed up my plans; what am I to do now?" Rather, when his people forced a detour on him, God devised a new route which, starting from where they were, still led to his ultimate will for their lives.

Sovereignty also permits a wilderness that is the result, not of another's sin, but of Satan's direct attack on God's people. There are times and places that the story of Job seems to play out all over again in the lives of God's faithful children: Satan saying, *"Turn him over to me; he's mine to test;"*[9] and

---

5. Gal 6:7. Cf. Rom 1:18–27.
6. Num 13:1–33.
7. Num 14:1–38.
8. Josh 7:1–26.
9. Cf. Job 1:6—2:5.

God responding, *"Very well, but not more than he can bear."*[10] Yet, even when permitting satanic aggression, which can temporarily knock us off our feet or off our course, God is very much at work, making a way for his chosen to recover and return to the path of his ultimate will. In other words, detours do not detour God. That is the thing we must not forget about sovereignty. Detours do not detour God.

Joseph may represent the clearest example of that truth. Not every detail of Joseph's life was scripted by God, any more than every detail of our lives is. An honest read of the story convinces me that the lion's share of Joseph's trouble was the result of sins by others, though some may possibly have been the result of his own pride. Flaunting those dream-stories in his brothers' faces—could he not see the consequences? Personally, I doubt the sincerity of Joseph as a seventeen-year-old. He did not, for example, draw dad aside and ask, "Do you think God is trying to tell me something through these dreams?" Instead, he said to his brothers, on at least two occasions, "Hey, guys, listen to this . . .."[11]

Then again, maybe Joseph was sincere and completely innocent in the whole affair. Maybe he was merely affirming, as had Moses and Abraham before him, the truths that God had spoken or shown. Maybe every bit of blame should lie at the feet of his brothers. I was not there, and I do not know. Either way, I firmly believe that God's will was to use Joseph as the savior of Israel. But I also believe that the route Joseph took to get to that place was not the same route God originally had in mind—a route, a plan, hinted at in those dreams. Those plans were subverted, perhaps in some way by Joseph's own pride, but definitely by the sin of his brothers and, once in Egypt, by the sin of a seductress, the wife of Joseph's master. Satan's attempts to stop God's will from being fulfilled in and through Joseph's life are evident through an entire string of events related in Genesis 37–41.

Satan, it seems, did not like Joseph's dreams any more than did Joseph's brothers. Hence, the forced detours. But, again, detours do not detour God. Faced with a series of detours, each of which had the potential to stop his divine plan dead in its tracks, God turned to what some theologians who work in big words and phrases call his "circumstantial will."[12] Put simply, God adapted to his environment. He reconfigured the route, via the hand he was dealt, and still got Joseph to where he wanted him to be. God's plan

---

10. Job 2:6. Cf. 1 Cor 10:13.

11. Gen 37:2–11.

12 A good and simple read on this topic is Leslie Weatherhead's *Will of God*, where the author differentiates between the *intentional* will of God (God's ideal plan for us); the *circumstantial* will of God (God's plan within certain circumstances); and the *ultimate* will of God (God's final realization of his purposes).

was not prevented because of a series of unexpected, puny detours—which, by the way, appear *anything but* puny to our finite eyes. They are, in fact, *nothing but* puny to God.

Faced with a circumstance that he had probably never *intended*—Joseph locked away in prison and forgotten—God used that imprisonment to get Joseph to Pharaoh. On the surface of the story, God already had a way in the works—Joseph in Potiphar's house and quickly moving up the ranks—and it is not too difficult to see how that would have ultimately led to the same end. The point is, however, that God countered every detour with a reroute and still got Joseph in place to save the Messianic line when that line most needed saved. Joseph's wilderness time, like the wilderness time of so many in Scripture, was not so much *planned* by God as it was *permitted*. Even the detours, whether imposed by others or by Satan, were rerouted and used by God to accomplish his ultimate will.

There is such a thing as God's sovereign permitting of a wilderness. Other times, however, God does more than merely *permit* a wilderness; he *purposes* one. Occasionally, he sovereignly leads his children into a wilderness of his own making. He charts a pilgrimage, which his children might never have charted or chosen for themselves and makes it the route by which they become everything and possess everything he desires.

The Hebrew people's initial wilderness time—the eighteen months or so between leaving the Nile and reaching the Jordan—was devised by God to meld a slave people into a nation, imprint a new law on their minds and hearts, and, in effect, reintroduce himself to them. It was in every way a sovereign, divinely purposed wilderness.

God also purposed a wilderness for his son Jesus.[13] It is possible that Satan's testing of Jesus followed a scenario similar to that of Satan's testing of Job—Satan to God: *"Let me have him to test;"* God to Satan: *"Alright, but I get him back in forty days"*—but whatever Satan's involvement in that wilderness, it was from beginning to end a place and a period of God's sovereignty. Jesus, remember, *"was led by the Spirit into the desert"*[14] and was led there *"to be tempted by the devil."*[15] From that sovereign, God-purposed wilderness, Jesus emerged perfectly oriented to his father's will, thoroughly equipped to see his work through to completion, and—Luke added—walking *"in the power of the Spirit."*[16]

---

13. Matt 4:1–11.
14. Matt 4:1.
15. Matt 4:1.
16. Luke 4:14

There are times when we are led into a wilderness by the Spirit (as was Jesus) or by a clear call from God (as was Israel). For lack of a better term, we could call those experiences *purposed* wildernesses. Other times we are forced into desert places by burdensome circumstances[17] or through the sins of others.[18] For lack of a better term, we could call those experiences *permitted* wildernesses. Whether purposed or permitted, a wilderness provides few answers for those who wander its often-severe stretches. God's sovereign will is infrequently shared with desert travelers. Like Abram of old, we must be content to journey toward a land God will *one day* show us.[19] But not now. A wilderness has "far more to do with trust than with certainty."[20]

What that means at the practical level of Christian and church is well-stated by J. W. Stevenson in his moving memoir as pastor of a small village church in Scotland during the dicey days before World War II:

> This is our calling—to go out with decisive step even while we are in hesitancy, to go to the act of thanksgiving before we are healed, to distribute Christ's bread to the hungry before we know it will be sufficient. It is not for us to learn certainty but to learn to trust ourselves to God, and to do what we know He is expecting of us while we are still uncertain; to commit ourselves to Him hour by hour through our very weakness, through the very circumstances which would otherwise be for our hurt, the mischances, the limitations—so that all things begin to work together for good. There can be no circumstance so frustrating that it cannot be made the means of committing us more closely to Him.[21]

In a sentence, wilderness travelers do not see or know everything God does. In truth, we see and know very little, except that the terrain is hard, the conditions harsh, and faithfulness is required.

Living in a wilderness can be like living on a single face of a Rubik's Cube. That six-sided puzzle with movable faces and rows was quite the rage

---

17. As were Hagar (Gen 16:1–16; 21:8–21), David (1 Sam 23:7—27:3; 2 Sam 15:1—19:8; 1 Chr 12:8—21:29), Elijah (1 Kgs 18:16—19:21), Hezekiah (2 Chr 32:24–31), and Job (Job 2:1–3).

18 As was Joseph (Gen 37:12–30).

19. Gen 12:1.

20. Taylor, *Leaving Church*, 170. Taylor's entire quote reads: ". . . I had arrived at an understanding of faith that had far more to do with trust than with certainty. I trusted God to be God even if I could not say who God was for sure. I trusted God to sustain the world although I could not say for sure how that happened. I trusted God to hold me and those I loved, in life and in death, without giving me one shred of conclusive evidence that it was so."

21. Stevenson, *God in My Unbelief*, 148.

in the 1980s. Each face of the cube had three rows of three squares (three rows of red, of yellow, of blue, and so on), and the whole thing was so put together that you could turn an entire face clockwise or counterclockwise and any row of squares horizontally or vertically. The purpose was to shift the colors by twisting rows and faces so that, in the end, each side of the cube was comprised of its own single color.

I tend to think of our wilderness treks in such terms. It is routinely hard to see a pattern, a rhyme or reason, to what God is doing through our desert days. It is helpful, at least for me, to remember that we live on, and therefore see, only one side of the cube. Had we eyes to view the remaining five faces, we would see that all the twisting and turning, all the shifting of rows and changing of colors, far from representing senseless or even sadistic behavior on God's part, represent instead the labor of wise, purposeful, and loving hands. The pattern God weaves, we seldom see. The work God performs, we rarely understand. Often, God "calls us to trust him when we're missing big pieces of the puzzle and he isn't giving answers."[22] Yet, God regularly orchestrates his perfect will through circumstances that confound us, and he routinely does his finest work through our fiercest trials.

The same sovereign Lord who oversaw Joseph's life oversees our lives. Through all the twisting and turning of events, through all the surprising obstacles and sudden dead ends, he weaves a pattern and a way that gets us from where we are to where we most need to be to serve his ultimate will. What we often interpret as an absent God who has abandoned us to the elements is, in fact, an ever-present God who is purposefully working in our lives so that we might become everything and possess everything he desires.

In her marvelous treatment of the Old Testament book of Ruth, a narrative told from the perspective of Naomi—a woman whose wilderness agonies included the death of her husband and both sons, as well as the loss of her social status, income, and societal protection—Carolyn Custis James addressed the issue of wilderness perspective:

> . . . it would be nice to board a spacecraft and look at our own lives from above the earth's atmosphere—to be able to see the end from the beginning and how all the smaller pieces of our stories fit into the bigger story God is weaving. From the ground, about all we can see is where we happen to be at the moment— the pain and regrets, the losses, the broken-down lives. From the human vantage point, we only see bits and pieces of what he is doing, and sometimes we, like Naomi, can't see anything that helps us make sense of what is going wrong in our lives.

22. James, *Gospel of Ruth*, 57.

If Naomi had the benefit of heaven's perspective on what was happening in her life, she would see that the painful path she was traveling was not a dead end. What appears from Naomi's point of view to be a very private grief and deeply personal struggle with God is actually a crucial piece of a larger master plan. Those who already know how her story turns out have seen that God is giving Naomi a key role in events that ultimately lead to the birth of Israel's mighty King David, and beyond that to the birth of Jesus—the clearest, strongest evidence that God cares more than anyone imagines about what happens to us here on earth. Earthbound Naomi would never know how big a role God was giving her. She doesn't even realize yet that God is using suffering to equip her for the pivotal role of raising a child who just happens to be the grandfather of Israel's future king.[23]

That is the nature of a sovereign wilderness. Discerning the many facets and features of such a wilderness is difficult, if not impossible. Knowing, for example, how long the trek will last, where a twist or turn might take us, why the pain must be so intense, or what God has in mind at any given mile marker, are matters we are seldom privy to as we walk its puzzling terrain. God usually treats our wilderness as his own private affair and is not prone to fill in missing details. At least, that seems to be the evidence of the biblical record. God knows what we do not. That is the bottom line. He knows, and that is sufficient. The specifics are in his hands, not ours.

What *is* in our hands is faithfulness. A wilderness demands a walk of faith. The tricky, often treacherous terrain requires a conscientious walk of trust and obedience. God does not suspend his demands for faithfulness in a wilderness. He did not do it for Israel or for Jesus, and he has no intent of doing it for us. Faithfulness, though essential in every walk of life, is especially crucial in the wild, where confusion and disorientation reign. Without a faith-walk, we easily lose our bearing. Faithfulness, like a gyroscope, keeps us properly oriented.

As a youth, I worked one summer at a factory in my hometown. One day the maintenance man led me to the roof to assist in repair work. Handing me a tool belt, he stepped onto a wooden plank which led from the roof we were on to the roof of the next building, calling to me, "Come on!"

I had walked two-by-fours previously, but never two-by-fours suspended between buildings with nothing but concrete below. It was not that a misstep had not mattered before; it had. I could have lost my balance and possibly twisted an ankle or skinned a knee; maybe even have broken a bone. But a misstep now—doing a highwire act between rooftops—had

23. James, *Gospel of Ruth.*, 131.

more serious and threatening consequences. I could lose my balance, fall to the concrete below, and be seriously hurt. I could even die. That day I found myself facing a walk of faith, where the slightest misstep could get me killed.

In an oasis and a wilderness alike, *all* missteps matter. That is a given. Whether we are walking barefoot in cool grass or sandaled on hot sand, ordering our steps is always vital. Whether God's people are camping at Elim or trudging through Sinai, faithfulness is always crucial. But an oasis is more like walking a plank lying flat on a roof, while a wilderness is more like walking a two-by-four between high buildings. It is much easier to balk at or refuse all together a faith-demanding step when faced with the prospect that even the tiniest misstep could be our undoing. A wilderness is more prone than is an oasis to bring us face-to-face with immediate life-and-death situations.

A wilderness demands a walk of faith.

It is not that missteps do not matter in an oasis; they do. It is not that ordering our steps does not matter in an oasis; it does. Faithfulness is always and everywhere crucial. But Israel taking a misstep amid the springs and palms of Elim was not as immediately life-threatening as taking a misstep amid the sands of Sinai and becoming the dinner entrée for a party of vultures. Faithfulness, always urgent and imperative, may be even more so in a wilderness.

A wilderness demands a walk of faith—not two-by-fours-securely-on-the-roof faith, but two-by-fours-spanning-buildings faith.

In a wilderness, where abandoning faithfulness can be a recurring temptation, we must be especially resolute about maintaining a walk of trusting obedience. Anyone who has walked a severe wilderness knows that obedience is not easy, but it is essential. Like Job, when the going gets especially tough, we must not depart from the commands of God's lips.[24] To do so can prove fatal. In a wilderness—whether one of sovereignty or of sin—every misstep, like every right step, has immediate and decisive consequences. Because God is God, because God is sovereign *of* and *in* a wilderness, out of every test and trial of our lives, he will have the victory, if we remain faithful.

The apostle Peter wrote:

> Pure gold put in the fire comes out of it proved pure; genuine faith put through this suffering comes out proved genuine. When Jesus wraps this all up, it's your faith, not your gold, that God will have on display as evidence of his victory.[25]

---

24. Job 23:12.
25. 1 Pet 1:7, *Message*.

THE SIN WILDERNESS

For Israel, a wilderness was what stood between the nation's rebellion and its reconciliation. It was that stretch of territory and time which began in disobedience on the banks of the Jordan[1] and ended only when God was ready to lead his people out and on. Unlike the wilderness Jesus endured millennia later, which was sovereignly orchestrated by God, Israel's wilderness was its own fault, the result of sin.

Unlike a sovereign wilderness, which finds its source in God (his wisdom and will), a sin wilderness finds its source in us (our rebel hearts and stubborn wills). As there is a wilderness which is God's doing and not the consequence of our sin, so there is a wilderness which is, at its heart, a portion of the interest we pay on our sin.

America's first influential African American poet, Paul Lawrence Dunbar, expressed the out-and-out extortion of a sin wilderness, when he wrote:

> "This is the debt I pay
> Just for one riotous day,
> Years of regret and grief,
> Sorrow without relief.
>
> Pay it I will to the end—
> Until the grave, my friend,
> Gives me a true release—
> Gives me the clasp of peace.
>
> Slight was the thing I bought,
> Small was the debt I thought,
> Poor was the loan at best—
> God! But the interest!"[2]

1. Num 14:1–23.
2. Dunbar, "Debt."

The Hebrew children could relate to that, paying forty years' worth of interest on a moment's worth of rebellion at the Jordan. David as well, on a pair of occasions, ignored the small print and ended up paying long-term, hefty interest on what had initially looked like a cut-rate bargain that would put no strain on his budget. And what about the this-world judgment and long periods of exile which God forced on his people that were the direct result of sin? The Old Testament narrative streams with stories of sin wildernesses.

As a rule, whether those desert times are more severe than ones of God's sovereignty, they seem to last much longer, sometimes stretching for generations. And they do not end—or so it appears—until God decides they have run their purposeful course. We may be hurry-up ready for a wilderness to end, but the biblical record reveals that it will not end until God has accomplished his endgame goal. That truth is enough to make us wish the wilderness stories were not in the Old Testament, to dismiss them as antiquated, to call them overstated scare tactics to keep people in line, or to see them as aberrations of God's character which were corrected by the time the New Testament was written. At the very least, it is enough to make us think that we do not really need those unsophisticated, unscientific, uncomfortable stories. But we do need them.

One of the reasons we need the Old Testament desert stories of Israel and others is that they are invaluable reminders of how costly sin is, of how high a price must be paid for carelessness and unfaithfulness, of how exorbitant is rebellion's interest and what a heavy toll it exacts from those in its debt. To view Israel's sin wilderness as simply an interesting but ancient tale with little, if any, contemporary value is to miss its clear and critical message about sin and its consequences. *"Even if it was written in Scripture long ago,"* counseled the apostle Paul, *"you can be sure it's written for us."*[3] About the specific details of Israel's wilderness journey, he wrote: *"These are all warning markers—DANGER!—in our history books, written down so that we don't repeat their mistakes. Our positions in the story are parallel—they at the beginning, we at the end—and we are just as capable of messing it up as they were."*[4] To Paul, all of Scripture's narratives, definitely Old Testament desert stories, were essential examples and lessons for the people of God. He knew, and felt it important for us to know, that:

> *Every part of Scripture is God-breathed and useful one way or another—showing us truth, exposing our rebellion, correcting our*

---

3. Rom 15:4, *Message*.
4. 2 Cor 10:11–12, *Message*.

mistakes, training us to live God's way. Through the Word we are put together and shaped up for the tasks God has for us.[5]

A vital truth of those long-ago desert days is that sin routinely results in a prolonged wilderness and its interest eats away at our lives. If we do not respond promptly and properly to a wilderness of sin, our payments never touch the principal of our rebellion. That, of course, translates into a long, hard stretch of time.

Israel's death march through the desert was costly and the interest excessive. On one occasion, the arid earth even cracked open and swallowed two hundred fifty Israelites. About the same number were consumed by heaven-sent fire and nearly fifteen thousand more died in a plague that followed—all the result of the community's sin.[6] By far, however, the steepest interest was paid by those who were twenty years or older when the Hebrew children left Egypt. Of that multitude, only two—Joshua and Caleb—entered Canaan. All others died in the wilderness.[7]

Judgment can be, and often is, severe in a wilderness of sin. It was for Israel. How difficult it must have been for those Hebrew children, having received the law at Sinai and standing at long last on the edge of promise, to hear God say, *"tomorrow you must turn back and travel through the wilderness."*[8] They had just left that hard place—none too soon in the minds of most—when they were abruptly ordered to retreat. The very act of turning back must have seemed costly enough in itself to Israel, but there was more to come, hefty interest yet to be paid:

> *In this desert your bodies will fall—every one of you twenty years old or more who was counted in the census and who has grumbled against me. Not one of you will enter the land I swore with uplifted hand to make your home, except Caleb son of Jephunneh and Joshua son of Nun. As for your children that you said would be taken as plunder, I will bring them in to enjoy the land you have rejected. But you—your bodies will fall in this desert. Your children will be shepherds here for forty years, suffering for your unfaithfulness, until the last of your bodies lies in the desert. For forty years—one year for each of the forty days you explored the land—you will suffer for your sins and know what it is like to have me against you.*[9]

5. 2 Tim 3:16-17, *Message.*
6. Num 16:1-50.
7. Num 14:20-35; Ps 95:7b-11; Heb 3:7-19.
8 Num 14:25, *Modern Language Bible.*
9. Num 14:29-34.

On its surface, the sin that sent Israel back to the wilderness might have seemed small to many in camp, but the interest was about to eat them all alive: *"When Moses reported this to all the Israelites, they mourned bitterly. Early the next morning they went up toward the high hill country. 'We have sinned,' they said. 'We will go up to the place the Lord promised'."*[10] God had dealt with feigned repentance before. In Egypt, Pharaoh had become adept at it.[11] God had not been duped then and was not duped this time around. He knew the hearts of his people as he knew the heart of Pharaoh, and he could instantly tell remorse from repentance. Hearts bent on sin will not be healed by God's yielding to dreams of a Promised Land. Some hearts can only be healed through a wilderness. Other hearts may never be healed at all. A heart that can hurt can be healed.

To genuinely grieve over and repent of our sin, to agonize over how profoundly we have hurt God and to recalibrate our hearts to his will, is to position ourselves where God can heal our hearts. But if we are looking for a quick remedy, expecting a wink-of-the-eye recuperation period, then we are in for massive disappointment. The testimony of Scripture's many desert stories is overwhelming that the finished product of a whole and healthy heart, beating once more in sync with God's will, is the result of intentional and intense wilderness therapy.

We slip into rebellion, as did Israel, quickly and easily, and prefer to slip out of it, then into repentance and recovery, the same way. If given the choice, we would almost certainly opt for a swifter, simpler way, but God seems always to prefer the Sinai route. God, as every wilderness trekker learns, is not the elected leader of a democracy.

It might help to think in terms of bauxite, iron and coal. If allowed to vote on whether to experience great heat and pressure over prolonged time, those raw materials might well turn thumbs down on the whole process. But if they did, they would miss the transforming process that produces something beautiful and better—aluminum, steel and diamonds. Take away the process and the product is lost.

Without a wilderness forcing us to come to terms with sin, not merely at the surface of our being but also at its very core, there would be no such things as spiritual growth and maturity, no such thing as Christlikeness. Ultimately, God would have failure-to-thrive infants on his hands. Desert heat, plus desert time, plus desert pressure combine to purge and purify our

---

10. Num 14:39–40.
11. Exod 8:8, 29; 9:27–28; 10:16–17.

minds and hearts while transforming us into the type of people God longs for us to be.[12]

A wilderness ordeal often becomes God's chosen process to eradicate sin so that a holy heart might be formed within us. I am not talking about the forgiveness of our sins leading to the salvation of our souls. Obviously, God has, in Jesus, provided a way for us to be forgiven of sin and free of its eternal consequences. I am talking, instead, of those sins—many of them habitual and ingrained, many of them long-term residents in our rebel hearts—that must be dealt with by God, here and now, before we can become everything and possess everything he desires. Those sins seldom go away for long and seem immune to sudden flashes of conviction, confession, and repentance. It routinely takes a wilderness to dredge up those sins from the cellars of our souls and send them packing for good. The process is painful but essential if God is to have what he seeks. Take away the process and the product is lost.

God does not grant voting rights to kingdom citizens, and for good reason. That reason has nothing to do with his being a tyrannical despot, but everything to do with his being an omnipotent lover who knows what is best and works what is best for those he loves. The wilderness process is not for his sadistic pleasure, but for our spiritual perfection. It is not an attempt to ruin us, but to refine us, restore us, remake us. Historically, God's people persist in thinking that a slap on the hand and a do-not-do-that-again reminder, instead of a stint in a wilderness, should do the trick. Being grounded for a while, rather than given to the desert, should produce the finished product God wants. We expect our departure from sin and our arrival at spiritual maturity to be easy and quick, perhaps even instantaneous. Biblically, those are unrealistic expectations.

I am convinced, from decades of Scripture study and living in Christian community, that true spiritual growth forms primarily, not by sudden lurches and leaps in wide-open spaces under clear, bright skies, but more like stalactites and stalagmites form, by steady drips and drops over long

---

12. There is nothing quick or easy about spiritual formation (growth into Christlikeness). There are no shortcuts to becoming the people God longs for us to be. For example, the maturity of which the apostle Paul wrote happens over prolonged time, indicated by his references to people growing (Eph 4:11–16) and fruit ripening (Gal 5:22–26), to mention only a pair of analogies. Change—if we are talking serious, metamorphosis-like change, and we *are* talking such change whenever we speak of being transformed into the likeness of Jesus—is not as simple as changing from work clothes into dress clothes for an evening out on the town. As one of Kathryn Stockett's characters says in *The Help*, "And Miss Skeeter asking don't I want to change things, like changing Jackson, Mississippi gone be like changing a lightbulb." Stockett, *Help*, 28. Spiritual formation is, in truth, the process of a lifetime.

stretches of time in deep darkness. We might rather have it otherwise, but Scripture seems insistent on that point.

Anne Lamott wrote:

> I wish grace and healing were more abracadabra kinds of things; also that delicate silver bells would ring to announce grace's arrival. But no, it's clog and slog and scootch, on the floor, in silence, in the dark.
>
> I suppose that if you were snatched out of the mess, you'd miss the lesson; the lesson is the slog. I grew up thinking that lessons should be more like the von Trapp children: more marionettes, more drindls and harmonies. But no: it's slog, bog, scootch.[13]

We prefer as little distance as possible between confession of sin and victory over it, and as little as possible of the slog, bog, and scootch. We want to get home where we belong a fraction-of-a-second after leaving where we do not belong. Better yet, in the words of Judy Delton, we would like to experience *"arrival without leaving home."*[14] We embrace a spirituality of shortcuts and convenience, having convinced ourselves that God does too. In an insightful assessment of the modern church, Sue Monk Kidd wrote, "When it comes to religion today, we tend to be long on butterflies and short on cocoons."[15] But did you ever try to produce a butterfly without a cocoon, or to rush the creature out of its chrysalis? Attempt to shortcut the process of metamorphosis and just see what happens. No, do not, because Annie Dillard already told us what happens.

In her book *Pilgrim at Tinker Creek*, she shared an experience from her grade school classroom:

> Once, when I was ten or eleven years old, my friend Judy brought a Polyphemus moth cocoon. . . . The teacher kept the cocoon in her desk all morning and brought it out when we were getting restless before recess. In a book we found what the adult moth would look like . . . a mighty wraith, a beating essence of the hardwood forest, alien-skinned and brown with spread blind eyes. This was the giant moth packed in the faded cocoon. . . .
>
> We passed the cocoon around; it was heavy. As we held it in our hands, the creature within warmed and squirmed. We were delighted and wrapped it tighter in our fists. The pupa began to jerk violently, in heart-stopping knocks. . . . We kept passing it

---

13.. Lamott, *Grace (Eventually)*, 50–51.
14. Delton, Introduction to *Most Common Writing Mistakes*, 1.
15. Kidd, "When The Heart Waits," *Whittenburg Door* (March/April 1991).

around. When it came to me again it was hot as a bun; it jumped half out of my hand. The teacher intervened. She put it, still heaving and banging, in the ubiquitous Mason jar.

It was coming. There was no stopping it now, January or not. One end of the cocoon dampened and gradually frayed into a furious battle. The whole cocoon twisted and slapped around in the bottom of the jar.... It emerged at last, a sodden crumple....

The chemical that coated his wings like varnish, stiffening them permanently, dried and hardened his wings as they were. He was a monster in a Mason jar. Those huge wings stuck on his back in a torture of random pleats and folds, wrinkled as a dirty tissue, rigid as leather. They made a single nightmare clump still racked with useless, frantic convulsions.[16]

At recess, in the cold of the concrete schoolyard, someone finally set the moth free. Dillard concluded: "He heaved himself down the asphalt driveway by infinite degrees, unwavering. His hideous crumpled wings lay glued and rucked on his back, perfectly still now, like a collapsed tent."[17]

Wilderness time, like cocoon time, must run its course. To take matters into our own hands, to attempt to circumvent or shorten the process, is to invade a sacred domain and invite tragedy. In the words of Jay Kessler, "If you assist a moth from a cocoon, or a bird from an egg, you endanger its life. The incubation time and thrashings of birth are necessary for growth and strength. By interrupting the process, you may unwittingly create a deformed monster."[18]

There is a lot of thrashing, banging, heaving, and violent jerking in a sin wilderness. God, however, always keeps the endgame in view, and is not about to interrupt the process. He is waiting on and working toward an entirely new thing—a "new creature" is what the apostle Paul called it[19]— which only careful, purposeful time, heat, and pressure can produce. Some things should not be rushed, cannot be rushed, if we are to reach the best of all possible ends. In the same way, for example, that we would not rush a surgeon removing a malignant tumor but would expect her to stay at it long enough to make certain that all cancer was eradicated and a life of health and wholeness lay before us, we must not rush God, whose wilderness

---

16. Dillard, *Pilgrim at Tinker Creek*, 61–62.
17. Dillard, *Pilgrim at Tinker Creek*, 62.
18. Kessler, *Growing Places*, 111–12.
19. 2 Cor 5:17.

surgery seeks to remove our rebel hearts and replace them with new hearts, healthy and holy hearts, hearts that do his will.[20]

If God were dealing with something merely cosmetic, like removing a pimple from our nose or a wart from our toe, that would be another thing entirely. When dealing with something as ingrained and deadly as sin, however, God is probing far beneath the surface, deep within our hearts, souls and psyches to the very wellspring of our rebellion. Some things simply cannot be cured with the age-old prescription "take two tablets and call me in the morning." Some things, like habitual, ingrained sin, defy easy remedies and convenient over-the-counter concoctions. Instead, they require the burning radiation of a desert sun and the skillful scalpel of the wilderness surgeon.

A wilderness for sin is often as imperative as surgery for cancer. Like all serious surgery, a wilderness is painful and its recuperation period lengthy, but it is often our only hope of healing. Because a wilderness deals with as terminal a thing as sin, its treatment must be invasive and radical. That makes a sin wilderness, like any serious surgery, a fearful, risky, dangerous thing. God, of course, far from being a good-old-boy offering a cheer-up slap on the back, is the surgeon holding the scalpel and getting down to life-and-death business.

As Barbara Brown Taylor admitted, however, that image of God is no longer in vogue.

> For many Christians I know, the idea of divine dangerousness went out of fashion shortly after the book of second Kings was written, or the book of Amos at the very latest. In the traditional understanding, Jesus put an end to all that by volunteering to satisfy God's wrath, and since then those who follow him have had nothing more to fear from God. God has become a great friend who would like to get to know us better, if we can find the time. And if we cannot, then God loves us anyway. 'The fear of the Lord' has become as outdated as an ephod.[21]

---

20. Jer 31:23–34; Ezek 36:22–38.

21. Taylor, *Leaving Church*, 189. In his creative work *If God Kept a Diary*, 60, Collin Morris entered the following paragraph into the Divine's Diary: "There is a prudent element in all religion. Deep beneath all the rituals, liturgy and fine sentiments there lurks a desire to domesticate me, to turn away in advance of my wrath. It is the tragic illusion of the earnestly religious that they not only think this possible but also that they have accomplished it. They begin to treat me as though I were a great cuddly moth-eaten lion without teeth. I can tell when they lose their respect and begin to presume—their imagery gets less primitive and their language more philosophical; fear gives way to urbanity. I cease to be the hissing serpent or ravening wolf or swooping eagle and become the ground of being or the unmoved mover or the great first cause—titles to be argued

But listen well to those from Scripture days onward who have endured a sin wilderness to come forth restored and remade, transformed into something new, nobler and far better than before, and they tell the tale of an almost indistinguishable distance between their fear of God and his love for them. Taylor wrote that many, from Bible days and times since, experienced encounters with the Divine that:

> ... included glimpses of the God who is as far above them on the food chain as an eagle is to a mouse. When they will talk about this at all, they do not speak like mice whose bones have been picked clean. They speak like mice who have been lifted high into the heavens where they have seen themselves, the world, and the lives they lead with a terrible new clarity. Set down again, they cannot look at anything the same way they once did, which means that they cannot live the same way either. Because their fear proved to be the means of their transformation, they do not want to get over it. Their time aloft has brought them as close to an eagle as most of them will ever get, which makes their terror appropriate. Their fear of the Lord and the Lord's love of them are two windows on the same reality.[22]

There is an element of great grace in a sin wilderness—a severe grace, to be sure, but one that leaves us transformed by the fearful and fearsome love of God. Ultimately, of course, it is better to avoid a sin wilderness altogether. Obedience is always preferable to disobedience, and not needing a wilderness to deal with sin is always better than needing one because of sin.

As a child, growing up with 1950s television programming, I was mesmerized by the weekly heroics of Lassie, a collie who was always saving the day by saving someone or something. I vividly remember an episode where Lassie felt sorry for a prize horse that was locked in a barn and, so, let it out. The rest of the program showed the horse, as well as little Timmy (who had gone out in search of the horse), facing edge-of-your-seat danger, not only from inhospitable terrain, but also from a ferocious mountain lion, which just happened to be on the prowl.

In the end, of course, Lassie saved the day—and the horse, and Timmy—and everyone was doting on the dog and singing her praises right before the closing credits rolled. Even with a seven-year-old's inexperienced logic, however, something did not add up to me. I remember asking my mom, "Why are they so happy with Lassie? She's the one that let the horse

---

about rather than to instil (sic) awe." Morris, *If God Kept a Diary*, 60.

22. Taylor, 189–90.

out in the first place. If she hadn't done that, nobody would have been in any danger."

"Well, she saved the horse . . . and little Timmy."

"Yeah, I know, but she's the one that put the horse and Timmy in danger to begin with."

The horse was back in the barn, the door securely shut, and everyone was praising Lassie. Another happy ending allowing us to rest easy for another week. But something within me was saying to the dog, "Don't you ever open that door and let that horse out again!" I understood my mother's point and I was glad that Lassie saved the horse. But I thought then, and still think, that it would have been better had Lassie not caused the problem in the first place. A lot of drama and trauma, as well as life-and-death danger could have been avoided had Lassie simply repressed the urge to open the door.

In that TV episode from long ago is a lesson for every one of us. I have personally benefited from every sin wilderness I have walked. They have served me well when I have needed them most. I have learned, I have grown, I have become a better person, I have become more like Jesus. I have emerged from every sin wilderness wiser and stronger than when I entered. In truth, we are never meant to exit a wilderness the way we entered it, but always better, stronger, purer. We are meant to come out changed. Sin wildernesses have consistently changed my life for good, for God. I have always emerged different, more like Jesus than I was when I had entered the desert. When needed, a sin wilderness has been a savior and a sanctifier in my spiritual journey. However—and this is imperative to grasp—I have not emerged from that desert as wise or as strong as I would have been had I never needed it. It is much more important that I obey in the first place than it is that I benefit from a sin wilderness. Obedience is always preferable to disobedience. Keeping the door shut against sin is always better than opening the door to sin. Not needing a sin wilderness is always better than needing one.

When we need a sin wilderness, though, it is a true gift of grace from God. Those who remain faithful to God in and through such a wilderness, those who repent and recalibrate their hearts to his will as they wait on him to lead them out and on, will always find grace in the wilderness.[23] God never abandons his people during their desert days, but always makes a way for them, a way to sustenance and strength, to refreshment and new life[24] that they might become everything and possess everything he desires.

---

23. Jer 31:2.
24. Isa 43:19.

THE SYSTEMIC WILDERNESS

The systemic wilderness stood between the initial enslavement of the Children of Israel in Egypt and their ultimate emancipation from Egypt long years later. As a wilderness, it was not so much a *place*, like the desert of Sinai would become for the People of God, as it was a self-perpetuating *system* deeply imbedded within and throughout Egyptian life, from government and business to education and leisure. As such it assured the ongoing oppression and suppression of the Hebrew people in Pharaoh's realm. Today we would call it *systemic evil*.

Personally, I can best make sense of systemic evil by thinking in terms of the physical evil we know as cancer. Cancer is caused by cells which possess damaged DNA and thus become abnormal. A cell's DNA is often referred to as its *knowledge*. When that knowledge is adversely impacted, when the DNA code is compromised, causing it to *forget*, terrible things can happen. There came a fateful day in Egypt when *"a new king, who did not know about Joseph, came to power."*[1] Out of that forgetfulness came a radical change in attitude toward that ever-increasing population of foreigners in the land. *"The Israelites have become much too numerous for us,"* Pharaoh warned. *"Come, we must deal shrewdly with them or they will become even more numerous and, if war breaks out, will join our enemies, fight against us and leave the country."*[2] As a result, the Israelites were systematically dehumanized, becoming mere chattel. They were promptly put under taskmasters and forced into slavery,[3] exploited and oppressed in numerous ways, including building entire cities as monuments to Pharaoh's ego.[4]

With that initial decision by Pharaoh to treat Israel differently, as fundamentally inferior to Egyptians, the now-deviant cell began dividing.

1. Exod 1:8.
2. Exod 1:9–10.
3. Exod 1:11a.
4. Exod 1:11b.

Then, like any malignancy, it spread into surrounding tissue, before finally metastasizing and racing to the furthest reaches of Body Egypt until no segment of society remained unaffected.[5] The disease eventually became so pervasive that its side effects, like the disease itself, became normalized and unthinkingly accepted, even protected, as part and parcel of Egyptian life.[6] The rub was, at least from the Hebrew point of view, that in order to be a workable, enduring system, the disease had to benefit the privileged and exploit the disenfranchised. As long as that balance was properly maintained, nothing much would change for Israel in Egypt.

Once the system became ingrained—firmly rooted in the stories and structures of Egypt, in the lives and living of Egyptians—it took on a life of its own. Repeatedly through the book of Exodus, Pharaoh and all who paid him homage—variously referred to as his *"officials,"*[7] his *"people,"*[8] the *"Egyptians"*[9]—act in seamless concert, as one, until they are routinely spoken of collectively as "Egypt,"[10] distinct from other clear references to the physical country of Egypt.[11] At that point, the system was running the show. What was experienced by Israel in Egypt was not a *sovereign* wilderness or a *sin* wilderness so much as a *systemic* wilderness.

In a systemic wilderness, the system runs the show, allowing evil to grow and spread virtually unchecked. As it spreads, evil picks up strength; as it grows, it stockpiles energy. Eventually, it fuels itself. What makes it possible for evil to constantly refuel itself, what makes a systemic wilderness so insidious and successful, is that the system itself is so massive and powerful that most of its individual parts see themselves as insignificant, as unrelated to the whole, as making no contribution in terms of consequences, as being so far removed from the actual evil itself as to seem no part of it.

Imagine a society where you work as a domino flicker. You show up at the domino factory every day, flick a solitary domino, go home, then repeat the simple process the following day. And so it goes six days a week, fifty

---

5. Exod 1:12b.

6. Exod 1:12b-14.

7. Exod 7:11; 8:4, 9, 24, 29, 31; 9:14, 30, 34; 10:1, 6, 7; 11:3, 8; 12:30; 14:5 (not exhaustive).

8. Exod 1:9, 22; 8:4, 9, 29, 31; 9:14, 15, 27 (not exhaustive).

9. Exod 1:12, 14; 3:9, 20–22; 6:5–7; 7:5, 18, 21, 24; 8:21; 9:6, 11; 10:2; 11:3; 12:23, 27, 33, 35–36; 14:9–10, 12–13, 18, 23, 25–27, 30–31 (not exhaustive).

10. Exod 11:1, 3; 12:13; 14:5. There are scholars of the opinion that the word choice and grammar of the author in those Scriptures, and several others, suggest that the term "Egypt" is used, not in the sense of the country or the land of Egypt, but in the specific sense of the people known collectively as "Egypt."

11. Exod 8:7, 16–17, 24; 9:9, 22–25; 10:15, 19; 13:16 (not exhaustive).

weeks a year, for your entire working life. It is somewhat boring—okay, *very* boring—but you are extremely well paid, and the job demands an incredibly small portion of your day, so you are happy. The domino you flick stands just outside a curtain that is as thin as air but as dark as pitch. You cannot see what, if anything, is on the other side of the curtain. And the darkness does something no other darkness does—it deadens all sound. You cannot see or hear what your domino does after you flick it. You just clock-in, flick the domino, clock-out and go home. Oh, and get your fat paycheck on Fridays.

Unbeknownst to you, on the other side of the curtain, are thousands of living, breathing dominos—with lives to live, little dominos to raise, and dignity to maintain—that the government has strategically set to topple whenever you flick your lifeless domino into the dark and then go home. Of course, your ignorance of what transpires on the other side of the curtain does not change the results from what you do. Every day, your little act of flicking topples thousands of living dominos hoping that this is the day they are finally able to stand and remain standing. Once more, however, your indifferent act has toppled them into chaos. And just when the dominos behind the curtain think the government is bringing order into their lives, by picking them up, lining them up, and giving them a chance, that very order becomes the means of chaos and the guarantee that their lives will never change.

Yet, as a trusted and trusting employee, you never think to ask, "What does the domino do after I flick it?" "Are there any real results to my flicking the domino?" "Does the domino make a negative impact in any way?" The questions are never raised because the flick of a single domino seems so far removed from the evil you hear about and occasionally see in the world, that there could be no possible cause-and-effect. And if someone were to insist, "You are involved in committing a great evil," your honest, heart-felt response would be, "That is not possible. All I do is flick a single lifeless domino." That is the problem: the whole of the system obscures the role of the individual.

The personal element has effectively been removed. The problem is structural. It is self-perpetuating. It is complex. It is cyclical. It is diabolical. It is evil. It is a systemic wilderness. And it was killing Israel before God showed up in Moses.

Obviously, Pharaoh was the mind behind the system, and the entire empire kowtowed to his whims and will, but the system itself ran on the 1500 BC equivalent of perpetual motion, illustrated by another kind of "flicking." It is as if Pharaoh flicked a coin and watched it spin into a blur on a tabletop. But *this* coin, instead of steadily losing energy—slowing predictably and finally falling into a dead-stop—kept spinning. Forty seconds.

Forty days. Forty years. Forty decades. It was fueling itself, feeding off itself. It may take a spin to get a systemic wilderness started but it eventually runs on its own accumulated energy—perhaps the closest thing to perpetual motion known to humankind.

In Scripture, there are three great empires that stand apart as paradigms of systemic evil: the Egyptians of Old Testament history, the Romans of the New Testament era, and the Babylonians, which the writer of Revelation singled out as a *universal* symbol of such evil.[12] The common denominator of that unholy trinity is that each grew into a self-perpetuating evil, enslaving and dominating, suppressing and oppressing people, particularly those deemed inferior and who, as a result, became disenfranchised minorities in the *literal* sense of that term—they were deprived of a franchise, that is, of certain legal rights, or of some privilege or immunity. In Old Testament days, that meant the Hebrew people.[13] In New Testament times, that meant primarily Christ-followers. For those reasons, both Jews and Christians—others as well—could be said to have endured a systemic wilderness.

Closer to our time, that could mean any number of people groups around the globe, including but not limited to Jews who were subjected to the holocaust, blacks who were subjected to apartheid, and Christians facing imprisonment and even martyrdom in many government-sanctioned, anti-Christian cultures. In such cases, normal citizens are caught up in the machinery and machinations of the system-in-power and may be distanced enough from the heart of evil itself to feel uninvolved and innocent of any personal wrongdoing. As Peter Storey insightfully pointed out, ". . . we have learned to let our institutions do our sinning for us."[14] And when we become the victim of institutional sin—evil that is truly evil and truly systemic—we are forced into a wilderness of someone else's choosing, a systemic

---

12. Rev 14:8; 16:19; 17:5; 18:2, 10, 21.

13. Obery M. Hendricks, Jr., wrote, "The term 'Hebrews' itself . . . is primarily a sociopolitical identity—specifically a class identity—-rather than a religious identity. In the Hebrew language, the term 'ibri,' or 'Hebrew,' means literally, 'he crossed over,' which reflects the Hebrews' status as 'outsiders' to Egyptian society. Moreover, the use of 'Hebrews' as a term of social or class description seems to be related to the early Semitic term 'hapiru,' which most scholars believe also connoted outsider class status in the ancient Near East. The sense of 'outsider' is reflected by the Exodus narrative in its own presentation of the Hebrews as in every way outcasts and aliens to the social and political mainstream of Egypt. Indeed, the book of Exodus graphically portrays the Hebrews as a despised and socially marginalized class. The ethic of compassion for the 'ger,' or 'alien stranger,' that permeates the Hebrew Bible from this point has much to do with the Hebrews' treatment in Egypt." Hendricks, Jr., *Politics of Jesus*, 15.

14. Storey, *God in the Crucible*, 153.

wilderness that can devalue, dehumanize and destroy with the full approval and weight of the culture in which we live.

In a search for what is needed in such a time as that, we would do well to consider the story of that systemic wilderness which Scripture defines as Egypt.

Pharaoh's attempt at ethnic cleansing—or, at least, ethnic population control—began with instructions to midwives that when assisting Hebrew women in childbirth, they were to *"observe them on the delivery stool, if it is a boy, kill him; but if it is a girl, let her live."*[15] That is when the storyteller identified the midwives as Shiphra and Puah,[16] then added, *"The midwives, however, feared God and did not do what the king of Egypt had told them to do; they let the boys live."*[17] When Pharaoh found out what they had done—or *not* done—he summoned them and demanded, *"Why have you done this? Why have you let the boys live?"*[18] Pharaoh knew that the system could eventually breakdown if even one or two people did not toe the line, did not do the solitary thing they were told to do, did not perform their job. Such insubordination was a chain reaction waiting to happen, and Pharaoh would have none of it. When confronted, Shiphra and Puah lied, and not just to *anyone* either, but to the king. *"Hebrew women are not like Egyptian women;"* they explained, *"they are vigorous and give birth before the midwives arrive."*[19] That story relates the first act of civil disobedience in the Exodus record. But not the last.

Making matters more distressing for the Hebrews, *"Pharaoh gave this order to all his people: 'Every boy that is born you must throw into the Nile, but let every girl live.'"*[20] What was originally the king's mandate to be carried out by midwives—death for all newborn males—now became a more wide-spread law, which was incumbent on all his people. As far as Pharaoh was concerned, the slipping between the cracks that happened, for whatever reason, under Shiphrah and Puah's watch, would not be repeated.

But that was before a certain married Levite woman gave birth to a son. Her name, we learn later, was Jochebed.[21] Ignoring the king's decree, she successfully hid the infant for three months,[22] but when that was no

15. Exod 1:16.
16. Exod 1:15.
17. Exod 1:17.
18. Exod 1:18.
19. Exod 1:18.
20. Exod 1:22.
21. Exod 6:20.
22. Exod 2:2.

longer feasible, *"she got a papyrus basket for him and coated it with tar and pitch. Then she placed the child in it and put it among the reeds along the bank of the Nile."*[23] A temporary, stopgap measure at best—a basket large enough to hold a three-month-old would probably stay afloat less than a week. So the mother stationed her daughter within purview of the hiding place to see what would happen to the baby.[24] It marked the story's second act of civil disobedience.

In the end, it was not the current or crocodiles that laid claim to the child; it was instead the Princess of Egypt, who also defied the king's command in another, yet shocking act of civil disobedience, this one emanating from the very palace of Pharaoh.

> *. . . Pharaoh's daughter went down to the Nile to bathe, and her attendants were walking along the river bank. She saw the basket among the reeds and sent her slave girl to get it. She opened it and saw the baby. He was crying, and she felt sorry for him. "This is one of the Hebrew babies," she said.*
>
> *Then his sister asked Pharaoh's daughter, "Shall I go and get one of the Hebrew women to nurse the baby for you?"*
>
> *"Yes, go," she answered. And the girl went and got the baby's mother. Pharaoh's daughter said to her, "Take this baby and nurse him for me, and I will pay you." So the woman took the baby and nursed him. When the child grew older, she took him to Pharaoh's daughter and he became her son. She named him Moses, saying, "I drew him out of the water."*[25]

Though no one but God knew it at the time, the birth of Moses was the dawn of Israel's deliverance from the systemic wilderness that was Egypt. In no way minimizing the spiritual realities of the Exodus, it remains primarily a liberation event with spiritual overtones, rather than the other way around. When, at the burning bush, God explained himself to Moses, he did not speak in what we might consider spiritual terms: "The worship of the Israelites has moved me" or "The faithfulness of the Israelites has impressed me" or "The Israelite's passionate pursuit of me has made me want to set them free." Rather, God spoke in more political terms, using words and images describing the Israelites' *"misery," "crying," "suffering,"* and *"oppression"* as well as his own seeing, hearing, concern, and commitment to their rescue.

> *The Lord said, "I have indeed seen the misery of my people in Egypt. I have heard them crying out because of their slave drivers,*

23. Exod 2:3.
24. Exod 2:4.
25. Exod 2:5–10.

> and I am concerned about their suffering. So I have come down to rescue them from the hand of the Egyptians and to bring them up out of the land into a good and spacious land, a land flowing with milk and honey—the home of the Canaanites, Hittites, Amorites, Perizzites, Hivites and Jebusites. And now the cry of the Israelites has reached me, and I have seen the way the Egyptians are oppressing them. So now I am sending you to Pharaoh to bring my people the Israelites out of Egypt."[26]

It is all too easy to spiritualize that story, to play down the social and political aspects that are so obviously prominent. Actually, more than prominent. God gives Moses no additional reason for what he is about to do. When pressed further, God simply says what he said before, only more succinctly, instructing Moses to inform the elders of Israel, *"The Lord, the God of your fathers—the God of Abraham, Isaac and Jacob—appeared to me and said: 'I have watched over you and have seen what has been done to you in Egypt. And I have promised to bring you up out of your misery in Egypt . . . ."*[27] What happened in Egypt when God showed up in Moses was, in the words of Obery M. Hendricks, Jr., "the root event from which the fundamental meaning of Judaism and the entire Judeo-Christian faith tradition flows."[28] It was clearly "a political event—the liberation event that was the exodus."[29]

A systemic wilderness is unique. Whereas the outcome of a sovereign wilderness is in God's hands and the outcome of a sin wilderness is largely in our hands, the outcome of a systemic wilderness is in the hands of a sometimes hard-to-put-a-finger-on but well-established, fully functioning, commonly accepted, self-perpetuating *system*, ably bolstered by *"rulers . . . authorities . . . the powers of this dark world and . . . the spiritual forces of evil in the heavenly realms."*[30] Therefore, ways of responding in other wildernesses—repentance and return in a sin wilderness, purposeful waiting on God in a sovereign wilderness—may not be all that is needed in a systemic wilderness. In fact, much more *will* be needed. That is why the apostle Paul, after identifying the principalities and powers that make up a system of evil, calls God's people to enter the fray, engage the evil and bravely fight with weapons both defensive and offensive:

> *Therefore put on the full armor of God, so that when the day of evil comes, you may be able to stand your ground, and after you have*

26. Exod 3:7–10.
27. Exod 3:16–17a.
28. Hendricks, Jr., *Politics of Jesus*, 14.
29. Hendricks, Jr., *Politics of Jesus*, 14.
30. Eph 6:12.

> *done everything, to stand. Stand firm then, with the belt of truth buckled around your waist, with the breastplate of righteousness in place, and your feet fitted with the readiness that comes from the gospel of peace. In addition to all this, take up the shield of faith, with which you can extinguish all the flaming arrows of the evil one. Take the helmet of salvation and the sword of the Spirit, which is the word of God. And pray in the Spirit on all occasions with all kinds of prayers and requests. With this in mind, be alert and always keep on praying for all the saints.*[31]

In a sentence, a systemic wilderness does not resolve itself. Had everyone in Egypt, from Midwives to pregnant women, simply acquiesced to the king's order, had no one—not Shiphra, Puah, Jochebed, Miriam, or the Princess of Egypt—courageously exercised civil disobedience, opting instead to simply sit around praying and waiting for God to do that thing God does . . . sometimes, there would have been no Moses the Deliverer. The Exodus is a story of the collective deliverance of a disenfranchised people from a systemic wilderness, ultimately made possible, on one hand, by God unashamedly taking the side of the oppressed and, on the other hand, by ordinary but courageous people engaged in civil disobedience, potentially at the risk of their own lives.

In a systemic wilderness, courageous, peaceful civil disobedience is needed to break the stranglehold of sin that grips the system and, in turn, grips the people.

Also needed, and clearly seen in the Exodus story, is the crucial blend of truly prophetic words and actions, which intentionally confront the heart of the particular systemic evil.

Moses, having four decades earlier fled Egypt as a felon, now returned as a prophet of God, armed with words and deeds which he brought forcefully against the system. He wasted no time confronting Pharaoh, placing before the king the ultimatum from God: "*This is what the Lord, the God of Israel, says, 'Let my people go' . . . .*"[32] It was a message Moses returned to persistently and repeated tirelessly, even though Pharaoh refused to yield,[33] the plan backfired and made matters far worse for Moses' countrymen,[34] the Israelite foremen turned on him in anger,[35] and God seemed to not do

---

31. Eph 6:13–18.
32. Exod 5:1.
33. Exod 5:2.
34. Exod 5:4–18.
35. Exod 5:19–21.

what he had promised.³⁶ In spite of it all, Moses remained ever faithful to his prophetic role, always speaking and acting against injustice and oppression, always confronting the heart of the evil that held God's people cruelly enslaved, and always proclaiming God's word and will to be the standard by which to judge all the doings and sayings of the system.

Moses spoke prophetically, pronouncing God's judgment on Egypt and its gods if Pharaoh persisted to be stubborn and stiff-necked and if the People of God remained enslaved and oppressed by the system. He also acted prophetically, bringing pressure to bear on Pharaoh in areas where the king and the Egyptians were most vulnerable and most personally invested. All of it in an effort to break the hold the systemic wilderness had on Israel and to set the people of God finally and forever free. In the end, Pharaoh wore down and relented, the system itself began to self-destruct, and Israel walked away free from what had been a generations-long systemic wilderness.

During the dark days of what was the systemic evil of Nazi Germany, Dietrich Bonhoeffer spoke of the need for the church to cross the borderline that stood between confession and resistance. To confess that God, not nations or governments or leaders or systems, rules the world; to confess that Jesus alone—not Hitler—is Lord; but then fail to resist those powers and persons, those structures and systems that seek to usurp divine authority, is unthinkable. Confession without resistance is not appreciably different from cooperating with the usurping powers. If that borderline separating confession and resistance was not intentionally and committedly crossed, the systemic evil could never be overcome.

There is a time and place where merely verbally confessing the truth of God is insufficient. It is possible, even necessary at times, to resist by confession, to stand our ground and say in the face of great evil, "Jesus is Lord . . . over everything or nothing."³⁷ But there also come times when, to be most effective against evil, we must boldly confess by resistance.³⁸ If you are uncomfortable with the word "resistance," then substitute "peaceful

---

36. Exod 5:22–23.

37. The imagery is that of Eric Metaxas. The direct quote reads, "All his life, Bonhoeffer had applied the same logic to theological issues that his father applied to scientific issues. There was only one reality, and Christ was Lord over all of it or none." Metaxas, *Bonhoeffer*, 361.

38. Metaxas, *Bonhoeffer*, 361. For the entire concept, I am indebted to Eric Metaxas, who wrote, "Thus we were approaching the borderline between confession and resistance, and if we did not cross this border, our confession was going to be no better than cooperation with criminals. And so it became clear where the problem lay for the Confessing Church: we were resisting by way of confession, but we were not confessing by way of resistance." Metaxas, *Bonhoeffer*,161.

civil disobedience." Either way, as the late William Sloane Coffin said in a message delivered at Harvard Divinity School in 1999, "Let Christians remember how Jesus was concerned most for those society counted least and put last. Let us all remember what Martin Luther King Jr. and Gandhi never forgot—how frequently compassion demands confrontation."[39] Confronting systemic evil with prophetic words and actions, as Moses did, and as Jesus did, is essential for its overthrow.

Another element that runs like a thread through the Exodus narrative and, like the first two elements, is essential if we are to endure a systemic wilderness to the ultimate glory of God is that of faithful suffering.

Those who are victimized by systemic evil—be they Hebrews, black people, women, the poor, or whoever else knows the terrible weight of an unjust, unfairly balanced system—will indeed suffer, just as did Jews in Pharaoh's Egypt and Christians under the thumb of Imperial Rome. They may suffer even more if they resist or peacefully disobey. What sets God's people apart from other wilderness-bound people is not their suffering, but their *faithful* suffering. To remain faithful in suffering—faithful to God, faithful to the way of Jesus, faithful to the word—is the hallmark of the Christian, and results in our good, in the good of others, and in the glory of God.

Peter Storey, who endured the systemic wilderness of South Africa apartheid, reminds us that "there is power in faithful suffering."[40] He wrote:

> Where most religions offer escape from suffering and increase in comfort, the Christian faith makes this astounding claim. The Christian Bible speaks of "going to Jerusalem, there to suffer much." It speaks of "taking up a cross," and of "being given a share in Christ's suffering."
>
> That is hard to understand and even harder to live; but if you want to know whether God is alive, you must go, not to where all is well, but into the places of brokenness and suffering. . . . It is where the crosses of this world are planted that we still find God.[41]

God is always found, as well as honored, in places of faithful suffering. And because God is there, impact will always be made, if we remain faithful. Faithful while working, of course; faithful in prophetically, peacefully, compassionately and courageously confronting systemic evil; and faithful in spite of suffering that may come our way. When the People of God remain

---

39. Coffin, *Harvard Divinity Today* 2 (Summer 2006): 6.
40. Storey, *God in the Crucible*, 80.
41. Storey, *God in the Crucible,*, 80–81.

faithful in suffering, the God of the People will prove faithful in making an impact.

"Don't ask me to explain it," wrote Storey, "but faithful suffering is never wasted. Somehow it allows this world to discover how closely God is with us."[42] And, so, he advises, "never underestimate the words that God can speak through your life when you suffer for godly truth, compassion, and justice. Through such lives, the word of God speaks."[43]

Long years of faithful suffering by the Hebrew people became cracks in the dam which eventually gave way under the steady pressure of Moses, enabling the Israelites to ride a wall of water into promised freedom. Somehow, in divine ways we cannot fully grasp, all those long days and nights of faithful suffering by ordinary women and men empowered Moses, generations later, to fulfill his role in God's great drama, his role as Liberator of Israel. In truly mysterious ways, by standing *against* the edict of Pharaoh and *for* God's truth as they knew it, Shiphra and Puah, Jochebed and Miriam, perhaps even Egypt's young princess, unwittingly prepared the way for the freedom of God's long-enslaved people. Their roles made Moses' role possible. Without their roles, Moses would have had no role. Without the former, there would not have been the latter. Once more quoting Storey, "Never underestimate the importance of ordinary people standing for the truth because they also enable others to play their part."[44]

Playing our part in God's drama, particularly in the context of a systemic wilderness, can be costly, and often is. I have wondered what it might ultimately have cost Shiphra and Puah. I know what it cost the deacon Stephen,[45] and how his martyrdom was probably the genesis of Saul's conversion.[46] It is easy for me to recall the price paid by people like Mahatma Gandhi, Dietrich Bonhoeffer, Martin Luther King Jr., and countless others—men and women, young and old—whose names and faces are forever etched in my conscious. And, of course, there is Jesus. I know what such a stand, what such persistent disturbance of in-place powers-that-be, what such prophetic words and actions, what such faithful suffering cost Jesus.

They are all blood-in-the-streets proof that a systemic wilderness does not resolve itself. But proof as well that a systemic wilderness can indeed, if we remain faithful, end in a celebration of freedom.

---

42. Storey, *God in the Crucible*, 82.
43. Storey, *God in the Crucible*, 84.
44. Storey, *God in the Crucible*, 130.
45. Acts 7:1–60.
46. Acts 8:1.

WILDERNESS AS CALL AND CHOICE

If we had our druthers, there are deserts we would rather not enter, but avoid altogether. I have no desire even to skirt the extreme edge of a sovereign wilderness like Abraham knew when he bound his son Isaac and stood ready to slay him.[1] And as to Israel's forty-year meandering trek through the sin wilderness of Sinai,[2] no thank you. I'll take a pass. As we know, however, when we sin ourselves into a wilderness or when God sovereignly forces us there, our druthers have no say in the matter. But that is not true of every wilderness.

There are some deserts we are compelled to enter, either by a direct call from God or by a more indirect call—something like a stirring in the heart that steadily intensifies until it becomes, first, an irresistible urge and, then an intentional choice to step into a wilderness alongside another or others. There are certain wildernesses, and a systemic wilderness can be one, that we enter willingly. We make a personal choice, we answer a divine call to walk and work with others so they do not walk and work alone.

The image immediately conjured up in my mind is that of a *paraclete*—the Greek term the apostle John alone used to describe a chief role of the Holy Spirit in a believer's life,[3] quoting Jesus' promise to send the Spirit to *step in alongside* his followers for counsel, comfort, encouragement and support.[4] Practically, a paraclete is *"one called alongside"*[5] who, in turn, becomes *"one who steps in alongside"*—who walks the path, bears the burden, joins the struggle, fights the battles, takes the blows *with us*.

---

1. Gen 22:1–19.
2. Num 14:34.
3. John 14:16, 26; 15:26; 16:7; 1 John 2:1. The word is translated variously as "counselor," "comforter," "encourager," "exhorter," and "advocate."
4. John 14:16, 26; 15:26; 16:7.
5. The Greek word *parakletos* is comprised of *para* ("alongside") and *kletos* ("to call").

Much of what it means to be people who are led by the Spirit is that we step in alongside those who are in distress, we join them in their places of sin and suffering, we refuse to allow them to walk any wilderness alone. The apostle Paul began his second Corinthian correspondence with a great burst of praise that sounds the same theme:

> *Praise be to the God and Father of our Lord Jesus Christ, the Father of compassion and the God of all comfort, who comforts us in all our troubles, so that we can comfort those in any trouble with the comfort we ourselves have received from God. For just as the sufferings of Christ flow over into our lives, so also through Christ our comfort overflows. If we are distressed, it is for your comfort and salvation; if we are comforted, it is for your comfort, which produces in you patient endurance of the same sufferings we suffer. And our hope for you is firm, because we know that just as you share in our sufferings, so also you share in our comfort.*[6]

Stepping in alongside has always been and will always be proper Christian behavior, a large part of what it means to be a Bible-believing, Jesus-following, Spirit-obeying community. To leave someone stranded in his or her own personal wilderness or to ignore the plight of those whose wilderness is communal, whether we are paralyzed by fear or by our desire for personal comfort, is a fundamental failure of staggering magnitude. Since Jesus has stepped in alongside us in our sins and the Spirit has stepped in alongside us in our struggles, how can we not step in alongside others in their sins and struggles? In the words of Dietrich Bonhoeffer:

> If we want to be Christians, we must have some share in Christ's large-heartedness by acting with responsibility and in freedom when the hour of danger comes, and by showing a real sympathy that springs, not from fear, but from the liberating and redeeming love of Christ for all who suffer. Mere waiting and looking on is not Christian behaviour. The Christian is called to sympathy and action, not in the first place by his own sufferings, but by the sufferings of his brethren, for whose sake Christ suffered.[7]

How can we not be there for others when God has been there for us in Jesus, in the Spirit, in our sisters and brothers? As Count Helmuth von Moltke wrote during the systemic evil of the Nazi holocaust, "What shall I

---

6. 2 Cor 1:3–7.
7. Metaxas, *Bonhoeffer*, 447.

say when I am asked: And what did you do during that time? . . . How can anyone know these things and walk around free?"[8]

Much of my fifty-plus years as a pastor has been spent intentionally sharing wildernesses with others. Often, I have been invited to step into those deserts; sometimes, I have intervened and stepped in uninvited. But, in either case, I was compelled to step in so that the person or persons would not be alone or without that small portion of help and encouragement I could provide.

Stepping in is the Christian thing, the Spirit thing, the Jesus thing, the God thing to do. We have an entire Bible, precept after precept and story after story, announcing that, and an entire church history affirming it. Christians are compelled to step in alongside.

It need not be a big step; just our step.

Peter Storey reminds us that,

> Somewhere, there are situations and people who only you can touch, places where only you can intervene . . . .
> You say, "Who me? Really?"
> Yes, you! I'm not necessarily talking about the big moments that make the headlines, where great statesmen reach out to each other across years of hatred and division—remember when Anwar Sadat first set foot on Israeli soil and held out his hand to Menachem Begin? Those are great moments of intervention in history and thank God for them—but I don't believe that's where the action usually is. It is more likely to be at street level, in the hands of ordinary people like us.[9]

Carolyn Custis James points to "ordinary people like us" as the way in which the gospel moves with power in this world, from the happiness of our daily existence to the holocaust of a systemic wilderness. The power of the gospel is unleashed by the humble, hopeful activity of "God's people engaged in simple yet extraordinary acts of hesed."[10] James properly defines "hesed" as,

> . . . one of the most potent words in the Old Testament. . . . a strong Hebrew word that sums up the ideal lifestyle for God's people. It's the way God intended for human beings to live together from the beginning—the "love-your-neighbor-as-yourself" brand of living, an active, selfless, sacrificial caring for one another that goes against the grain of our fallen nature.

8. Metaxas, *Bonhoeffer*, 393.
9. Storey, *God in the Crucible*, 99–100.
10. James, *Gospel of Ruth*, 117.

Two parties are involved—someone in desperate need and a second person who possesses the power and the resources to make a difference. Hesed is driven, not by duty or legal obligation, but by a bone-deep commitment—a loyal, selfless love that motivates a person to do voluntarily what no one has a right to expect or ask of them. They have the freedom to act or walk away without the slightest injury to their reputation. Yet they willingly pour themselves out for the good of someone else. It's actually the kind of love we find most fully expressed in Jesus. In a nutshell, hesed is the gospel lived out. . . .

Hesed can be boiled down to this: Someone cares and has freely made it their business to look after me.[11]

Christians are compelled to step in alongside.

It need not be a fearless step; just a faithful step.

We tend to think that if we are bold, we are fearless. We are inclined to assume, for example, that when the first Christians were filled with boldness,[12] that meant they were no longer afraid. I have trouble believing that. Some situations those Jesus-followers faced would doubtlessly have produced fear. After all, their peace and comfort, not to mention their families, futures and lives, were on the line. Some were facing boycotts, loss of jobs and confiscation of property; others were staring poverty, persecution and martyrdom in the face. I don't think that being bold meant they were not afraid; rather, I think it meant they were unafraid of being afraid, that they accepted fear as the barrier it was and broke through it to the other side. Their fears did not stop them from saying or doing what they must. *That*, to me, is biblical boldness.

If I had stepped into the thick of the South Africa struggle against apartheid or into the heart of racial hatred in the southern United States in the 1950s and 60s, I am confident I would have been sweating bullets, maybe even dodging them. But I pray I would have been bold, doing and saying what needed done and said, even if it meant giving up my life. That, I think, is the true measure of our boldness.

Ultimately, as Carolyn Custis James insists, "The God in whom we confess faith invites us to participate with him in the completion of his program for the world. His preferred method of getting things done is to work through his image bearers. We aren't spectators to what God is doing in the world, but participants."[13] Stepping in is not optional for followers of Jesus.

---

11. James, *Gospel of Ruth*, 114–117.
12. Acts 4:29–31.
13. James, *Gospel of Ruth*, 133.

Whether a wilderness is one of sovereignty, sin or systemic evil; whether the specific wilderness-bound pilgrim is suffering as a result of a self-inflicted spiritual wound, a sovereign season from the hand of God, an addiction that holds him or her enslaved, or a systemic evil that holds an entire people in bondage, Christians are compelled to step in alongside. Whether we are talking the people of God's kingdom or the people of this planet, we do not leave our sisters and brothers alone in a wilderness.

There are times we are compelled to step in alongside by a call from God.

Moses is probably the quintessential example of that. The liberation of the Hebrew people from their long slavery to Pharaoh was due to Moses stepping into the systemic wilderness that Egypt had become and coming alongside his brethren. He was compelled, having answered a direct call from God.[14]

It seems a safe assumption that Moses would never have returned to Egypt without an unmistakable call from God. He had left Egypt in panic and fear, as a wanted man, his picture hanging in every post office of the land.[15] He ran to where he thought all maps ended, met a woman, got married, raised a family, and settled into a shepherd's life in Midian.[16] All the Bible really says about those days was that they were a *"long period"*[17]—about forty years in all. In that span of time, Egypt had doubtless become a fading memory to this man in exile.[18] It took an exceptional encounter with God[19] to get Moses off his father-in-law's farm in Midian and onto the road to Egypt, and even then Moses doggedly dug in his heels, fighting against the whole idea, trying his best to convince God that he was the wrong man for the job,[20] and that the whole divine plan would not work anyway.[21] Eventually, Moses realized he was up against the call of God and that it was futile to resist. He piled his wife and kids onto the donkey and headed back to Egypt.[22]

The rest is liberation and salvation history.

---

14. Exod 3:7–10.
15. Exod 2:11–15.
16. Exod 2:15–22.
17. Exod 2:23.
18. Exod 2:22.
19. Exod 3:1–10.
20. Exod 3:10–12; 4:10–17.
21. Exod 3:13—4:9.
22. Exod 4:18–20.

The solution to Moses' dilemma—should he believe who he knows himself to be or believe who God says he is? Should he stay in Midian or return to Egypt?—as well as the solution to the dilemma of the enslaved Children of God was to be found only in Moses answering God's call. "The solution," wrote Dietrich Bonhoeffer, "is to do the will of God, to do it radically and courageously and joyfully."[23] In the end, Moses' reluctance to answer God's call did not matter; it mattered only that he ultimately answered God's call with a "yes" and stepped into the systemic wilderness with Israel.

Sometimes, a call from God comes, and we are compelled to step in alongside.

Other times, we are compelled to step in alongside by a clear choice.

Jesus is the quintessential example of that. The liberation of the human race from slavery to Satan was due to Jesus stepping into the sin wilderness that our world and our lives had become, and taking his stand with us in the struggle. He was compelled, having chosen to make his life an offering to God.

With some of the most poignant and powerful words in Scripture, the apostle Paul told the story of Jesus' incarnation in this way:

> *Your attitude should be the same as that of Christ Jesus:*
> *Who, being in very nature God,*
> > *did not consider equality with God*
> > > *something to be grasped,*
> *but made himself nothing,*
> > *taking the very nature of a servant,*
> > *being made in human likeness.*
> *And being found in appearance as a man,*
> > *he humbled himself*
> > *and became obedient to death—*
> > > *even death on a cross!*
> *Therefore God exalted him to the highest place*
> > *and gave him the name that is above every*
> > > *name,*
> *that at the name of Jesus every knee should*
> > *bow,*
> > *in heaven and on earth and under the earth,*
> *and every tongue confess that Jesus Christ is*
> > *Lord,*
> > > *to the glory of God the Father*[24]

---

23. Mataxas, *Bonhoeffer*, 471.
24. Phil 2:5–11.

Peter Storey encourages us to never forget that "the cross was raised not only by humankind's sin. It was raised because God determined to come amongst us, to stand with us, to suffer with and for us. Jesus died not only as a victim but as a participant in something deep and profound."[25] Jesus was God-with-us,[26] God-in-flesh,[27] God pitching his tent with us[28] and moving into the neighborhood.[29] He was our *paraclete*—the one who stepped in alongside, walked the path, bore the burden, joined the struggle, fought the battle, and took the blows *with us*.

Helmut Thielicke once said something about how you can't learn war in a theater. That is the only way I have known war; I have never served my country in uniform. I know war only by means of movies and books, television documentaries and stories my father told. I am only a theater soldier and, therefore, no soldier at all. Jesus, however, was no mere theater soldier. He knows war and our fiercest battles first-hand. He shared the foxholes and the front lines of those battles with us. *With us*. He stepped in alongside. No one required it of him. It was his own free choice of his own free will, a choice which his heart compelled him to make.

The rest is our salvation history.

Jesus, more than anyone else, was a man for others, even though the others were the least, the lonely and the lost. Like no one else, he identified with them, with all of us, in our sin and suffering, and did so willingly and lovingly, fully and radically. So much so, in fact, that he shared his life with us and laid down his life for us. We were *his people*, and in ways we do not yet fully understand.

Obery M. Hendricks, Jr. wrote:

> Rose Businge, the thirty-six-year-old Ugandan nurse who founded Meeting Point International, a relief organization in Kireka, explains that the Kireka women believe that "those who are suffering, they belong to us. They are our people. Their problems are our problems. Their children are like our children." Their motto is "One Heart," which Businge explains means, "The heart of [humanity] has no race." It moves to another human being wherever the suffering.[30]

---

25. Storey, *God in the Crucible*, 137.
26. Matt 1:23.
27. John 1:1, 14.
28. John 1:14.
29. John 1:14. *The Message* reads: "The word became flesh and blood, and moved into the neighborhood."
30. Hendricks, Jr., *Politics of Jesus*, 110.

That is the nature of a Christlike life. That is a lifestyle that cannot be forced upon a person, but only taken up by a person who chooses the way of Christ. Stepping in alongside others in their sin and suffering, stepping into even the rage and hell of a systemic wilderness, may mean suffering for us—possibly death—just as such a choice meant for Jesus, and for many others. But "those who suffer faithfully discover God in new and deeper ways and can become mediators of God to (the rest of) us."[31]

Sometimes, it is necessary that we suffer *from* something (our sins or those of others) in order to become everything and possess everything God desires. Other times, we may be called to suffer *for* something (stepping in alongside those victimized by systemic evil) that God's truth and God's way might ultimately prevail. Often, doing the latter is dangerous. It can be like trying to stand against the sea surge from a massive hurricane. To suffer *for*, *alongside* the victimized and disenfranchised is routinely painful, is mostly a losing battle, and can be—as history has too often proved—deadly. But to suffer *faithfully* for such things because of a determined choice or an unequivocal "yes" to God's call means, as Peter Storey explains, that "God can speak words through us that can never be silenced."[32]

In this matter of *choosing* to step in alongside others, Storey also wrote, "The deepest and most profound suffering comes, not as a chance blow, or out of poverty or oppression, nor even as a consequence of obedience. It comes as a free choice, when we choose freely to suffer with another, and the only thing that holds us is love."[33]

Sometimes, a choice must be made, and we are compelled to step in alongside.

Because one person—Moses—said "yes" to God and stepped in alongside the sins and sufferings of others, the result was freedom and new life, hope and a promise for the Hebrew people. Because one person—Jesus—chose to step in alongside the sins and sufferings of others, the result was healing and wholeness, forgiveness and newness.

That stepping-in was the story of our salvation.

It still is.

---

31. Storey, *God in the Crucible*, 81.
32. Storey, *God in the Crucible*, 83.
33. Storey, *God in the Crucible*, 84.

CAN AN OASIS BE A WILDERNESS?

In his commentary on the book of Genesis, Leon Kass wonders about Israel (Jacob) as he journeys to Egypt following news that his beloved son Joseph is actually alive, not dead as he was told,[1] and that the once idle dreamer is not just scraping by, but has actually risen to second in command, behind only Pharaoh himself:[2] "Old Israel goes to Egypt on his own terms. But will he like what he finds there? Will Israel and his people be able to preserve their identity and independence in Egypt?"[3]

Israel, determined to see Joseph before closing his eyes in death,[4] gathered all his belongings and all his kin and headed for Egypt via Beersheba.[5] The presence of his resurrected-from-the-dead son in Egypt transformed Israel's journey there from a famine-spawned last-ditch effort for his clan's survival[6] into a pilgrimage of promise, delight, blessing and hope.[7]

Once arriving at Beersheba—where so much of significance in the life of Abraham's tribe had occurred[8]—God spoke to the aging patriarch: *"I am the God of your father. Don't be afraid of going down to Egypt. I'm going to make you a great nation there. I'll go with you down to Egypt; I'll also bring*

1. Gen 45:26a.
2. Gen 45:26b; 41:40–44.
3. Kass, *Beginning of Wisdom*, 615.
4. Gen 45:28.
5. Gen 46:1.
6. Gen 42:1–2.
7. Gen 46:1.
8. Both Abraham and Isaac made pivotal covenants at Beersheba (Gen 21:22–34; 26:26–33); Abraham went and stayed there following the marvelous deliverance of Isaac in the mountains of Moriah (Gen 22:19); Isaac famously found water there (Gen 26:32); God appeared to Isaac there (Gen 26:23–24); Isaac built an altar there and there he *"pitched his tent"* (Gen 26:25); and from Beersheba he set out on a journey, made camp, slept on a pillar of stone, dreamed about angels ascending a descending a ladder, and had a life-changing encounter with Yahweh (Gen 28:10–22).

you back here. And when you die, Joseph will be with you; with his own hand he'll close your eyes."[9]

That is a remarkable, hope-filled promise. But to anyone aware of the history of Abraham and his descendants with the land of Egypt, those words of God are somewhat surprising.

Abraham had sojourned in Egypt, after his call from God[10] but before he had entered into covenant with him,[11] traveling south and settling there because of a severe famine in his land.[12] While in Pharaoh's domain, and as a precaution, Abraham passed off his wife as his sister, worried that her beauty could lead to his murder by someone who desired her.[13] As it turned out, Pharaoh desired her and subsequently took her into his palace, keeping Abraham alive and lavishing him with much wealth.[14] When, as a result of taking Abraham's wife, God *"inflicted serious diseases on Pharaoh and his household,"*[15] Egypt's king returned Sarah to Abraham and sent them both packing.[16]

Following that harrowing episode, Abraham and his descendants steered clear of Egypt. When once again there was famine in the land, Abraham's son Isaac headed south toward Sinai, seemingly bound for Egypt, but stopped in Gerar, presumably to see if Philistine King Abimelech had means to help.[17] Probably because Abimelech could not assist in any practical manner, and since Isaac was on his way to Egypt anyway, the Lord appeared to Abraham's son and said:

> *Do not go down to Egypt; live in the land where I tell you to live. Stay in this land for a while, and I will be with you and will bless you. I will give you all these lands and will confirm the oath I swore to your father Abraham. I will make your descendants as numerous as the stars in the sky and will give them all these lands, and through your offspring, all nations on earth will be blessed, because Abraham obeyed me and kept my requirements, my commands, my decrees and my laws.*[18]

9. Gen 46:3–4, *Message*.
10. Gen 12:1–4.
11. Gen 15:1–20.
12. Gen 12:10.
13. Gen 12:11.
14. Gen 12:12–16.
15. Gen 12:17.
16. Gen 12:18–20.
17. Gen 26:1.
18. Gen 26:2–5.

The result was that *"Isaac stayed in Gerar."*[19]

That was not the last time God stopped his chosen ones from traveling to Egypt. The last time was years later. Fearful of the king of Babylon[20] and not trusting God's promised deliverance from his hands,[21] the Jews asked Jeremiah for a word from the Lord about whether they should stay in the land or leave for Egypt.[22] Jeremiah prayed for guidance.[23] Ten days later, God answered.[24] Then Jeremiah, being Jeremiah, passed along the unpopular word:

> . . . *he will have compassion on you and restore you to your land.*
>
> *However, if you say, "We will not stay in this land," and so disobey the Lord your God, and if you say, "No, we will go and live in Egypt, where we will not see war or hear the trumpet or be hungry for bread," then hear the word of the Lord, O remnant of Judah. This is what the Lord Almighty, the God of Israel says: "If you are determined to go to Egypt and you do go to settle there, then the sword you fear will overtake you there, and the famine you dread will follow you into Egypt, and there you will die. Indeed, all who are determined to go to Egypt to settle there will die by the sword, famine and plague; not one of them will survive or escape the disaster I will bring on them." This is what the Lord Almighty, the God of Israel, says: "As my anger and wrath have been poured out on those who lived in Jerusalem, so will my wrath be poured out on you when you go to Egypt. You will be an object of cursing and horror, of condemnation and reproach; you will never see this place again."*
>
> *Oh remnant of Judah, the Lord has told you, "Do not go to Egypt."*[25]

Isaiah also spoke sternly to God's people who saw in Egypt and Pharaoh the fulfillment of all their longings:

> *"Woe to the obstinate children,"*
>   *Declares the Lord,*
> *"to those who carry out plans that are not*
>   *mine,*
>   *forming an alliance, but not by my Spirit,*
>   *heaping sin upon sin;*

19. Gen 26:6.
20. Jer 42:11a.
21. Jer 42:11b-12.
22. Jer 42:1–3.
23. Jer 42:4.
24. Jer 42:7.
25. Jer 42:12b-19a.

*who go down to Egypt
    without consulting me;
who look for help to Pharaoh's protection,
    to Egypt's shade for refuge.
But Pharaoh's protection will be to your
        shame,
    Egypt's shade will bring you disgrace.
Though they have officials in Zoan
    and their envoys have arrived in Hanes,
everyone will be put to shame
    because of a people useless to them,
who bring neither help nor advantage,
    but only shame and disgrace."*

*An oracle concerning the animals of the Negev:
Through a land of hardship and distress,
    of lions and lionesses,
    of adders and darting snakes,
the envoys carry their riches on donkeys' backs,
    their treasures on the humps of camels,
to that unprofitable nation,
    to Egypt, whose help is utterly useless.
Therefore I call her
    Rahab the Do-Nothing.*

*Go now, write it on a tablet for them,
    inscribe it on a scroll,
that for the days to come
    it may be an everlasting witness.
These are rebellious people, deceitful children,
    children unwilling to listen to the Lord's
        instruction.
They say to the seers,
    'See no more visions!'
and to the prophets,
    'Give us no more visions of what is right!
Tell us pleasant things,
    Prophecy illusions.
Leave this way,
    get off the path,
and stop confronting us
    with the Holy One of Israel!'"*[26]

---

26. Isa 30:1–11.

On one level it seems strange that God would earlier encourage Israel to make his way to Egypt after telling Abraham, and much later his exiled people, to have nothing to do with Egypt. On another level, though, the stories make sense. Each is distinctive—describing different people in different places at different times. So, it is probably not too surprising after all that Israel was permitted to go to Egypt while others were not. Still, there is something about Egypt that should—and biblically *does*[27]—produce a degree of wariness, not only on the part of the Jewish people of the times and of the prophets who followed, but also on the part of modern readers of those ancient Bible stories.

Kass's earlier question about Israel appears relevant to all times when God's people were in Egypt: "Will Israel and his people be able to preserve their identity and independence in Egypt?" The loss of those twin essentials represented the true danger of Egypt for the people of God—forgetting who they were and forgetting to whom they belonged. That is certainly true of Israel's kin as their story unfolds in Genesis 42–50.

In the thick of a terrible, widespread famine,[28] *"Jacob learned that there was grain in Egypt."*[29] He hurriedly sent his sons, with the exception of his youngest, Benjamin,[30] southward with a precise purpose: *"Go down there and buy some for us, so that we might live and not die."*[31] It was a desperate move by a desperate man staring starvation in the eyes. At that moment, Egypt meant to Israel and his clan food and drink in an otherwise parched and lifeless wilderness; sufficiency in a place of far-as-the-eye-could-see scarcity; hope and a future for a once healthy lineage now hungry and struggling to survive. Egypt was to God's people everything an oasis is to people facing death in the desert.

Egypt was not, however, an oasis to Israel in some purely metaphorical way, but in a way that actually, historically saved the lives of the people of God and preserved the line that brought the Messiah Jesus into the

---

27. It is the ambiguity of Egypt that seems to fuel the Bible's—particularly the Old Testament's—wariness about the land. It is both of place of refuge and a place of oppression, a place of release and a place of enslavement, a place of hope and a place of despair, a place of triumph and a place of defeat, a place of life and a place of death, a place to flee to and a place to flee from, an oasis and a wilderness. Particularly during the Hebrew children's long enslavement there, which seems to color all later references to the land, Egypt becomes synonymous with all that is opposed to God—an entity, a nation, a land, a place not to be trusted, and not to be allowed to shape, as it seems so capable of doing, the minds, hearts, and souls of God's people.

28. Gen 41:53–57; 42:5.

29. Gen 42:1.

30. Gen 42:4.

31. Gen 42:2.

world. Remember: It was in Egypt that the Hebrews not only survived but thrived.[32] Yet Egypt was more often than not, in the minds of Old Testament prophets and authors, a double-edged sword—in this case, particularly, a saving oasis; but in most cases, a potentially lethal wilderness.

For Israel, Egypt was both a blessing and a curse, both an oasis and a wilderness; or, to perhaps say it better, Egypt started as a blessing and ended as a curse, began as an oasis but became a wilderness to Israel. By ultimately going to Egypt, "Jacob unwittingly starts the process that will bring him and his people to Egypt . . . for four hundred years."[33] At first welcomed and allowed their freedom in the land,[34] the people of God were eventually

---

32. Gen 47:27. See also Exod 1:6–10: *"Now Joseph and all his brothers and all that generation died, but the Israelites were fruitful and multiplied greatly and became exceedingly numerous, so that that land was filled with them. Then a new king, who did not know about Joseph, came to power in Egypt. 'Look,' he said to his people, 'the Israelites have become much too numerous for us. Come, we must deal shrewdly with them or they will become even more numerous and, if war breaks out, will join our enemies, fight against us and leave the country.'"* Nicholas Perrin, in *The Exodus Revealed*, 24–25, saw in Israel's fertility a mark of their obedience to God's creation command, and in Pharaoh's efforts to curb that fertility a bringing of God's curse on Egypt and its king: "Here is also a theological point. When we think back to the very beginning of Israel's story—that is, back to the creation story itself—we remember Yahweh's benediction and mandate to Adam and Eve. 'God blessed them, and God said to them, 'Be fruitful and multiply, and fill the earth and subdue it; and have dominion over the fish of the sea and over the birds of the air and over every living thing that moves upon the earth'" (Genesis 1:28). The same mandate for multiplication is repeated three times in the story of Noah (Genesis 8:17; 9:1, 7). Later, when Yahweh confirms his covenant with Abraham, one of the key promises in the covenant was his progeny's fruitfulness (Genesis 17:6). Promises of fruitfulness also follow Isaac (Genesis 26:22; 28:1–4). When the patriarch's descendants come to Goshen in the land of Egypt, they follow their forefathers' lead for 'they were fruitful and multiplied exceedingly' (Genesis 47:27). Thus when Pharaoh expresses his dismay over the expanding demographic sector known as 'the Israelites,' he is reacting to a well-established pattern within the biblical story that had its roots in one of Yahweh's very first commands to Israel (that is, when Israel was in Adam). The Israelites' fertility was a mark not only of their obedience to that creational mandate but also to God's blessing them even in the midst of their estranged existence. Meanwhile, as the well-versed ancient readers of Torah would have understood almost immediately, Pharaoh's resistance to this population trend made him a marked man. Think of it: Israel's fruitfulness was a direct result of Yahweh's blessing. In attempting to impede Israel's growth as a nation, Pharaoh was in fact cursing God's people (indeed the Hebrew notion of 'curse' entails the notion of restriction or confinement). Israel's God had already promised Abraham, 'I will bless those who bless you, and the ones who curse you I will curse' (Genesis 12:3). Again, the attentive reader would have been well aware: If Yahweh's promise to Abraham were trustworthy, then Yahweh was bound to curse the same Pharaoh who had cursed Israel."

33. Kass, *Beginning of Wisdom*, 574.

34. Gen 46:31—47:12.

resented and, in time, cruelly enslaved and oppressed.[35] As a result, Egypt became, for Old Testament prophets, the textbook example of an oasis becoming a wilderness for the people of God.

When Israel and his extended family eventually arrived and settled into Egypt, they found that Joseph had been settled in long enough that he had assimilated into Egyptian culture, much as a meal is taken into the body, digested, absorbed into the tissues, and becomes part of the body—first feeding it, then fueling it, finally becoming it. When Israel at long last saw Joseph with his own eyes, he recognized not only a son who was, as it were, risen from the dead, but also one who was thoroughly Egyptianized.[36]

Egypt always assimilates its own—whether citizens or aliens, settlers or sojourners. Joseph seemed a clear example of that, something that was not in the least lost on Israel. Married to an Egyptian, the daughter of a priest;[37] fashioning a home and raising a family in Pharaoh's shadow;[38] enjoying power and receiving praise throughout the land;[39] the self-proclaimed *"father to Pharaoh, lord of his entire household and ruler of all Egypt;"*[40] his former life an indistinct, fading memory;[41] his current life in a pagan empire both successful and prosperous[42]—all of it gave Israel pause. So much so, in fact, that as he anticipated his death, the patriarch engaged in two extraordinary acts.

In the latter of the two acts, Israel, from his deathbed, while speaking his final and fully authoritative family blessing, claimed Joseph's Egyptian born sons, Ephraim and Manasseh, as his own. *"Now then,"* he informed Joseph, *"your two sons born to you in Egypt before I came to you here will be reckoned as mine; Ephraim and Manasseh will be mine, just as Reuben and Simeon are mine. Any children born to you after them will be yours; in the territory they inherit they will be reckoned under the names of their brothers."*[43]

---

35. Exod 1:6–22.

36. "From the start, Jacob is on the alert regarding both Egypt and Joseph. In three stages, we watch Jacob gradually and reluctantly come to realize that Joseph is permanently lost to him and to the way of Israel and that his choice of Joseph as his replacement was a mistake. In the first episode, the reunion of Jacob and Joseph, we will see the first sign of Jacob's reserve toward his beloved but Egyptianized son and the prospective cultural antagonism of Egypt toward Israel." Kass, *Beginning of Wisdom*, 621.

37. Gen 41:45, 50.
38. Gen 41:50–52.
39. Gen 41:41–44.
40. Gen 44:8.
41. Gen 41:51.
42. Gen 41:52.
43. Gen 48:5–6.

The move was as bold as it was stunning. Israel was, in effect, adopting his grandchildren, forcing Joseph to relinquish his parental rights.[44] But the old man was not finished. He promptly placed his hands on his grandchildren and, as he did, blessed their father Joseph. As significant as the words spoken was the placement of Israel's hands. Though what follows is, in fact, the blessing of Joseph,[45] it is important to realize that since Israel's hands rested on Ephraim and Manasseh, and not on Joseph, the family blessing would be carried on through Joseph's sons, not through Joseph himself. The blessing of Joseph is actually the blessing of his sons.

Israel's blessing over Ephraim and Manasseh, however, came with a twist. All went according to prescribed protocol—Joseph having placed Ephraim on his father's left and Manasseh, the oldest, on Israel's right—until Israel, always the trickster, reverted to Jacob-of-old and crossed his arms, placing his right hand on the younger and his left hand on the older, thereby transferring the primary blessing to Ephraim.[46] That was not what Joseph wanted, but what Joseph wanted was no longer the issue. It was now Israel's call.

By that time, however, Joseph was more than what the *New International Version* terms *"displeased."*[47] The entire ceremony was making Joseph sick—literally. The Hebrew word is *wayyera*—*"and it was noxious"* to Joseph, who physically took hold of his father's right had to put it on the head of Manasseh, saying, *"No, my father, this one is the firstborn; put your right hand on his head."*[48] Yet, again, that was no longer Joseph's but Israel's call. *"I know, my son, I know,"* said Israel. *"He too will become a people, and he too will become great. Nevertheless, his younger brother will be greater than he, and his descendants will become a group of nations."*[49] And the deed was done.

It may be more than possible—in fact, it seems to me probable—that Israel saw Joseph as so completely Egyptianized, so fully assimilated into

---

44. I believe that those who interpret this story as Joseph receiving a double portion of Israel's inheritance through his sons, focus on a single scene while missing the panoramic fullness of what had happened, what is happening and what is yet to happen to the children of Israel in Egypt. I believe that Israel blesses Joseph's sons, not in order that Joseph will receive a double portion, but to keep Joseph from receiving any portion at all, his son having become, in the old man's estimation, hopelessly Egyptianized. Thus, the blessing of Israel is passed on to Israel's grandsons, whom he in essence adopts.

45. Gen 48:15 — "Then (Israel) blessed Joseph *and said* . . . ."
46. Gen 48:12–16.
47. Gen 48:17.
48. Gen 48:18.
49. Gen 48:19.

Egyptian life and culture, that he knew he could never extricate his son. If he could not save his son, however, he would at least save his grandsons. If Joseph was so Egyptian as to view the land of Pharaoh as a satisfactory substitute for the Land of Promise, then Israel would see that the promise was carried on, not through the paganized Joseph, but through Ephraim and Manasseh.

Israel may have been the only one in his family who understood the power of an oasis to become a wilderness, the power of a place of abundance like Egypt to become first addictive, then enslaving. For all his failing eyesight,[50] Israel nonetheless saw clearly the power exerted by such an oasis as Egypt over mind and heart, a power to produce amnesia in a resident and reshape loves and loyalties. Israel saw how easy Egypt made it for Joseph to forget who he was and where he was from, and the old man quickly assessed that his other sons and their families might similarly lose their identity and independence if they settled into the oasis, growing their roots too deeply in Egyptian soil.

Israel, though, was not the only person in Egypt perceptive enough to grasp that; so was Pharaoh. When Joseph's brothers received an audience with Egypt's king, they explained, *"We have come to live here awhile, because the famine is severe in Canaan and your servants' flocks have no pasture."*[51] The phrase *"live here awhile"* means "to sojourn" and refers to the temporary state of a resident alien. But, afterwards, when Pharaoh spoke to Joseph about the matter, he said, *"Your father and your brothers have come to you, and the land of Egypt is before you; settle your father and your brothers in the best part of the land. Let them live in Goshen."*[52] In other words, "Forget all that sojourning talk; have your family settle-in to the best that Egypt offers." Pharaoh was shrewd. Like Israel, he knew the pull and power of the oasis he ruled; he knew how the game was played, how the rigged system worked. If he could turn sojourners into settlers, he could speed up and all but ensure their complete assimilation into the Egyptian way of life.

From father Israel's perspective, his son Joseph was irrefutable evidence of that reality. The old man grasped the game and the system, and he knew how to rig either or both—the proof in the pudding from his younger days, when he had played the game and worked the system as well as anyone. He knew that if he did not get his children out of Egypt soon, he might never get them out. Already, Israel, shrewd as ever, had set a plan in motion.

---

50. Gen 48:10.
51. Gen 47:4.
52. Gen 47:5–6a.

Already, the old conniving Jacob had reared his head and was hedging his bet.

In the former of the two extraordinary acts, Israel demanded from Joseph a solemn oath (Hebrew: *hishav'ah li*) that he would bury his father, not in Egypt, but at the old family cemetery in Canaan:

> *"If I have found favor in your eyes, put your hand under my thigh and promise that you will show me kindness and faithfulness. Do not bury me in Egypt, but when I rest with my fathers, carry me out of Egypt and bury me where they are buried."*
> *"I will do as you say,"* he said.
> *"Swear to me!"* he said. *Then Joseph swore to him, and Israel worshiped as he leaned on the top of his staff.*[53]

Not only did that request show Israel's resolve to never assimilate into Egyptian culture and to never embrace Joseph's new way of life, but it also revealed the shrewdness, trickery and deception of that part of Israel which remained ever Jacob. In fact, the only other recorded instance of Jacob demanding a solemn oath was from his brother Esau who, in a moment of desperation, promised to hand over his birthright. Now the aging Israel demanded, this time from his son, a "deathright" as well: "When I die, get me out of this place and take me back home." In the language of the day, Israel was specific. "Don't order it done, like you did when you brought me here, but do it yourself." The language is quite pointed and specific: *"(You) carry me out of Egypt and (you) bury me where they are buried"*[54]—to which Joseph replied, and then swore at his father's insistence, *"I will do as you say."*[55]

Was there a twinkle in the old man's eyes? It was a Jacob moment if there ever was one: a sleight-of-hand, a putting-over-on, a shrewd move. When Israel died, Joseph had no choice; he must leave Egypt. He had sworn a solemn oath. Did the old man recall God's promise? *"I will go down to Egypt with you, and I will surely bring you back again."*[56] Was the old man, from his deathbed, participating in that promise, and in the even earlier promises to Isaac and Abraham? When the patriarch died, what could his family in Goshen do but follow Joseph as part of the funeral cortege to Canaan, as part of an exodus from Egypt? Not quite as massive as the one four centuries later, but an exodus nonetheless. Israel seemed intent on playing

---

53. Gen 47:29–31.
54. Gen 47:30a.
55. Gen 47:30b.
56. Gen 46:4.

his part in the fulfillment of a long-cherished promise.[57] *"Free at last! Free at last! Thank God Almighty, we are free at last!"*

But was there freedom to be had, or even wanted?

When Israel died, Joseph sent word to Pharaoh of his father's passing; adding, *"My father made me swear an oath and said, 'I am about to die; bury me in the tomb I dug for myself in the land of Canaan',"*[58] then requesting, *"Now let me go up and bury my father; then I will return."*[59]

As to freedom being *had*, when Pharaoh responded to Joseph's request, there was a hint of I've-been-backed-into-a-corner-and-what-can-I-do reluctance in his words. *"Go up and bury your father,"* he said, *"as"*—or, perhaps, better yet *"since"*— *"he made you swear to do."*[60] Pharaoh then followed that seeming reluctance with measures intended to ensure the entire funeral cortege would, in fact, return to Egypt: *"All Pharaoh's officials accompanied (Joseph)—the dignitaries of his court and all the dignitaries of Egypt—besides all the members of Joseph's household and his brothers and those belonging to his father's household."*[61] Not only that, but according to Genesis 50:9, *"Chariots and horsemen also went up with him. It was a very large company."* It was a show of respect for the father of a principal figure in Egypt and, equally, a show of strength to guarantee that principal figure would return to Egypt. As it turned out, Pharaoh's political savvy out-flimflammed Jacob. The result

---

57. Like mother, like son. See Gen 27:1–40. Jacob's mother Rebekah, after overhearing her husband Isaac's intent to give the family blessing to the oldest son Esau, shrewdly set a plan in motion to guarantee that that the blessing would not be given to the firstborn, but to the younger Jacob. In my mind, the story is often misinterpreted. Rebekah is not the villain in the story, but the hero. If anyone is attempting to thwart God's already disclosed plan, it is not Rebekah, but Isaac. Rebekah is not attempting to keep Isaac from doing the right thing, but to stop him doing the wrong thing. In truth, by preparing to pronounce the blessing on Esau, Isaac is acting in opposition to the clearly spoken word and will of God, which was revealed to Rebekah as a promise—a promise which directed that, contrary to the custom of the time and place, the older son would be subservient to the younger: *"Two nations are in your womb, and two peoples from within you will be separated; one people will be stronger than the other, and the older will serve the younger"* (Gen 25:23).In essence, with Isaac's plan in place to bless Esau, Rebekah saw the promise of God about to be dismissed, so she stepped in to bring about its fulfillment. It was a shrewd move on her part, hatched as it was, not out of a sinful and sinister heart, but out of a true heart's desire to see God's promise honored and fulfilled. Years later, in Egypt, with the promise of God once more hanging in the balance and the Promised Land about to be forgotten in favor of Pharaoh's land, Israel hatched an equally shrewd plot from equally pure motives to see God's promise to his people honored and fulfilled.

58. Gen 50:5a.

59. Gen 50:5b.

60. Gen 50:6.

61. Gen 50:7–8a.

was that Joseph and his kin were soon back under the king's watchful eye: *"After burying his father, Joseph returned to Egypt, together with his brothers and all the others who had gone with him to bury his father."*[62]

As to freedom being even *wanted*, when Joseph asked permission to leave Egypt, he assured Pharaoh *"I will return."*[63] As pledge of that promise, not everything or everyone belonging to Joseph left Egypt. Almost missed in the narrative are a dozen words—a subtle sentence—tacked on to the end of Gen 9:50: *"Only their children and their flocks and herds were left in Goshen"*—enough to serve as security for Joseph's return, and the return of all the children of Israel.

It seems that Pharaoh and Israel alone understood how the system worked, rigged as it was in favor of the house. The old man and his extended family might win here and there, now and then, but over time, the house always wins. To Israel, Joseph was proof of that. So, the man aptly named Jacob—"deceiver," "trickster," "charlatan," or perhaps even "high stakes gambler"—went "all-in" with a bold two-part gamble that was intended to get him and his descendants, Joseph included, out of Egypt. He might lose the shirt off his back in the process, but he would lose it trying to move his family toward a promise that Egypt made easy to forget.

It would take time, though. At the very least, Israel must wait long enough for the famine to end, otherwise the journey to Canaan would be a death march. He must also wait for the perfect moment; timing was everything. As it turned out, Israel waited seventeen years.[64] Finally, the opportune moment came. As Israel drew close to death, he saw his chance and seized it.[65] But it was too late. For Joseph, the comfort level of the oasis was too high. For Pharaoh, the risk of losing Joseph was too great. The high stakes gamble failed, and Israel's descendants remained in Egypt for centuries afterwards, losing their freedom on the heels of having lost their identity.

> (There was once) a little wave, bobbing along in the ocean, having a grand old time. He's enjoying the wind and the fresh air — until he notices the other waves in front of him, crashing against the shore.
>
> "My God, this is terrible," the wave says. "Look what's going to happen to me!"

---

62. Gen 50:14.
63. Gen 50:5.
64. Gen 47:28.
65. Gen 47:28–31.

> Then along comes another wave. It sees the first wave, looking grim, and it says to him, "Why do you look so sad?"
>
> The first wave says, "You don't understand! We're all going to crash! All of us waves are going to be nothing! Isn't it terrible?"
>
> The second wave says, "No, you don't understand. You're not a wave, you're part of the ocean."[66]

If I may draw a conclusion never intended by the weaver of that story, who told it with a positive twist, the children of Israel arrived in Egypt as a wave, distinct and free, but became in Egypt merely part of the ocean, homogenous and eventually enslaved. As both Pharaoh and Israel knew it would, the oasis did its work. Egypt always assimilates its own. An oasis—if we settle-in, forgetting our identity and forfeiting our independence—has the very real potential of becoming a wilderness where dreams of God's promise grow dim and eventually disappear.

To those like Joseph, "comfortable in his own place of exile,"[67] the oasis that was Egypt was not seen as a problem. How could such blessing and abundance be a problem? But the gambling Jacob saw clearly that, in the words of Kass, "All this prosperity and increase will make it very difficult for Israel to return as intended to the Promised Land when the famine ends. Why will Israel want to go back to the promises of the Promised Land from a place that already seems to fulfill those promises?"[68]

The old man Israel had at least given his children the chance to enter into freedom and promise. He had, in his own scheming way, put feet to what faith they had left. He had arranged to lead them, even in death, out of Egypt and into the Promised Land. Did he anticipate they would afterward return to Egypt? Regardless, they did. Instead of living in the Promise, Joseph and the rest died under Pharaoh's hold.

It is a down note on which the book of Genesis ends. It is a fitting note, I think, but nonetheless a down note. The author recorded simply, *"So Joseph died at the age of a hundred and ten. And after they embalmed him, he was placed in a coffin in Egypt."*[69] The symbolism, intentional or not, is pointed and powerful. That does indeed seem to be the end of the story. How does the long drama of Abraham, Isaac, Jacob and Joseph end? In Egypt . . . with an unmistakable period after *"in Egypt."* For four centuries more, God's people would remain *"in Egypt."* Whatever else might be said about God's Chosen who were once, briefly, as Jacob had hoped and schemed, out of

---

66. Albom, *Tuesdays With Morrie*, 179–80.
67. Kass, *Beginning of Wisdom*, 635.
68. Kass, *Beginning of Wisdom*, 635.
69. Gen 50:26.

Egypt, they were most definitely still *"in Egypt"*—and, in a very real sense, *"in a coffin in Egypt."* For four hundred more years, instead of living in the Promise that could have been theirs, they died in Egypt.

That is, potentially, the subtle but lethal danger of an oasis. It can become a wilderness when it disorients us and draws us away from God, triggering a forgetfulness of who we are and to whom we belong, promising fulfillment now instead of later, causing us to stop short of God's ultimate promise and to settle in rather than sojourn on. When that happens, when we remain in Egypt rather than living in the promise, then like Joseph and, ultimately, like the rest of the children of Israel, we may be free for a time, but we are never free as we are meant to be. In the words of Nicholas Perrin: ". . . freedom is not, as so many today seem to think, the ability to do anything we want, depending on our whims and personal cravings. Rather, true freedom is the ability to fulfill the calling that we have been given by God as created and redeemed humanity."[70]

The freedom to be who we were made and meant to be, who we were created and redeemed to be, can never be found in Egypt. Egypt is, after all, the Land of Pharaoh, not of promise. With Pharaoh, we may be free for a time, but we are never free to become everything and possess everything God desires. That freedom is ours only in promise.

---

70. Perrin, *Exodus Revealed*, 213.

SOJOURNERS OR WANDERERS?

Whereas an oasis[1] draws people by its abundance, a wilderness deters people by its lack, as well as by its stark terrain and severe conditions. Because of Egypt's bounty in protracted seasons of scarcity, multitudes of marginal people, like Israel and his family, sought refuge there and, in time, became settlers—moved in, took up residence, put down roots and became part of Pharaoh's nation on the Nile. A wilderness, by contrast, is not conducive to settling. In the wild, one is more prone to find sojourners or, perhaps, even wanderers, but seldom settlers.

Those in Scripture who found themselves passing through or embedded in a wilderness—due either to divine sovereignty or human sin—were, for the most part, either *wanderers* (dazed, disoriented, confused, floundering) or *sojourners* (steady, oriented, focused, resolute). The children of Israel, wilderness-bound for forty years, were very much wanderers, as were others, but only temporarily—David when pursued by Saul[2] and then by Absalom;[3] Job when attacked by Satan;[4] Elijah following his victory on Mount Carmel.[5] By contrast, Jesus, during his forty-day fast in the wild,[6] was very much a sojourner, as were others before him—Abraham when journeying from Ur,[7] Moses when plodding through Sinai.[8] Some desert

---

1. Either a literal fertile place in a desert or a figurative place like Egypt was to famine ravaged Israel. For the latter, see: Gen 41:53—42:2; 47:3-4a.
2. 2 Sam 23:7—24:22.
3. 2 Sam 15:1—18:33.
4. Job 1:6—2:10.
5. 1 Kgs 19:1-18.
6. Matt 4:1-11; Mark 1:12-13; Luke 4:13.
7. Gen 12:1-9.
8. Deut 2:1—3:20.

SOJOURNERS OR WANDERERS? 113

trekkers even blurred boundaries. Job, for example, was dazed but steady,[9] began in confusion but ended in clarity.[10]

When it comes to a wilderness, there are wanderers and there are sojourners. Which we are is determined, not so much by the wilderness we travel as by the heart we bring to the journey. Those whose hearts are unfixed and stray from God to surroundings and circumstances are overcome by fear and worry. They are soon wandering from place to place without clear focus or definite direction. Those whose hearts are fixed and stay with God are, by contrast, purpose-driven and walk in rhythm with God's leading, even though the steps they take may be painful. They are sojourning with God, toward God, and with the promise in view.[11] In Scripture, those who *wander* a wilderness—literally or figuratively—most frequently do so as a result of their own rebellion,[12] the rebellion of others,[13] the instigation of Satan;[14] or of life in a fallen world just happening;[15] while those who *sojourn* a wilderness—again, physically or metaphorically—most frequently do so in response to a clear call or a definite leading of God.[16] For those reasons, there tends to be more clarity of purpose among sojourners, while wanderers struggle more to grasp what is happening.

Wandering is the image most associated with Israel's wilderness days. The phrase "wilderness wandering" slips almost automatically from our lips

9. Job 1:13—2:10.
10. Job 42:1–6.
11. Cf. Phil 4:12–14 and Heb 11:13-16.
12. The nation of Israel is such an example. Num 32:10–13.

13. David, victimized by Absalom's rebellion, is such an example. See 2 Sam 15 where David describes his own state as one of wandering, saying to Ittai the Gittite, who had come to join his ranks, *"You only came yesterday. And today shall I make you wander about with us, when I do not know where I am going?"* (v. 20).

14. Job may be the classic biblical example of such a wilderness wanderer. See the entire book of Job, but especially 1:1—2:10; 3:12–13, 16–17; 26, 6:1–4 where the sufferer struggles to right himself in a severe wilderness that had cruelly stripped him of all that had defined him and seemed to expose as false most of what he had believed regarding God.

15. 1 Kgs 19:1–18.

16. Abraham was called by God to leave Ur and embrace a sojourner's life, becoming a nomad with flocks and kinfolk as he made his way to an unspecified land that God would one day reveal to him (Gen 12:1—4a). Moses was called by God to lead Israel from Egypt, which included a forty-year hitch in a vast and sometimes hostile wilderness (Exod 3:1—4:20). In obedience to God's call to take on flesh, humble himself and become obedient to death (Phil 2:7–8), Jesus first followed the Spirit into a wilderness, fasting forty days before winning a pivotal victory over Satan (Matt 4:1–11), and ultimately into the horror of Gethsemane and Calvary, which became our salvation (Heb 10:5–7; Phil 2:5–8; Matt 26:36—27:50).

and is readily understood to reference Israel's forty years in Sinai. In point of fact, however, Scripture uses that specific language sparingly. In probably the best-known such passage (Num 32:13), we are told that *"The Lord's anger burned against Israel and he made them wander in the desert forty years, until the whole generation of those who had done evil in his sight was gone."*[17]

Inherent within the word "wander" is the aspect of being lost or purposeless, directionless and drifting; of moving about without a fixed course or goal. A "wanderer" could be said to ramble, to meander, perhaps even to feel or grope one's way haphazardly, blindly, aimlessly. The word first surfaces in Genesis 4 when God passed sentence on Cain, who had killed his brother Abel: *"You will be a restless wanderer on the earth."*[18] In response, Cain insisted, *"My punishment is more than I can bear. Today you are driving me from the land, and I will be hidden from your presence. I will be a restless wanderer on the earth, and whoever finds me will kill me."*[19]

From the word's first appearance in the Old Testament text to its association with Israel's generation-long trek through the wilderness, "to wander" seems fundamentally tied to a person's or a people's sin and disobedience,[20] and does, by nature, produce restlessness—a restlessness that is not dependent on physical, geographical wandering. Cain, remember, became a city builder,[21] named the place after his son,[22] and presumably lived there. Can a settler remain a wanderer even while settled? Certainly. Such is the nature of sin. Prodigals wander with their hearts before their feet. The prodigal in Jesus' story, for example, had put a great distance between he and his father before he ever left home.[23] As Elie Wiesel pointed out, "Exile is not necessarily linked to geography."[24] Even should geographical wandering cease in favor of settling, restlessness remains. Like a Bach composition, the notes

---

17. Also Josh 14:10 and 2 Kgs 21:8.

18. Gen 4:12.

19. Gen 4:13–14.

20. The Hebrew word *ta'ah* in the qal stem means "to wander" and in the hiphil stem morphs into "to be led astray." The two images are intimately linked. So much so that always lurking behind the word "wander" is the idea of straying because of sin. The Old Testament word also describes the act of leading astray the blind (Deut 27:18) and can refer to someone "staggering" from drunkenness (Isa 28:7–8). It is a favorite word of the Prophets who apply it to those who stray from God's way. See Brown, *New International Dictionary of New Testament Theology*, 457–58.

21. Gen 4:17b.

22. Gen 4:17c.

23. Luke 15:11–13. The boy's simple demand for his inheritance, essentially a wishing for his father's premature death, demonstrates the vast distance that existed between father and son before the boy ever gathered his belongings and left home and family behind.

24. Wiesel, *Messengers of God*, 55.

keep sounding, the rest never comes. The wandering restlessness within can seem, at times, interminable, making it, at least from a wilderness perspective, *"more than (we) can bear."*

The word "wandering" denotes a life of restlessness;[25] a life with no fixed roots, no place to call home;[26] a life that is directionless and in need of guidance;[27] a life that has strayed from its past, from its God, and from God's word.[28] Wandering is, however, most often associated with a literal wilderness or with wilderness-like conditions.[29]

Regardless of the type of wilderness, when we allow circumstances to distract us, to divert our eyes and hearts from God, they can daze and disorient us, cloud and confuse us, leaving us unfocused and floundering. As a result, we end up like Israel and other desert trekkers—wandering.

Sojourning, on the other hand, is intentional and purposeful. The word describes someone traveling a specific direction with a clear destination in mind. Sojourners, always light on their feet, are passing through, moving on, sometimes staying in one place for a while,[30] but always temporarily, eventually striking camp and hitting the road once more.

Abraham was called to leave Ur and "sojourn"—literally; that is what the Hebrew word means[31]—until God said, "Stop! This is the place."[32] As a result, for most of his life, Abraham lived as a nomad. His traveling was not a sight-seeing trip, but his lifestyle, his answer to the call of God. Though occasionally trekking across long stretches of wilderness, Abraham was never a wanderer, but always a sojourner. Along the way, he grew a flock and grew a family, he became the great nation God had promised he would be.[33]

Moses as well, for all the time he spent in wildernesses, was never a wanderer, but always a sojourner. A careful reading of his biography reveals

---

25. Gen 4:12b.

26. Gen 20:13; Josh 14:10; Hos 9:17.

27. Zech 10:2.

28. 2 Kgs 21:8; Ps 119:10, 21, 118; Jer 14:10; Zech 10:2. A favorite image of Old Testament authors to describe the Hebrews' habit of turning aside from God's way and wandering from it is that of straying sheep (Ps 119:176; Isa 13:14; 53:6).

29. Gen 21:14; Num 32:13; Josh 14:10; Job 12:24; Ps 107:4, 40; Heb 11:37–38.

30. In the Septuagint, the Greek word *parepidemos* (one who sojourns) comes from the verb *parepidemeo*, which literally means *"to stay for a short time in a strange place."* The word "sojourner" is often translated "stranger," since it describes someone whose home is elsewhere but who is living as an exile in a land not his/her own, among a people not his/her own.

31. See Gen 12:1, 4.

32. Gen 12:1.

33. Gen 12:2–3.

a life carefully orchestrated by God to get him—one step at a time, each step of the way—to exactly that place he needed to be so as to prepare him for the key tasks of getting the Hebrew people out of Egypt, through Sinai, and into the Promised Land. Though for forty years his human flock, Israel, was routinely dazed, disoriented, confused, floundering and unfaithful, Moses remained, with rare exceptions, steady, oriented, resolute, focused and faithful.

Likewise, Jesus was a wilderness sojourner, not a wilderness wanderer. On the heels of his baptism,[34] Jesus followed the Spirit's lead into the wilderness[35] where, despite its dangers on one hand and its enticements on the other, Jesus was never distracted from God's goal for his life, never sidetracked from God's call, never unclear about God's purpose.[36] Concerning that wilderness sojourn, Matthew wrote:

> *After fasting forty days and forty nights, he was hungry. The tempter came to him and said, "If you are the Son of God, tell these stones to become bread."*
>
> *Jesus answered, "It is written: 'Man does not live on bread alone, but on every word that comes from the mouth of God'."*
>
> *Then the devil took him to the holy city and had him stand on the highest point of the temple. "If you are the Son of God," he said, "throw yourself down. For it is written:*
>
> *'He will command his angels concerning*
>   *you,*
> *and they will lift you up in their hands,*
>   *so that you will not strike your foot against a stone'."*
>
> *Jesus answered him, "It is also written: 'Do not put the Lord your God to the test'."*
>
> *Again, the devil took him to a very high mountain and showed him all the kingdoms of the world and their splendor. "All this I will give you," he said, "if you will bow down and worship me."*
>
> *Jesus said to him, "Away from me, Satan! For it is written: 'Worship the Lord your God, and serve him only'."*
>
> *Then the devil left him, and angels came and attended him.*[37]

At several different levels, Jesus' forty-day wilderness sojourn parallels Moses' forty-year Sinai sojourn. Abraham's, however, stands apart. Primarily, Abraham was not "exiled" to a wilderness, as both Moses and Jesus were, but chose the wilderness as his place of growing flocks and family strong

---

34. Matt 3:13—4:1.
35. Matt 4:1.
36. Matt 4:1–11.
37. Matt 4:2–11.

enough to sustain his tribe. There he settled for stretches until the needs of his flock necessitated moving on. For Abraham, the wilderness was not a test, but where he pitched his tent as he became a great nomadic patriarch on his way to the land God would one day show him.

What Abraham does share in common with Moses and Jesus, however, is his clarity and purposefulness—identifying marks of one who is in no way a wanderer, but in every way a sojourner. Even in his taxing-the-imagination test, the call from God to sacrifice his son Isaac,[38] Abraham does not waver, but follows God's call with great clarity and purpose, determined to faithfully obey regardless of personal cost, reasoning that, if worse came to worse, once the deed was done, God could raise Isaac from the dead.[39]

Moses and Jesus, despite being in the wild for different reasons than Abraham, demonstrate similar clarity of purpose. Neither wavers but follows God's call and faithfully obeys regardless of personal cost, with complete and utter confidence in God. They are sojourners, not wanderers, and that is how it is meant to be. That is how God's people are meant to traverse a wilderness.

As I write this chapter, my youngest son and his wife have just concluded a sojourn of sorts through a long personal desert. Nine months earlier, they purchased their dream home, spent one night in it, were awakened in the middle of the night and told that the river was flooding, and they must evacuate the next morning. They did, and the river overran that entire rural subdivision. It was one of those once-in-a-century floods. The beautiful, long-awaited dream home flooded, necessitating months of demolition, a complete gutting of the inside, and the eventual restoration of the house. Having sold their previous house, and now without any residence of their own, they were forced to move in with a friend, who generously offered his house to them. They eventually moved back into their dream house . . . just in time for Hurricane Harvey to hit, and the whole scenario played out again. Though living out of suitcases in a house that was not theirs, they never wavered or wandered, never lost their focus or determination, but were always aware of the ongoing work that would one day, as promised, get them into the house that would be their home. They were ever sojourners—doing what work they must, trusting the work another was doing—until they arrived at their intended destination.

The more I read Scripture, the more I am convinced that we are meant to walk a wilderness in that manner—not as wanderers acquiescing to the elements, turning our focus inward, barely shuffling across the sand in

38. Gen 22:1–2.
39. Heb 11:19.

"poor-me" despondency, but as sojourners still hearing the call of God, still seeing the promise ahead, still believing that there is an end, a destination, a place that is truly our home, *"whose architect and builder is God."*[40]

When it comes to a wilderness, there are wanderers and there are sojourners. Which we are is determined, not so much by the wilderness we travel as by the heart we bring to the journey.

We may be led into a wilderness because of our "wandering"—as Israel was—but we are never meant to wander a wilderness. We are meant to sojourn. It is not always easy, for sojourning requires a great deal of trust and perseverance, and sometimes a hanging-on-for-our-life faith, but it remains the only way to travel. We are not meant to spend our days in confusion (dazed and disoriented, floundering and unfaithful), but in clarity (oriented and focused, resolute and faithful), knowing that God is, as promised,[41] doing his work and working his will so that we can become everything and possess everything he desires.

---

40. Heb 11:10.
41. Rom 8:28.

PART IV

MORE THAN MEETS THE EYES

"We can end up with a view of God that is more like a fairy godmother—showing up from time to time to wave a sparkling wand and bring a little magic into our lives. Or like a superhero waiting in the wings for just the right moment to step in and rescue us from disaster. A view like this doesn't begin to come to terms with how complex, mysterious, and completely unpredictable God actually is or with his overarching agenda for our broken world or for our individual lives.

There is, of course, a certain benefit to limiting God's involvement in our lives to these occasional sightings. This way we can keep God at a comfortable distance from the awful things that happen to us and the tragedies we hear about in the daily news. If God only makes positive appearances, then we're spared from having to deal with awkward questions about why bad things happen under his watch. Yet, while I certainly don't want to take anything away from the notion that there are pleasant places in life when God's hand is evident (I rejoice in them myself), at the same time, it's scary to think God is somehow absent at crucial moments and from crises when we need him most."[42]

CAROLYN CUSTIS JAMES

---

42 James, *Gospel of Ruth*, 126

FOR OUR GOOD

The word *katartidzein* appears several times in the Greek New Testament and is translated variously in our English texts as *prepare, restore, equip, train,* and even *discipline*. Originally, *katartidzein* described the action of repairing a torn fishing net or setting a dislocated bone in a person's arm. At its heart, the word describes the process of taking something damaged and restoring it to its intended usefulness.[1]

Both Paul and Peter thought of the word in terms of *restoration*. Paul wrote to the church in Galatia, *". . . if someone is caught in a sin, you who are spiritual should restore him gently,"*[2] while Peter encouraged the far-flung persecuted church with the assurance that *"the God of all grace, who called you to his eternal glory in Christ, after you have suffered a little while, will himself restore you and make you strong, firm and steadfast."*[3]

Elsewhere, Matthew and Mark used the word in its sense of *preparation*, telling of James and John *"preparing their nets"*[4] while Paul wrote to the Ephesian Christians, *"It was (Jesus) who gave some to be apostles, some to be prophets, some to be evangelists, and some to be pastors and teachers, to prepare God's people for works of service, so that the body of Christ may be built up . . . ."*[5]

---

1. William Barclay wrote: "In classical Greek it has a wide variety of meanings, all of which can be gathered together under one or other of two heads. (i) It means 'to adjust, to put in order, to restore.' Hence it is sed of pacifying a city which is torn by faction; of setting a limb that has been dislocated; of developing certain parts of the body by exercise; of restoring a person to his rightful mind; of reconciling friends, who have become estranged. (ii) It is used of 'equipping or fully furnishing someone or something for some given purpose.' So it is used of fitting out a ship and it is used of an army, fully armed and equipped, and drawn up in battle array." Barclay, *New Testament Words*, 168–69.

2. Gal 6:1.

3. 1 Pet 5:10.

4. Matt 4:21; Mark 1:19.

5. Eph 4:11–12.

The author of Hebrews preferred the image of *equip*, praying for his readers, *"May the God of peace . . . equip you with everything good for doing his will,"*[6] and Paul spoke of *supply* when he wrote to the Thessalonians, *"Night and day we pray most earnestly that we may see you again and supply what is lacking in your faith."*[7]

The common denominator in all those uses of the word *katartidzein* is the idea of returning to its intended usefulness something that has been damaged or is not functioning as it should. Today we might best understand *katartidzein* in terms of *therapy*.

As I write this chapter, I have started therapy for a painful left shoulder that has lost a significant percentage of its mobility and, if left in its current damaged condition, will become a *frozen* shoulder, requiring surgery. My therapist is a friend who, despite that friendship, persists in putting me through great pain on a twice-weekly basis. Wrapping my shoulder in heat to begin our sessions and in cold to end them feels wonderful, but it is the hour-and-a-half between those two feel-good episodes that can be agonizing. As if that in-office pain were not enough, she gave me a series of exercises to do at home twice each day. The worst of the ten sets requires that I place my forearm on a table, keep my palm flat and my elbow in place as I bend down and away to the point of significant pain and hold that position for five seconds. I repeat the process nine times.

At our last session, I told her, "I don't like you very much." "Therapy *is* painful," she smilingly reminded me, "but it is for your own good." She was right. Already, pain is diminishing, mobility is returning, and I am on my way to a fully functioning left shoulder. Therapy is *katartidzein* to me—a sometimes agonizing process which has produced intense pain and reduced me to tears more than once, but is restoring my damaged shoulder to its intended usefulness, though not overnight.

A wilderness is like that. In the hands of God, the master therapist, a wilderness is healing and recuperative, strengthening and restorative. Those parts of us which have been damaged by sin or simply need to be fortified are the focus of his work. Unless we are Jesus—and we are not—God uses wildernesses of sin and sovereignty to get us functioning as we were meant to function. A wilderness is for our own good. Like therapy, it is that which stands between our injuries and inadequacies on the one hand and our healing and wholeness on the other. It stands between our current state of limitation and impairment, which is bad for us, and our coming state of freedom of movement and proper function which is good for us.

---

6. Heb 13:20–21.
7. 1 Thess 3:10.

In Israel's case, a wilderness stood between the tormenting restraints of Egyptian bondage, which was never intended as their ultimate destination, and the welcome freedom of the Promised Land, which God had always planned for them. In God's providence, there was but one way for those Hebrew children to come into their greatest good, and that was through a wilderness. Whenever God leads his people into a wilderness, it is always for their ultimate blessing. For that reason, God always has the endgame in view, and that endgame is always for our good, our healing and wholeness, our becoming and possessing. *"I know the plans I have for you,"* he announced through the prophet Jeremiah, *"plans to prosper you and not to harm you, plans to give you hope and a future."*[8] The apostle Paul concurred: *"We know that in all things God works for the good of those who love him, who have been called according to his purpose."*[9]

Of course, those are easy truths to *"Amen!"* while listening to an upbeat sermon, but difficult truths to believe and embrace in the clutches of an incapacitating wilderness. There are times, when desert winds whip the sand like tiny spikes of glass, that our eyes are tightly closed and unable to see the hand of God anywhere along those lengthy and lonely stretches. In such periods, Max Lucado's advice rings true: "When you can't trace God's hand, trust his heart."[10] The heart of God always beats for the good of his children. Even in a debilitating desert, he desires only our best, only our ultimate good.

Again, the therapy image is helpful. Therapy is not my idea of how to spend four free hours each week. Sitting in Starbucks with my wife seems a far better use of time—and, I might add, much more enjoyable. But when you are on the brink of a frozen shoulder and hoping to avoid surgery, therapy moves to the top of the time-use list. Not only that, but that great inflictor of pain, the therapist, becomes your new best friend, because she is working for your ultimate good and is giving you something Starbucks cannot—a normal and fully functional shoulder. But that is seldom our attitude toward a wilderness while we walk its tormenting terrain.

More often than not, we become grumblers and gripers after the fashion of wilderness-bound Israel. We desire to halt the therapy, believing the patient knows better than the therapist; confident that Egyptian home remedies and over-the-counter potions from Pharaoh's pharmacy will do the trick and have us the picture of health in no time. Meanwhile, we disregard the Great Therapist whose diagnosis alone is accurate and whose treatment

---

8. Jer 29:11.
9. Rom 8:28.
10. Lucado, *Eye of the Storm*, 154.

alone is healing. Hustled by fast hands and smooth talk under the desert sun, we buy advertised easy solutions and bottles of snake oil from passing caravans of charlatans, while ignoring the trusted therapist whose shingle over the office door reads:

> *To those who love God,*
> *who are called according to his plan,*
> *everything that happens fits into a pattern for good.*[11]

For good. Our good. Always and only for our good.

An intriguing question, in light of the Bible's many wilderness stories, is simply this: What would have happened, or *not* have happened, to certain persons or groups had they never known a wilderness? Would Abraham ever have been our father in the faith without the wilderness that was Moriah? Probably not. As Soren Kierkegaard pointed out, "Abraham is not what he is without his dread,"[12] without his wilderness. But Abraham's is not the only story of someone *becoming* via desperate desert days. Would Israel ever have been a nation, a people for God's renown? Would David ever have been a man after God's own heart? Would Moses ever have been . . . well, Moses? Would Saul the persecutor ever have been Paul the apostle without a stint in Arabia that lasted twice as long as his stay at any church? Though Scripture gives no specific answers to those questions, we *do* know that a wilderness always serves God's purpose, a purpose which includes our greatest good. To bypass a wilderness is to miss elements essential to our spiritual walk and mission. That being true, I think it is safe to say that, at least to some degree, without a wilderness, there would be a deficiency in our lives that would make a fundamental negative difference in our faith-walk.

If Jesus *had* to pass through the wilderness, as he *had* to pass through Samaria,[13] then the inference is that had he missed the wilderness, he would have missed something essential to his spiritual ministry, and his spiritual life would have lacked a crucial element. I know how hard it is for many to think of Jesus in those terms. The idea of a developing Jesus, who needed to learn and grow and mature, is a foreign concept to many Christians. Such a picture does not jive with the Jesus we have come to know and love. The traditional Vacation Bible School Jesus was full-blown and full-grown from the start. He never wondered or questioned or struggled. He never wept until

---

11. Rom 8:28, *New Testament in Modern English*.
12. Kierkegaard, *Either/Or*, 1: 341.
13. Matt 4:1; John 4:4. The word used by John and translated *"had"—"he had to go through Samaria"*—implies a strong moral imperative, a profound and irresistible inner compulsion, and is often used in John's gospel of the urgent necessity to undertake a divine mission (John 3:14; 9:4; 10:16; 12:34; 20:9).

Lazarus died and never hurt until Gethsemane hit. He was perfectly mature by the age of twelve, when the graph of his spiritual life abruptly plateaued, like the line going straight on a hospital heart monitor. The biblical record, however, reads differently. Of Jesus, the author of Hebrews wrote:

> *While he lived on earth, anticipating death, Jesus cried out in pain and wept in sorrow as he offered up priestly prayers to God. Because he honored God, God answered him. Though he was God's Son, he learned trusting-obedience by what he suffered, just as we do. Then, having arrived at the full stature of his maturity . . . he became the source of eternal salvation to all who believingly obey him.*[14]

Mark Harris wrote, "Jesus of Nazareth lived with nerves raw to the sharp edges of life. He wore no suit of armor. He is Emmanuel, not immune or indifferent to our pain, but 'God with us' in our pain."[15] Scripture is firm in its stance that Jesus' sorrow and suffering became—in ways we cannot completely comprehend—agents of grace in the process of Jesus *becoming* Jesus.

It seems that no one, not even Jesus, is zapped with instant trusting-obedience. It seems that everyone, even Jesus, becomes and possesses everything God desires via a wilderness. That seems to be why the Spirit *threw out* Jesus into the desert. That is as valid a translation of the Greek word *ekballei* in Matthew 4:1 as the traditional *led* or *drove*. In fact, it is probably a far more accurate description of what happened to Jesus. Every sojourner of a severe wilderness to whom I have spoken says *that* is what it felt like. God just threw them out, dumped them in the desert, like last week's unwanted trash, and then forgot about them. Whoever thinks about trash once it is thrown out?

During the darkest days of my life, in the most oppressive wilderness I have ever known, that is precisely how it felt. It was as if God had hauled me out to some deserted dump, as far from him as east is from west, tossed me onto a pile of smoldering rubble, walked away and left me on my own. Then, adding insult to injury, he forgot about me. I have never felt more alone or lifeless. One thing I knew with certainty: my life was over.

There are stories in Scripture of people who felt that way. Job and Naomi are agonizing examples. Of that forlorn and seemingly God-forsaken pair, Carolyn Custis James wrote, "Naomi and Job share a fundamental

---

14. Heb 5:7–10, *Message*.
15. Harris, *Companions for Your Spiritual Journey*, 27.

equality in that they have both lost everything. Their lives are in ruins, and their souls are drowning in grief."[16]

When Naomi, upon her return to Bethlehem after losing her husband and both sons, spoke to old friends, we are permitted not only to hear her words, but also to feel the pain and poverty of her heart. *"'Don't call me Naomi,' she told them. 'Call me Mara, because the Almighty has made my life very bitter. I went away full, but the Lord has brought me back empty. Why call me Naomi? The Lord has afflicted me; the Almighty has brought misfortune on me.'"*[17]

Naomi means *pleasant*; Mara means *bitter*. The wilderness had wrought a fundamental change in the life of this widow and grieving mother. Though Ruth returned from Moab to Bethlehem with her, Naomi was nonetheless utterly alone, dumped by God at a place she never dreamed of in her worst nightmares, a place that was truly, at least in her estimation, God-forsaken, just as *she* was. Carolyn Custis James summarized succinctly:

> Naomi's words say it all: "I am empty" (see Ruth 1:21). Once brimming with life and dreams for the future, she is drained of hope and meaning. Her losses assault her value as a human being, her dignity as a child of God, her purpose in life. The culture will discard her; she believes God will too.[18]

Likewise, Job's words reveal intense pain, as well as the conviction that his life had ended, or that he at least wished it would end. In fact, Job went so far as to voice the belief that his fate would have been better had he never been born. It does not take reading between the lines to feel Job's incredible agony or to sense his despondency in view of the fact that life, for him, is over.

> *Why were there knees to*
> *receive me*
> *and breasts that I might be*
> *nursed?*
> *For now I would be lying*
> *down in peace;*
> *I would be asleep and at*
> *rest.*[19]
>
> *Or why was I not hidden in*

---

16. James, *Gospel of Ruth*, 57.
17. Ruth 1:20–21.
18. James, *Gospel of Ruth*, 59.
19. Job 3:12–13.

> the ground like a
>   stillborn child,
> like an infant who never
>   saw the light of day?
> There the wicked cease from
>   turmoil,
> and there the weary are at
>   rest.[20]
>
> I have no peace, no
>   quietness;
> I have no rest, but only
>   Turmoil.[21]
>
> If only my anguish could
>   be weighed
> and all my misery be placed
>   on the scales!
> It would surely outweigh the
>   sand of the seas— . . .
> The arrows of the Almighty
>   are in me,
> my spirit drinks in their
>   poison;
> God's terrors are marshaled
>   against me.[22]
>
> My days are swifter than a
>   runner;
> they fly away without a
>   glimpse of joy.[23]
>
> I loathe my very life.[24]

Holocaust survivor Elie Wiesel who, like Job, endured unimaginable suffering, took the extreme position that Job may have carried his feelings to the grave:

---

20. Job 3:16–17.
21. Job 3:26.
22. Job 6:2–3a, 4.
23. Job 9:25.
24. Job 10:1.

The last line of the book is also the last stroke of irony: "Vayamat iyov zaken useva yamim"—"And Job died an old man, saturated with years." This can be interpreted as: Saturated with life; he has had enough.[25]

Both Job and Naomi endured a frightening and indefinable wilderness. They felt forsaken and crushed at a deeply profound and personal level.

If Jesus did not share similar feelings when dumped in a wilderness to begin his ministry, he definitely did near the end, in the desert of Golgotha, screaming from the depth of his agony, *"My God, my God, why have you forsaken me?"*[26] It seems to me that if we feel like so much thrown-out trash in a wilderness, utterly alone and forsaken by God, then we are in good company. Key characters from Scripture have been there, done that. Jesus has been there, done that. He knows our feelings and fears, our *"loud cries and tears."*[27] That is not *all* Jesus knows, however.

Jesus knows that in a wilderness, despite sometimes intense feelings to the contrary, we are not utterly, or in any way alone; that God has not and will not discard and forget us. Jesus knows that a wilderness, for all its potentially excruciating pain, is essential if we are to be everything and possess everything God desires. For those who submit to its therapy, a wilderness is *katartidzein*—working the damaged and weakened parts of us (parts which if left as they are will be the ruin of us) and restoring us to our intended usefulness.[28] Because God is in it, a wilderness is for our good.

If Jesus embraced a wilderness as that which was for his good, as that which led him to become everything and possess everything God desires, then who are we not to submit to its divine therapy? That therapy, painful as it may be, is always and only for our good.

---

25. Wiesel, *Messengers of God*, 232.

26. Matt 27:46; Mark 15:34.

27. Heb 5:7.

28. As Edith Schaeffer wrote of God, *"He does not allow affliction to be wasted,"* but carefully uses it for our betterment. Schaeffer, Affliction, 160.

FOR OTHERS' GOOD

A wilderness is endured, not simply for our own good, but also for the good of others. As an encounter with a wilderness is meant to be a learning and growing experience, so is an encounter with a wilderness trekker. Those who weather a wilderness become witnesses to others. Through watching a desert traveler, even casual observers can discover that Yahweh is Lord.

"*The Egyptians will know that I am the Lord,*"[1] was God's encouragement to Moses as he stood with Israel at the fringe of the Red Sea with Pharaoh's army in hot pursuit. Deserts have a way of pinning backs against walls, but God has a way of making himself known and bringing himself glory in and through those who are up against it. God has never left himself without a witness[2]—not even in the most desperate, devoid-of-life desert.

Often—unquestionably in Israel's case—when it comes to seeing God at work in a wilderness and learning the lessons he teaches there, the observer can be more insightful than the traveler. A fascinating sidebar to Israel's exodus from Egypt and journey to the Promised Land is that others learned as much, perhaps more, from watching God's people travel as God's people learned by traveling. At the very least, others seem to grasp certain realities more quickly than did Israel. Routinely, the observer—early on, that meant the Egyptians—gained sudden, almost immediate insight into what God was doing while Israel arrived at the same understanding much later.

A single contrast may best illustrate that truth. Before the Hebrew ex-slaves had journeyed very far from Egypt, they panicked. Trapped between Pharaoh's hounding soldiers and the sea, and certain they would die, the Israelites decided to at least get in one last word, firing a final verbal salvo at Moses, the man they held responsible for the major mess they were now in—"*It would have been better for us to serve the Egyptians than to die in the desert.*"[3]

1. Exod 14:18.
2. Acts 14:17.
3. Exod 14:12.

Moses was quick to respond. *"Do not be afraid,"* he told the people. *"Stand firm and you will see the deliverance the Lord will bring you today. The Egyptians you see today you will never see again. The Lord will fight for you; you need only be still."*[4] In truth, however, Israel always struggled to be still, learning very late (and then repeatedly forgetting) that God would fight for and deliver them. It was a problem that persisted even on the other side of the Jordan.

On oath, God had promised the land of Canaan to the Hebrews. If they followed him faithfully, obeying his word, they would take possession of that promise. The land would be theirs. A dozen scouts were sent to explore the land and, after forty days, returned with details of unimaginable fruitfulness—displaying produce that words were inadequate to describe[5]—but also with doubts, at least in the minds of ten spies, that the land could be taken.[6]

Caleb summarized the minority report, insisting, *"We should go up and take possession of the land, for we can certainly do it;"*[7] later assuring the people, *"If the Lord is pleased with us, he will lead us into that land, a land flowing with milk and honey, and will give it to us."*[8] The people, however, were not convinced and sided with the majority that cautioned, *"We can't attack those people; they are stronger than we are. . . . The land we explored devours those living in it. All the people we saw are of great size. . . . We seemed like grasshoppers in our own eyes, and we looked the same to them."*[9] A remarkable response, considering that those same Israelites had earlier seen God deliver them from a world power and drown Egypt's elite charioteers in the Red Sea.

But such miracles seemed to make only fleeting impressions on God's Chosen People who, despite a series of astounding miracles wrought by Yahweh, made a habit of rebellion and disobedience, *"for they did not believe in God or trust his deliverance."*[10] For the most part, Israel seemed unable to discern the hand of God at work in their midst, and that lack of discernment made any belief or trust on their part short-lived at best.

By contrast, the Egyptians appeared much more discerning. When, for example, their pursuit had Israel pinned against the sea,

---

4. Exod 14:13–14.
5. Num 13:27.
6. Num 13:30–33.
7. Num 13:30.
8. Num 14:8.
9. Num 13:31–33.
10. Ps 78:22.

> *The Lord looked down from the pillar of fire and cloud at the Egyptian army and threw it into confusion. He made the wheels of their chariots come off so that they had difficulty driving. And the Egyptians said, "Let's get away from the Israelites! The Lord is fighting for them against Egypt."*[11]

As unbelievable as it sounds, the Egyptians, in their confusion, were more coherent than was Israel. They understood, and believed it down to their bootstraps, that what they saw was God at work on behalf of the Hebrews—an awareness that Israel grasped much more slowly. As the biblical record reads, observers learn as much, sometimes more, from watching God's people who are up against it as God's people learn in being up against it. At the very least, those trekking through a wilderness become witnesses—living testimonies of God—to those who observe.

Jesus picked up that theme with his disciples, saying near the end of his time with them, *". . . (People) will lay hands on you and persecute you. They will deliver you to synagogues and prisons, and you will be brought before kings and governors, all on account of my name."*[12]

Persecution and imprisonment are deserts in their own right and must have been frightening prospects for disciples of Jesus, many of whom experienced far worse than beatings or incarcerations; there were those who were martyred because of their faithfulness to Jesus. Those who hated the Way did terrible things to those who followed the one who *was* the Way. But the result of it all was exactly as Jesus had promised: *"This will result in your being witnesses to them."*[13]

God has never left himself, and *will* never leave himself, without a witness.[14] A wilderness, though it can most definitely skew our perspective of things, does not change the truth about God. God is truth and God speaks truth, no matter what lies a wilderness may tell us.[15] In the hands of God, a wilderness is for the good of others. Our journey of faithfulness becomes a witness to those who watch. That is an invaluable perspective for desert travelers.

A recurring refrain in the sermons and writings of E. Stanley Jones was the simple dictum "Don't bear trouble; use it." He saw in our trials and troubles—our many and varied desert journeys—that which was meant to be converted into something good, into something for God, into a testimony,

---

11. Exod 14:24–25.
12. Luke 21:12.
13. Luke 21:13.
14. Acts 14:17.
15. Rom 3:4.

into a means for God to touch the hearts of others. Terry Waite came to a similar understanding as he reflected on his prolonged period as an Iranian hostage:

> I have been determined in captivity, and still am determined, to convert this experience into something that will be useful and good for other people. I think that's the way to approach suffering. It seems to me that Christianity doesn't in any way lessen suffering. What it does is enable you to take it, to face it, to work through it, and eventually to convert it.[16]

Converting our wildernesses is a task we undertake alongside God, who by working in and through all things for our good and his glory,[17] constantly redeems what often appears too painful and meaningless to be redeemed, and then, astounding as it sounds, calls us to join in the redemption effort. It seems to me that Jesus was calling his disciples to follow his father's example and redeem even the most harrowing and hopeless desert. In fact, that was an example Jesus himself followed, praying from the depths of Gethsemane, with the weight of Calvary's cross pressing down on him, *"Now my heart is troubled, and what shall I say? 'Father, save me from this hour?' No, it was for this very reason I came to this hour. Father, glorify your name!"*[18] Jesus redeemed his most excruciating wilderness so that it might serve our good and God's glory. In many ways, as the martyr Thomas More pointed out, by walking a wilderness of suffering, Jesus taught us how to suffer, how to bear suffering, use suffering, and redeem suffering.[19] Through his own suffering, wrote More, "Christ wanted his own deed to speak out."[20] Alan Paton sounded a similar note in *Cry, The Beloved Country*, where one of his characters remarked:

> I have never thought that a Christian would be free of suffering. . . . For our Lord suffered. And I have come to believe that he suffered, not to save us from suffering, but to teach us how to bear suffering. For he knew that there is no life without suffering.[21]

---

16. Waite, *Taken on Trust*, 37.
17. Rom 8:28.
18. John 12:27–28a.
19. See More, *Sadness of Christ*, 1–17, where in a commentary on the passion narratives of the four gospels, More discusses what Jesus' own suffering teaches us about how to approach suffering that it might be truly transforming.
20. More, *Sadness of Christ*, 16.
21. Paton, *Cry, The Beloved Country*, 227.

When we work alongside God in redeeming a wilderness, we cannot gauge its impact but impact it will have. Accurately measuring that impact is always beyond us and remains the domain of the divine. Often what looks too barren to raise a single blade from the ground blossoms into a bumper crop that feeds many people. It happens in unexpected, unpredictable ways, but it happens, and happens repeatedly. Someone comes to saving faith, or to sustaining faith, because a lonely desert traveler, up against it and barely able to hang on, remains faithful.

The martyr Stephen remained faithful, even as a staccato of stones pelted his body. He even prayed audibly, as he was dying, *"Lord, do not hold this sin against them."*[22] I have wondered, as have countless others since Stephen's death, what role that fatal wilderness of Stephen's played in the life of a young man holding the cloaks of the executioners—a soon-to-be zealous persecutor of the church who, in time, was radically transformed into an apostle of Jesus named Paul.[23]

In an even older Scripture story, Rahab's truly mind-blowing statement, made to the Hebrew spies she was hiding, reveals the impact of Israel's wilderness experiences on the pagans of Jericho:

> *I know that the Lord has given this land to you, and that a great fear of you has fallen on us, so that all who live in this country are melting in fear because of you. We have heard how the Lord dried up the water of the Red Sea for you when you came out of Egypt, and what you did to Sihon and Og, the two kings of the Amorites east of the Jordan, whom you completely destroyed. When we heard of it, our hearts melted and everyone's courage failed because of you, for the Lord your God is God in heaven above and on earth below.*[24]

If Israel's forty years of trekking through the desert accomplished nothing else, it brought a thoroughly pagan woman to faith in Yahweh as the one true God. There was more to it than that, of course, because the impact of those wilderness days extended far beyond that single moment and that solitary woman. It was more far-reaching and all-inclusive than anyone at the time could possibly have imagined, for from Rahab's lineage came King David and, ultimately, the Messiah Jesus.[25] The divine context of a wilderness is always vaster than the severe stretch of territory we are traveling.[26]

22. Acts 7:60.
23. Acts 6:8—7:58.
24. Josh 2:9–11.
25. Matt 1:5–6, 16, 21.
26. Perrin, *Exodus Revealed*, 120: "By linking the imminent Exodus with the

The impact of a wilderness pilgrim reaches beyond the lost to make itself felt even among the saved. I am a more mature Christian and moving closer to the likeness of Jesus because of faithful desert nomads I have known. Some I have observed only at a distance, others I have known personally, but all have made a lasting impact for the kingdom of God in my life.

More than forty years ago, a friend of mine—a dear lady in a church where I pastored at the time—lost her husband, her son and her infant grandson in less than a twelve-month span. Her storms—emotional, financial, spiritual—were severe and would have scuttled many, but she never jumped ship. She died years ago, but I still bear in my life the powerful impact of her example as she struggled ever so wearily, but ever so faithfully, through those fierce and frightening storms. Her faithfulness has carried across the years and buoyed my own voyage through often storm-tossed seas, bringing me safely into the calm of God's presence and peace. In the process, I have experienced the truth of Macrina Wiederkher's words:

> "Your storm journey
> Like all hurricanes
> Leads you into the eye."[27]

I have also experienced what Peter Storey said about peace (*Shalom* in the Old Testament): "Shalom is more like the place where an experienced sailor steers, the very eye of the storm. He knows that there will be found in the midst of the roaring wind a place of balance, a place where one force is countered against the other and held in a remarkable equilibrium. There, in the center of the storm—shalom."[28] From such experiences, learned, as God so wonderfully orchestrates such things, from watching a lonely wilderness pilgrim, I have thus been able to buoy others through their own turbulent times.

A wilderness is endured for others as much as for ourselves. It is for their good as much as it is for our own. Beyond its personal impact through the days of our own lives, a wilderness is like God's word itself: *". . . for a future generation, that a people not yet created may praise the Lord."*[29]

Years ago, I attended the funeral of my friend Donna, who lost a grueling eight-year battle with cancer. I had grown to love her and her children, as I had her husband whom I first remember as a little kid running at

---

Abrahamic covenant, Yahweh's words in Exodus 6 frame the miraculous historical moment within a context that was larger than the immediate plight of the Israelites."

27. Wiederkehr, *Tree Full of Angels*, 49.
28. Storey, *God in the Crucible*, 96.
29. Ps 102:18.

break-neck speed around the church building where I pastored. Donna was famous for her "God stories"—testimonies of what God was doing in her life; testimonies to his greatness and grace, to his unfailing presence, peace, and provision. Even when her pain was its fiercest and her struggles the most intense, Donna never lost her grip on God, never surrendered her joy, never abandoned her walk of faithfulness. She could always be counted on for a story about what God was doing in her life.

The most powerful God story I ever heard, however, came not from Donna, but from the doctor who treated her through her entire ordeal with cancer, a petite Asian lady with a profoundly gentle spirit and loving heart. Her testimony at Donna's funeral was unforgettable. At their first meeting, after doctor and patient had discussed diagnosis, prognosis, and treatment, and as Donna was leaving the office, she stopped in the doorway, turned around and asked her doctor, "Do you believe in God?" "The question caught me by surprise," the doctor told us at the funeral, "and I answered the way I think most people like me would have answered. I said, 'Yes, I believe that there is a higher power in this universe that, in some sense, governs the affairs of our lives.'" Donna replied, "Well, I believe in God—in a personal and powerful God who will walk with me and see me through this battle with cancer."

In the ensuing years, the regular meetings between Donna and her doctor followed a predictable pattern. "We would spend twenty minutes talking about how she was doing, how the treatment was working, and dealing with any questions she had," explained the doctor. "Eventually, she would always ask me, 'Would you like to hear a God story?' and we would spend the rest of our time talking about God. In time, as I listened to all the God stories of this wonderful woman fighting such a fierce battle, that cold thing that was my heart melted, and I came to know and love the Jesus she knew and loved."

It was an incredible testimony—the kind God never leaves himself without. But none of us who listened to Donna's doctor that afternoon was prepared for the power of her final sentence. "Little did I know," she said, "that as I was saving Donna, she was saving me."

Never underestimate the eternal impact of a faithful walk through a wilderness.

FOR GOD'S GLORY

We do not so much confront a wilderness as God confronts us in a wilderness. That distinction is important. When we walk a wilderness, we encounter much more than simply the wilderness. We experience what Barbara Brown Taylor called, "the unscripted encounter with the undomesticated God."[1]— unscripted, at least, from our vantage point.

A wilderness is first and foremost an encounter with God. At the heart of every wilderness in Scripture is not the wanderer or sojourner, but the God of the Wilderness. Give voice to the deserts of Scripture—Midian and Arabia, Sinai and suffering—and they weave tales of Moses and Paul, of Israel, Job and others, but only incidentally. The main subject of those stories, of all such stories, is God. He is the key player, the chief character, the hero of the narrative, the heart of it all. It is God's wilderness more than it is anyone's wilderness. He invites, calls, leads, even forces people there. He wills, works, waits, and woos while he has them there. The desert is ever God's domain. A wilderness is always about him, always an encounter with him. God did not design a desert "so that we might merely meet him but so that we might encounter him—more exactly, be encountered by him."[2]

The centuries-long theological debate about whether God causes or allows a wilderness seems a moot point in light of the fact that to encounter a wilderness is to encounter God. Either way, like Jacob at Jabbock,[3] we are left alone to struggle with the God who confronts. The Jabbock for Jacob, like the desert for his descendants, was a place of divine encounter. God wrestled with Jacob until daybreak and with his descendants for long years. As was the case with Jacob, God seems to always be the aggressor, the initiator of the struggle.[4]

1. Taylor, *Leaving Church*, 171.
2. Perrin, *Exodus Revealed*, 12.
3. Gen 32:22–31.
4. Gen 32:24.

What is God up to with all that initiating, confronting, and wrestling? What does God gain from wilderness encounters with his people? In a word, *glory*. A wilderness is for God's glory.

Glory, as an ascription of praise, properly belongs to God.[5] He can receive glory from the most mundane and ordinary elements and events of our lives, if we offer them to him as our worship.[6] He can also receive glory from desert days well-lived, as his people remain faithful through their journeys, seeking even in hard and desperate times to be vessels for his glory.[7]

In Chiang Mai, Thailand, I once shared an evening with a group of university students from many Asian countries. One young lady, a deeply passionate Christian from China, spoke with me through the night and into the next day's dawn. Via a translator in the room, she gave a heartfelt account of extensive persecution against the church and told of friends and family who had been martyred for their faithfulness to Jesus.

The bulk of conversation centered on her father, a man nearly ninety years old. He was an itinerant evangelist who was so successful in conversion campaigns that he was often beaten and imprisoned by government officials. Six months prior to my visit with his daughter, the old man had been released from his prison cell but ordered to never again leave the limits of his village. No longer itinerant, but always an evangelist, he converted and baptized more than eight hundred villagers during the first half-year following his release. Though he was threatened daily with threats of torture and even death, though he was repeatedly flogged and jailed, he remained faithful to God's call on his life.

Only days before my arrival in Chiang Mai, he had written his daughter, asking her to return to China and help him. Because of his age, he no longer had the strength to disciple the droves of converts while keeping at the work of evangelism. He was hopeful that his daughter—fulfilling a lifetime dream by studying at a Christian college—would give up her studies, return to China and help with the work, he doing the evangelizing, she the discipling.

I left Chiang Mai for Singapore the next day and never knew what the young girl decided. But I do know that there are hundreds, probably thousands of Christians scattered across China today because one man stayed faithful through an intense and prolonged wilderness. By one man's faithfulness through genuinely tough times, God received glory. When a person remains faithful through a wilderness, God is always glorified.

---

5. Rom 4:20; 11:36; 16:27; 2 Cor 1:20; Gal 1:5; Eph 3:21; Phil 1:11; 2:11; 4:20; 1 Tim 1:17 represent an extremely small sampling from just the New Testament.

6. 1 Cor 10:31.

7. 2 Cor 4:4–12.

Not simply a wilderness, but all life and all living is for the glory of God. We literally exist for God's glory. According to the apostle Paul, everything God has done for us in Jesus is so that his glory might be praised.[8] Even the gift of the Holy Spirit is given *"to the praise of his glory."*[9] But more than merely *bringing* praise to God, we are meant to *exist*, to *be* for the praise of God's glory.[10] Marcus Barth wrote:

> We do not just say, recite, sing but become a praise to God's glory. Our total existence in good and evil days, from the cradle to the grave, our strength and weakness are included. We are to praise God's glory through our very existence—be it in the promised land or in exile, in positions of honor as held by Joseph and Daniel, or in the predicament of Jeremiah or Jonah.[11]

God desires a people who will praise him. Everything about our lives—the bad as well as the good, the pain as well as the joy, the wilderness as well as the oasis—is for the praise of God's glory. That is the reason we exist, the reason we are, the reason we find ourselves on this tiny planet spinning through space. No one understood that better than Jesus.

In John's gospel, more than any other, Jesus is shown interpreting all of life in terms of glorifying God. In fact, he did it so often and in such unexpected ways and places, that his words often tend to make us uncomfortable. We have even been known to discount some of his more difficult sayings. For example, Jesus and his disciples once encountered a man who had been blind from birth. It pushed a troubling question to the front of the disciples' minds: *"Rabbi, who sinned, this man or his parents, that he was born blind?"*[12] "Which is it—A or B?" "C," answered Jesus, telling his astonished disciples that this dreadful thing had happened, not because of anyone's sin, but *"so that the work of God might be displayed in his life."*[13]

What seemed important to Jesus was not what the man's blindness resulted *from*, but what it resulted *in*. Here was an opportunity for God to be glorified. Jesus might even have been going so far as to say that the man was born blind for the precise purpose of bringing glory to God. As with a lot of things Jesus said, those words, if that is their meaning, are unnerving and confusing—unless we remember that we exist for one purpose alone: God's

---

8. Eph 1:3–14.
9. Eph 1:13–14.
10. Eph 1:12.
11. Marcus Barth, *Ephesians*, 114.
12. John 9:1.
13. John 9:3.

glory. Put simply, if God can be glorified through us, our lives are fulfilled. Even a wilderness of blindness can be for the praise of God's glory.

On another occasion, Jesus was informed that his beloved friend Lazarus was gravely ill. Knowing in his heart that the young man was already dead, Jesus said to his disciples, *"It is for God's glory so that God's Son may be glorified through it."*[14] He stated it matter-of-factly, but the disciples' minds must have been reeling, searching for an explanation. Mine would have been. "How can the death of a dear friend, a young and vibrant disciple, possibly be for God's glory?" Jesus gave no explanation, but simply stated that it *was* for God's glory. We struggle with such statements—even when they come from the lips of Jesus—because they birth questions that defy easy answers or, for that matter, any answers at all. In the words of Joanna Adams:

> Because we are human, we want to know why; because we are only human, we cannot know why. The Scripture promises that someday we will know why, but that day is not today. God knows what we need today is not an explanation; what we need today is faith.[15]

Jesus was stretching his disciples' faith. To embrace all of life—even the worst of it—as being for God's glory, and to accept God being glorified in and through our life as our true fulfillment, is a stretch of faith indispensable for discipleship. The type of faith Jesus calls for recognizes that even a desert of death is meant for God's glory.

Carol was a friend of mine whose father died of cancer. She had earlier strayed into an immoral life, but with her father's passing, she spiraled even deeper into that lifestyle, putting a great divide between herself and the God she had once loved so fervently and served so faithfully. The climax came one bitterly cold winter night when she jumped from a bridge over the Mississippi River in a suicide attempt that failed. Then, by the grace of God—somewhat, I think, like the prodigal son in Jesus' story—she came to herself. She returned to her spiritual home and lived as a faithful child for the rest of her days. Her zeal and kingdom commitment were tireless and genuine. She was one of the most devoted followers of Jesus and one of the most powerful witnesses for him I have ever known. My life still bears the positive and powerful impact of her life.

Shortly after her new beginning, doctors discovered she had leukemia. It was well-advanced and they gave her only thirty days to live. She lived nearly two years after that prognosis. During those dark desert days,

---

14. John 11:4.
15. Adams, "Only Question," 268.

her living testimony all but shouted to passers-by. No one—believer or unbeliever—escaped the touch of that testimony, the impact of her life. I certainly did not. Carol spent a week in our home and with our church in February of 1977. It was a week that changed the lives of all who rubbed shoulders and souls with her. Soon afterwards, she took a major turn for the worse, and it became only a matter of time before Carol lost her battle with leukemia. In October of that same year, just three months before she died at the age of twenty, knowing that death was inevitable, she penned these words to be read at her funeral:

> My eternal prayer is that I'll see you all again in that home of glory. I look forward to that day when we shall be praising our heavenly father.
>
> I look upon this day as a blessing and a final answer to all of the prayers. All those days of pain and suffering are over. If what I've gone through has helped just one soul to turn to the Lord and has strengthened the faith of fellow brothers and sisters, then I have not suffered in vain.
>
> Faith in the Almighty will take you safely through all the storms of life. . . . We must pray for his will to be done and have faith in knowing he hears and answers. . . .
>
> If you don't have the Lord for your personal savior, then don't wait. Who knows what's going to happen tomorrow?
>
> As the lid of this box, which contains only the framework of my life, is closed, I shall be in heaven rejoicing and praising God. Be not sad, but rejoice, for I have been delivered into the hands of my Maker.

Even in death, the testimony of her faithfulness changed lives. It still does.

I wish you could have known Carol as I did. God could touch a person through her in a way that would change them forever. My life has never been the same since I watched her in and sometimes walked with her through that terrible desert. She taught me many things on her journey; among them that a desert is truly an amazing and redeeming place when entrusted to the hands of God. Carol's witness affirmed what Jesus taught his disciples about Lazarus: Even a wilderness of death is meant for God's glory.

But Jesus did more than simply interpret what happened to *others* in that light; he also interpreted what happened to *himself* in that light. As he approached the cross, he prayed to his father, *"I have brought you glory."*[16] His entire life was characterized by the truth that his life had only one purpose: The praise of God's glory. Even through the agony of Gethsemane,

---

16. John 17:4.

Jesus lived for the glory of God. Though his flesh cried for release from the impending suffering of the cross, he was willing to bear that cross to his death if it meant God's glory.

You can trace that truth through Jesus' prayers in the garden. He first prayed, *"Father, if it is possible, may this cup be taken from me. Yet not as I will, but as you will."*[17] It was a cry for release; it was a commitment to remain. Which would it be? Whichever God willed for his life. That is a prayer uttered only by one who knows that life has but one purpose: God's glory.

When Jesus prayed again, he seemed to know that release from the fatal wilderness of crucifixion was not possible. His change in wording is significant: *"My Father, if it is not possible for this cup to be taken away unless I drink of it, may your will be done."*[18] No one prays like that unless they know that ultimate fulfillment comes by allowing God to be glorified in and through their life.

In the end, Jesus knew he would not be delivered from death this side of the tomb. That awareness is evident in his words spoken to Peter about *"the cup the Father has given me"*[19] and his climactic prayer, *"Father, glorify your name."*[20] People don't talk like that—to either friend or father—unless they realize that a wilderness of suffering and death fulfills life's purpose if it brings glory to God.

A wilderness faithfully traversed always brings glory to God. If as profound a wilderness as death can be for God's glory;[21] if Jesus could say to his disciples of his approaching death, *"it is for your good that I am going away;"*[22] if Paul could say of dying, not simply that it is better than living, but *"better by far,"*[23] then the worst wilderness it is possible to walk can be redeemed and can result in good for us, good for others, and glory

---

17. Matt 26:39.
18. Matt 26:42.
19. John 18:11.
20. John 12:28.
21. John 21:19.
22. John 16:7.
23. Phil 1:23.

for God.²⁴ Even sudden death is sudden glory for daughters and sons of Yahweh.²⁵

What is the purpose of a wilderness? The same as the purpose of life: The praise of God's glory. And, so, with the apostle Paul we affirm:

> *Praise be to the God and Father or our Lord Jesus Christ, who has blessed us in the heavenly realms with every spiritual blessing in Christ. For he chose us in him before the creation of the world to be holy and blameless in his sight. In love he predestined us to be adopted as his sons through Jesus Christ, in accordance with his pleasure and will—to the praise of his glorious grace, which he has freely given us in the One he loves. In him we have redemption through his blood, the forgiveness of our sins, in accordance with the riches of God's grace that he lavished on us with all wisdom and understanding. And he made known to us the mystery of his will according to his good pleasure, which he purposed in Christ, to be put into effect when the times will have reached their fulfillment—to bring all things in heaven and on earth together under one head, even Christ.*
>
> *In him we were also chosen, having been predestined according to the plan of him who works out everything in conformity with the purpose of his will, in order that we who were the first to hope in Christ, might be for the praise of his glory. And you also were included in Christ when you heard the word of truth, the gospel of your salvation. Having believed, you were marked in him with a seal, the promised Holy Spirit, who is a deposit guaranteeing our*

---

24. This is not to imply that redeeming a wilderness into that which is for God's glory is easy. It is certainly more complex and complicated than the simple mental exercise, "Remember, one day you'll look back on this and laugh." In every era, the church and the Christian must—through personal holiness, faithful obedience, prayer, Scripture study, application, Holy Spirit guidance, community dialogue, speaking the truth in love, clear and uncompromising stands, and unflinching courage—discern the times and learn the means of redeeming injustice, agony, terror, pain, grief, and the many wildernesses that harass humanity. The purpose of the Bible's teaching on eschatology is not to make Christians content as they wait in hope for the coming kingdom; rather, it is to make us viable change-agents in the world here and now. The Bible and church history tell of many who, like Joseph, redeemed what others had meant for evil, turning it into good, and who, like William Wilburforce and John Woolman, used their positions and influence to help free others from injustice (slavery). When a Christian is rightly oriented toward God and others, the worst wilderness imaginable can potentially be redeemed and, thereby, transformed into that which is for our good, for others' good, and for God's glory. That is a general truth of the Bible's wilderness stories. The specific *how to* in the face of each wilderness, however, must be discerned by the obedient church.

25. As it was for Jesus himself. See Luke 24:26 where Jesus said to the Emmaus disciples, *"Did not the Christ have to suffer these things and then enter into glory?"*

inheritance until *the redemption of those who are God's possession—to the praise of his glory.*"[26]

Diagnosed with rectal cancer and given anywhere from thirty days to six months to live, a thirty-two-year-old Christian husband and father of three children spent long days living with Jesus in the pages of the twelfth chapter of John's gospel. When he emerged, his faith had been stretched, like that of the disciples of old. He picked up a pen and put his faith—and his gaps of faith—on paper:

> Jesus,
> > All I ever wanted was to do your will
> > and have your name glorified through me.
>
> I was ignorant
> > of shapes
> > > and forms
> > > > and times
> > > > > and places—
> > > > > > knowing not how you
> > > > > > would work the details
> > > > > > or
> > > > > > weave the fabric;
> > > > > > knowing only
> > > > > > what I wanted:
> > > > > > > to glorify you.
>
> **"The hour has come to be glorified."**
>
> But, Lord,
> > why?
> > > Why this way?
> > > > Why now?
> > > > > Why is this the hour?
> > I had no idea it would all work out this way.
> > > The shapes and forms
> > > are different than I anticipated;
> > > so is the time and place.
> > I am confused.
> > > **"My heart is troubled, and what shall I say?"**
>
> **"I tell you the truth,
> > unless a kernel or wheat falls to the ground**

---

26. Eph 1:3–14.

> *and dies*
> *it remains only a single seed.*
> *But if it dies,*
> *it produces many seeds."*

But, Jesus,
    how can this be?
        I have lived to glorify you;
        must I now die to do so?
Is this the hour?
    The hour I've been looking to,
        dreaming of,
            hoping for,
                living for?
Is this the hour?
    The hour when the seed must fall
        and die
            and come to life again
                as a bountiful harvest?
Is it time for the harvest?
    A harvest of seeds—
        many seeds
            unknown seeds
                unexpected seeds
                    unseen seeds;
                        seeds unable
                            to be harvested
                                by other means?
Is this the hour?
    the hour when
        finally
            completely
                perfectly
                    I do your will?
What shall I say?
    Father,
        save me,
            save me,
                save me,
                    save me from this hour?

"The man who loves his life will lose it,
while the man who hates his life in this world
will keep it for eternal life."

Lord Jesus,
    I cannot ask to be saved.
    I dare not ask for my life.
        For it has meaning
            Only as it is lived for you,
            only as it brings you glory.
    I cannot ask for a different way,
        An easier way.
    I dare not ask for another cup.
        For this is your cup,
            the one you placed in my hands,
                the one you drank from
                    so willingly;
        for this is your father's cup,
            the cup of his will,
                your will,
                    my will,
                    our will.
    And I, too, drink it willingly.
        I cannot refuse.
        I dare not say 'no.'
            For who knows?
            Who knows?
            O, Lord, you know
                whether

***"It was for this very reason
I came to this hour."***

***"Whoever serves me must follow me,
And where I am, my servant will also be."***

Dear Jesus,
    I follow. I follow.
    For this is the path you have chosen.
        The path you have walked.
            Not once despising it.
            No thought of shunning it.
    Upon this path
        I find your footprints.
    Upon this path
        I find your will.
    Upon this path
        I bring you glory.

> Upon this path
>   I share your suffering
>   That I may share your glory.
> Praise you, Jesus.
>   All I ever wanted was to follow you.
>   Whatever made me think that my desire
>   would lead me down a path
>   unfamiliar to you,
>   unknown to you;
>   a path you yourself
>   had never walked?
> Somehow, I think, I always knew
>   that following you
>   meant following you
>   even
>   unto
>   death.
> **"Father, glorify your name!"**
>
> **"My father will glorify the one who serves me."**
>
> Thank you, dear Jesus.
>   All I ever wanted
>   was to do your will
>   and have your name glorified through me."

I wrote those words in 1982. Even now, and every time I read them, I relive the experience and reaffirm what I learned through those dark and difficult times. A wilderness, like life itself, is for God's glory.

"Father, glorify your name!"

A TOUCH OF GRACE

When the prophet Isaiah gave a synopsis of the Hebrew children's arduous wilderness journey, he said of God, *"In all their affliction He was afflicted."*[1] That revealing glimpse into the heart of God casts a wilderness in fresh light. God knows—and *feels*—the distress of a desert. He experiences a wilderness as if he himself were the sufferer. Israel's were not the only bruised feet, burdened backs or broken hearts amid that desert expanse. God shared the affliction of his people. In all our wilderness experiences, we are never alone, and God is never aloof.

God's understanding of the deserts we walk is in no way academic or remote, but always up close and personal. Just as Jesus, by the grace of God, *"tasted"* death[2]—not in an isolated clinical sense or a detached objective sense, but personally, subjectively, emotionally and experientially—so God, as it were, *tastes* a wilderness.[3] He joins in the suffering and humiliation, the isolation and intensity, the burdens and battles of a wilderness. In the manner

---

1. Isa 63:9, *New American Standard Bible*.

2. Heb 2:9. I am indebted to Reardon, who pointed out that the author of Hebrews "speaks of Jesus' death not just as an objective and clinical fact, but as a matter of experience." He continues, "According to Hebrews, then, God's Son assumed, not simply human nature, but the existential burden of human experience. His was to be a full and felt solidarity, in which 'he is not ashamed to call them brothers, saying, 'I will declare Your name to my brothers' (Heb 2:11–12). For this reason, declares Hebrews, 'in all things he had to be made like the brothers' (2:17). These 'all things' particularly included the tasting of death." Reardon, *Jesus We Missed*, 154–55.

3. The Greek word in Heb 2:9 is *gensetai* and means "to taste or to partake of," "to come to know something (through first-hand experience)." Jesus' first-hand, experiential sharing of our flesh and our death follows the pattern of God's sharing in the sufferings of his wandering people, since "the experience of Jesus was consistent with God's known character and fixed purpose." (Lane, *Call to Commitment*, 47). As Jesus was a *"partaker"* of our flesh and blood (Heb 2:14), we also become *"partakers"* of his suffering (1 Pet 4:13). Whether our point of departure is the New Testament description of Jesus or the Old Testament description of God, we reach the same end: The sufferings of a wilderness represent a shared experience of the finite with the infinite.

of his son Jesus centuries later, he becomes like us in every way,[4] sharing our humanity,[5] and is not ashamed to call us his brothers and sisters.[6] Ultimately, it is through his own suffering that he is able to help us.[7] Ours is a shared wilderness. A child of God, who is beloved by God, never journeys or suffers alone, is never afflicted without God taking that affliction upon himself.

"*Grace came in the wasteland . . . to Israel,*"[8] was God's reminder to the prophet Jeremiah. That grace came in the form of one who was not only above and beyond the wasteland, holding absolute and sovereign control over it, but also one whose presence and provision sustained Israel every step of their journey and then safely delivered them into the land he had sworn on oath to give them. Because God is in it, a wilderness is a touch of grace. In fact, grace is written all over the story of Israel's exodus from Egypt, from the Sea to Sinai to the Land of Promise.

Just as God, by grace, delivered his people out of the kingdom of sin and into the kingdom of the Son he loves,[9] so God, by grace, delivered his children out of slavery in Egypt and into the freedom and delight of a new land. Repeatedly, God reminded his people of that great, singular act of grace—"*I am the Lord your God, who brought you out of Egypt, out of the land of slavery.*"[10] That *bringing out* theme resurfaces many times: When Moses addressed the people of God,[11] as well as in the words of David,[12] Solomon,[13] Samuel,[14] Daniel,[15] the Hebrew children,[16] an unnamed prophet,[17] and an

---

4. Heb 2:17.

5. Heb 2:14.

6. Heb 2:11.

7. Heb 2:18. See Lane: " . . . the exalted Son of God, who is now enthroned at God's right hand, is a person who actually shared our situation. He was fully human. His humanity was exposed to the full range of testing, just as ours is. He was made to be like us. He fully identified himself with us. For these reasons he is qualified to help us when our faith is severely tested." Lane, *Call to Commitment*, 43.

8. Jer 31:2, *Bible in Basic English*.

9. Col 1:13.

10. Exod 20:2. See also the following suggested but incomplete list: Exod 29:46; Lev 11:45; 19:36; 22:32–33; 25:38, 42, 55; 26:13, 45; Num 15:41; Deut 5:6; Josh 24:6; 1 Kgs 9:9; 2 Chr 6:5; Ps 81:10; Hos 11:1; Amos 2:10.

11. Exod 13:9; 16:32; 18:1; Num 20:16; Deut 6:12, 21; 8:14; 13:5, 10; 16:1; 20:1; 26:8; 29:25.

12. 1 Chr 17:21.

13. 1 Kgs 8:16, 21, 51, 53.

14. 1 Sam 10:18; 12:6.

15. Dan 9:15.

16. Josh 24:17; Jer 2:6.

17. Judg 6:8

angel of the Lord.[18] Even the New Testament author Jude felt it necessary to remind his readers *"that the Lord delivered his people out of Egypt . . . "*[19] The exodus marked *the* distinctive grace event in the Old Covenant history of God's chosen people.

Whereas God's deliverance of his people *out of* Egypt and *into* the Promised Land are seen as occasions of grace for which God is to be praised, a wilderness is often seen as an occasion of grief for which God is to be blamed. The Hebrews habitually blamed God, or his surrogate Moses, for the grief the wilderness brought them, and God often takes the blame today for the grief endured by wilderness-bound people. Praise is hard to come by when grace is in short supply—or, at least, when it seems in short supply. It is easy to spot grace in an exodus from Egypt or an entry into promise; not so easy when a desert is all but doing us in. Yet much of our failure to discern grace, especially in a wilderness, has to do with our somewhat limited understanding of that elusive but awesome gift of God.

Grace is not merely a *past act* of God (an *out of* blessing where God got us out of sin); not merely a *future promise* of God (an *into* blessing where God will get us into heaven); but grace is also a *present gift* of God (an *in between* blessing, a *right now* gift where God sustains us and sees us through whatever is our current wilderness). In other words, grace is not confined to past and future, but is also a present blessing.

A wilderness is a touch of grace; yet that grace is seldom as in-your-face as the Red Sea parting for Israel, then engulfing the Egyptian army[20] or as the Jordan opening a dry-as-bone path for God's people.[21] Many times a wilderness seems devoid of grace, even devoid of God.[22] We find ourselves echoing the feelings of the fictional Leah Price: "When I walk through the valley of the shadow the Lord is supposed to be with me, and he's not! Do you see him here?"[23] Grace, like God, though always present in a wilderness, is not always visible.

18. Judg 2:1.
19. Jude 5.
20. Exod 14:19–31.
21. Josh 3:14–17.
22. The statement by Paton in *Cry the Beloved Country*, 74, that "there are times, no doubt, when God seems no more to be about the world," rings true of nearly every wilderness traveler in Scripture—it certainly rang true of Jesus, whose tormented scream was awash in agony as he wondered aloud, *"My God, my God, why have you forsaken me?"* (Matt 27:46)—and it also rings true of nearly every wilderness-bound soul I have known. Inevitably, there come times—moments, hours, days, months, sometimes years—when we could, if we wanted, drive ourselves mad with the question, "Where is God?" or, more specifically, with the question of Philip Yancey, "Where is God when it hurts?"
23. Kingsolver, *Poisonwood Bible*, 309.

J. W. Stevenson wondered,

> ... why we often cannot see amongst us the unmistakable evidence of God—signs which would make any of us believe. We cannot look upon God; we can only look upon what God is doing.... Our eyes are darkened ... and (we) say we cannot see a sign of His redemption. There was no Providence visible on Calvary.[24]

There is something very much of Calvary in a wilderness. At Calvary, as Jesus was dying, women were mourning him, priests and passersby were mocking him, criminals were slurring him, injustice was crushing him, and darkness was engulfing them all. There was, on the surface, no providence visible, no grace to be seen. A wilderness, like Calvary, can severely restrict spiritual vision. Much of Isaiah's vivid description of the passion of Jesus reads like a wilderness devoid of grace, reads literally like Calvary:

> *He was despised and rejected by men,*
>   *a man of sorrows, and familiar with*
>   *suffering.*
> *Like one from whom men hide their faces*
>   *he was despised, and we esteemed him*
>   *not....*
> *we considered him stricken by God,*
>   *smitten by him, and afflicted....*
> *He was oppressed and afflicted ...*
> *he was led like a lamb to the slaughter ....*
> *By oppression and judgment he was*
>   *taken away.*
>   *And who can speak of his descendants?*
>   *For he was cut off from the land of the*
>   *living;*
>   *for the transgression of my people he*
>   *was stricken.*
> *He was assigned a grave with the wicked,*
>   *and with the rich in his death,*
> *though he had done no violence,*
>   *nor was any deceit in his mouth.*
>
> *Yet it was the Lord's will to crush him*
>   *and cause him to suffer....*[25]

---

24. Stevenson, *God in My Unbelief*, 68–69.
25. Isa 53:3, 4b, 7a, 7c, 8–10a.

Without knowing the rest of the story, without Isaiah filling in the blanks, that desert seems totally devoid of grace. God is supposed to be there; do we see him? In that mess? In that horror? I do not—unless, perhaps, he is present in some sadistic sense. Isaiah, with those discerning eyes of a prophet, saw what others could not see, what even many of us, with trained spiritual eyes, have trouble seeing. He saw grace in a wilderness of great suffering, grace where no providence was visible to anyone else:

> "Surely he took our infirmities
>   and carried our sorrows...
> But he was pierced for our transgressions,
>   he was crushed for our iniquities;
> the punishment that brought us peace was
>   upon him,
>   and by his wounds we were healed.
> We all, like sheep, have gone astray,
>   each of us has turned to his own way;
> and the Lord has laid on him
>   the iniquity of us all....
>   and though the Lord makes his life a
>   guilt offering,
> he will see his offspring and prolong his
>   days,
>   and the will of the Lord will prosper in
>   his hand.
> After the suffering of his soul,
>   he will see the light of life, and be
>   satisfied;
> by his knowledge my righteous servant
>   will justify many,
>   and he will bear their iniquities.
> Therefore I will give him a portion among
>   the great,
>   and he will divide the spoils with the
>   strong,
> because he poured out his life unto death,
>   and was numbered with the
>   transgressors.
> For he bore the sin of many,
>   and made intercession for the
>   transgressors."[26]

---

26. Isa 53:4a, 5–6, 10b–12.

Isaiah weaves as one the minor and major keys of Jesus' life, shocking us with the presence of so much sorrow and so much grace fitting into the same passion song. As Isaiah sings that song—in fact, as all of Scripture tells the story—grace trumps sorrow. Only the grace of God exceeded the sorrow of Jesus at Calvary, but the grace wasn't nearly as discernable as the sorrow. Suffering in no way precluded grace at Calvary. Suffering in no way precludes grace in a wilderness, either the ancient one Israel knew or the modern ones we know. Still, in the dread and darkness of our own private desert, when our heart is full of pain and our eyes are full of tears, we grope to find even the faintest flicker of grace.

"Suffering," wrote Carolyn Custis James, "is a sacred meeting place between God and his child, where faith is fighting to survive and God's goodness"—I might add, his *grace*—*"comes into question."*[27] That is the place and the moment that calls most for faith. Faith trusts God's grace to be at work even in a wilderness. Faith trusts God's grace to be at work even when it cannot be seen or felt.

J. W. Stevenson described a wilderness-like occasion for his church and explained, "we were perplexed, not because God had not been there, but because he had."[28] God's presence can sometimes be as perplexing as his absence, especially when it is joined to so much pain and suffering. One would think that God's presence and so much pain could not share the same space, that his presence would, in fact, banish pain as light does darkness. But Calvary—and a host of wilderness narratives—show otherwise. It is a troubling, perhaps terrifying mystery. Yet, as Stevenson went on to say, "The mystery lay heavy upon us, but it was the mystery of God dwelling with his people, not the mystery of their being forsaken."[29]

The mystery of pain and suffering in a wilderness is the mystery of God's presence, not his absence. Faith trusts *that*. Faith trusts God to be God, and to be present, even when all we sense is his absence. Faith trusts that, because God is in a wilderness, even suffering is a gift of his grace. Even a wilderness is an occasion of grace as God uses its often-harsh realities to make us more fully his than we could possibly be without them.

Without that kind of trust, without that kind of faith, we can all too quickly transition from questions to complaints to doubts to unbelief, as did Israel. All those instances of infantile behavior and temper tantrums thrown by Israel in the wilderness—and there were several such events—were viewed as much more serious matters by God. They were tantamount

---

27. James, *Gospel of Ruth*, 85.
28. Stevenson, *God in My Unbelief*, 72.
29. Stevenson, *God in My Unbelief*, 72.

to rebellion and unbelief. The author of Hebrews, beginning with a quote from Psalm 95, succinctly summarized the actions of Israel in such terms, using the very words *rebellion* and *unbelief*:

> *"Today, if you hear his voice,*
> *do not harden your hearts*
> *as you did in the rebellion,*
> *during the time of testing in the desert,*
> *where your fathers tested and tried me*
> *and for forty years saw what I did.*
> *That is why I was angry with that generation,*
> *and I said, 'Their hearts are always*
> *going astray,*
> *and they have not known my ways.'*
> *So I declared on oath in my anger,*
> *'They shall never enter my rest'."*
>
> *See to it, brothers, that none of you has a sinful, unbelieving heart that turns away from the living God. But encourage one another daily, as long as it is called Today, so that none of you may be hardened by sin's deceitfulness. We have come to share in Christ if we hold firmly till the end the confidence we had at first. As has just been said:*
>> *"Today, if you hear his voice,*
>> *do not harden your hearts*
>> *as you did in the rebellion."*
>
> *Who were they who heard and rebelled? Were they not all those Moses led out of Egypt? And with whom was he angry for forty years? Was it not with those who sinned, whose bodies fell in the desert? And to whom did God swear that they would never enter his rest if not to those who disobeyed? So we see that they were not able to enter, because of their unbelief.*[30]

The apostle Paul sounded the same note in his letter to the church at Rome, contrasting the unbelief of the Children of Israel (*"What if some did not have faith? Will that lack of faith nullify God's faithfulness?"*)[31] and their subsequent wavering into rebellion, with the exemplary faith of Israel's father Abraham, who *"did not waver in unbelief regarding the promise of God, but was strengthened in his faith and gave glory to God, being fully persuaded*

---

30. Heb 3:7b-19.
31. Rom 3:3.

that God had the power to do what he had promised."[32] Later, in that same correspondence, Paul spoke of Israel being *"broken off because of unbelief."*[33]

In Israel's case, unbelief was as simple as not trusting God's presence to be there when needed and, in the same vein, not trusting God's grace to provide—whether deliverance from Pharaoh's advancing army at the Red Sea, or victory on the other side of the Jordan, or food and drink in an otherwise provision-less wilderness. At the bottom line, Israel did not trust God's grace to be present and active when they were up against it and in fear for their lives.

Perhaps Israel wondered as I have sometimes wondered, as maybe you have also wondered, how presence could fit into the same space with so much absence, how grace could fit into the same space with so much suffering—even though that space was as vast as Sinai. How can grace and suffering co-exist; more than that, how can they intertwine? Yet, Scripture assures us, and the record of the wandering people of God affirms, that through the distress of that entire generation-long wilderness, *"grace came . . . to Israel."*

Grace seldom stands alone in Scripture but is regularly in tandem with suffering. Though often unrecognized, grace is always unfailing, always present and active, at work on behalf of God's people. Sorrow and grace are closely, even carefully intertwined in a wilderness. God frequently uses a wilderness and its suffering as the conduit for his grace. As Henri Nouwen wrote, using the imagery of Jesus in Gethsemane:

> The "cup of sorrows" and the "cup of joys" cannot be separated. Jesus knew this, even though in the midst of his anguish in the garden, when his soul was "sorrowful to the point of death" (Matthew 26:38), he needed an angel from heaven to remind him of it. Our cup is often so full of pain that joy seems completely unreachable. When we are crushed like grapes, we cannot think of the wine we will become. The sorrow overwhelms us, makes us throw ourselves on the ground, face down, and sweat drops of blood. Then we need to be reminded that our cup of sorrow is also our cup of joy and that one day we will be able to taste the joy as fully as we now taste the sorrow.[34]

---

32. Rom 4:20–21.

33. Rom 11:20.

34. Nouwen, *Can You Drink*, 49. Nouwen's reference to Jesus needing an angel to remind him is taken from Luke 22:43 where, after Jesus prayed, *"Father, if you are willing, take this cup from me; yet not my will, but yours be done"* (Luke 22:42), we read, *"An angel from heaven appeared to him and strengthened him."*

Perhaps that is part of what the author of Hebrews had in mind when writing of our hearts being *"strengthened by grace."*[35] As, by faith, we trust God's grace to be at work in the deep and profound sorrows of our lives; as, by faith, we trust God's grace to use the harsh realities of a wilderness to make us more fully God's than we could possibly be without them; as, by faith, we trust God's grace to bring us safely to that time and place where "we will be able to taste the joy as fully as we now taste the sorrow;" our hearts are strengthened and a life of radical faith becomes possible. As Richard J. Foster wrote, "Our hearts will be 'strengthened by grace,' so that we might live more freely with God. . . . Grace is the activity of God in our lives, the reality of God pouring into us more than we could ever do on our own."[36]

The apostle Paul went to the next level when he suggested that we could take the somewhat radical step and actually *"rejoice in our sufferings, because we know that suffering produces perseverance, perseverance character, and character, hope. And hope does not disappoint us, because God has poured out his love into our hearts by the Holy Spirit, whom he has given us."*[37] Because grace is present, we can rejoice even in a wilderness.

Grace is as much a part of wilderness terrain as are barrenness and brokenness. Sometimes that grace can seem as harsh as the desert itself, like surgery can seem as harsh as the disease itself. Other times grace is noticeably gentle. It has been known to come in soft and subtle ways, strengthening our hearts through our long desert affliction. Either way, grace is present. Either way, grace is saving and sustaining.

My friend Phil lost his wife Donna, also a dear friend, to aggressive breast cancer. When she was diagnosed on the afternoon of September 18, 1991, the couple was expecting their third child. The next day, doctors delivered the baby before performing a radical mastectomy on Donna. But the prognosis was frightening. "The cancer will attack again in two-to-five years," came words framed in matter-of-fact finality, "and when it does, there is nothing more we can do. It will take your life." On Saturday morning, March 5, 1994, Donna died.

Near the end, while Donna was still somewhat alert but barely able to communicate, and as her husband bent over her bedside listening to her fading, raspy voice, she said to Phil, "Suffering is a gift of grace that allows you to let go of me and me to let go of you." I saw grace in a wilderness that morning though I had been blind to it only minutes before. Up to that point, it represented a version of faith and trust with which I was largely

---

35. Heb 13:9.
36. Foster, *Life with God*, 193–94.
37. Rom 5:3–5.

unfamiliar. "In this version," wrote Barbara Brown Taylor, "there were no formulas, no set phrases that promised us safe passage across the abyss. There was only our tattered trust that the Spirit who had given us life would not leave us in the wilderness without offering us life again."[38]

In the years since, I have tried to keep my eyes open for grace in those places where, in the words of Julia Cameron, "we cannot feel so much as a trickle of grace."[39] I have intentionally, consistently sought grace in such a wasteland—that grace of which Donna spoke to Phil, that grace of which God spoke to Isaiah. I am spotting it more and more in the deserts of my life, as well as in the deserts of others. I am spotting it enough to know that it is there—hidden in plain sight, perhaps, but always there; always arriving in time to help, just as the author of Hebrews assured us it would;[40] always present in the dry bones and empty shells of our lives, ready to offer life again, ready to breathe into us and make of us something new.[41] "Even when there's nothing left but rubble," wrote Carolyn Custis James, "God is mysteriously at work in the mess."[42] The God of the mess—I like that. I am a mess, a lot of the time, maybe most of the time; *probably* most of the time. But *this* God—Yahweh, the God of Christian Scripture—does more than stand over the mess; he stoops into it, gets up to his knees and elbows in it, and makes our mess his own.

The God of the mess, the God of our deserts, feels every wilderness as if he himself were a wanderer. To personalize Isaiah's words, *"In all our affliction, he is afflicted."* Because God is not just with us in a wilderness but is with us in a wilderness *in that way*—working in and with the mess to bring us hope and a future—even suffering is a touch of grace, and grace in the form of suffering is one of the greatest blessings of our lives.

We might do well to embrace the prayer of Thomas a Kempis:

> Your grace is with me. It is my strength, my counsel and my help, more powerful than all my enemies, and wiser than all the worldly-wise.
>
> Your grace is the teacher of truth, the master of discipline; it brings light to the heart and solace in affliction; it banishes sorrow, dispels fear, nourishes our devotion and moves us to tears

---

38. Taylor, *Leaving Church*, 178.
39. Cameron, *Artist's Way*, 170.
40. Heb 4:14–16.
41. Ezek 37:1–10.
42. James, *Gospel of Ruth*, 51. "God is moving forward," wrote Nicholas Perrin, "even through the suffering of his people," (*Exodus Revealed*, 120).

of repentance. What am I without it but a withered tree, a bit of dry timber to be cast into the fire?

Grant, therefore, O Lord, that Your grace always go before me, be ever at my back, keeping me ever intent upon good works to be done, through Jesus Christ, Your Son and my Lord. Amen."[43]

---

43. Thomas à Kempis, *Imitation of Christ*, 223.

A WORD OF LOVE

It is shocking to me the number of times the God of the Wilderness describes himself as a jilted lover or as a husband whose wife, Israel, has been unfaithful. It is a recurring Old Testament theme, particularly in the writings of Jeremiah and Ezekiel, as well as through the entire prophecy of Hosea. The Hebrew text repeatedly accuses God's people of adultery (*naaph*[1]) and whoring or prostitution (*zanah*[2]) while bound exclusively to him. Though such unfaithfulness on the part of his beloved hurts and angers God, it is his passionate and pursing love that is preeminent in the stories of God and Israel's stormy relationship. In some of the most moving soliloquies of the Old Covenant,[3] God speaks as a lover wooing his beloved or as a husband winning back his wife.

The story of Hosea is particularly striking and stands as a parable of God's love for his unfaithful people. The prophet married a woman who became unfaithful to him and eventually left him and their children. Despite her prostitution and adultery, as well as her longing for love elsewhere, God called Hosea to love her still, to seek her out, and to bring her home.

> *The Lord said to me, "Go show your love to your wife again, though she is loved by another and is an adulteress. Love her as the Lord loves the Israelites, though they turn to other gods..."*
> *So I bought her for fifteen shekels of silver and about a homer and a lethek of barley. Then I told her, "You are to live with me many days; you must not be a prostitute or be intimate with any man, and I will live with you."*[4]

1. Jer 3:9; 9:2; 29:23; Hos 2:2.
2. Exod 34:15–16; Ezek 6:9.
3. Jer 3:6—4:4; Ezek 16:1–63; Hos 2:2–23.
4. Hos 3:1–3.

In that same narrative, Israel is paralleled to Hosea's wife Gomer and is pictured saying, while walking away from God:

> "I will go after my lovers,
>   who give me my food and my water,
>   my wool and my linen, my oil and my
>   drink."[5]

The Message translation captures for modern hearers the true spirit of unfaithful Israel, which found grass greener away from God: *"I'm off to see my lovers! They'll wine and dine me, dress and caress me, perfume and adorn me!"*

Regardless of the translation used, however, what is particularly revealing is God's response to Israel's repeated acts of unfaithfulness. He plots a way to win back his wife's love.

> *Therefore I am now going to allure her;*
>   *I will lead her into the desert*
>   *and speak tenderly to her.*
> *There I will give her back her vineyards,*
>   *and will make the Valley of Achor a*
>   *door of hope.*
> *There she will sing as in the days of her youth,*
>   *As in the day she came up out of Egypt.*
>
> "In that day," declares the Lord,
>   "you will call me 'my husband'."[6]

Commenting on Hosea's prophecy, James Luther Mays wrote of the word "allure" or "entice" (*pathah* in Hebrew), used in verse fourteen:

> (It) means to persuade irresistibly, to overwhelm the resistance and will another. The verb is used for the seduction of a virgin (Ex. 22.16) and for the divine constraint which holds a prophet powerless (Jer. 20.7). Like a lover who plots to be alone with his beloved, Yahweh will take the woman into the wilderness.... In the wilderness, Yahweh will "make love" to Israel; the expression is literally "speak to her heart," and we can feel its proper context in the speech of courtship by looking at its use in the talk of a man to a woman whose love he seeks (Gen. 34.3; Ruth 2.13; Judg. 19.3).... The passion of God becomes visible—a passion

---

5. Hos 2:5b.
6. Hos 2:14–16.

that does not hesitate at any condescension or hold back from any act for the sake of the beloved elect.[7]

Perhaps better than anyone else in Scripture, prophets such as Hosea, Ezekiel and Jeremiah understood a wilderness in terms of love. In their estimation, deserts represented a divine refusal to let us get away with sinning. Just as God loved Israel enough to not let them get away with rebellion and loved David enough to not let him get away with adultery and murder, so God loves us enough to not let us get away with our particular brand of sinning.

Sinning, like all forms of unfaithfulness, damages relationship. The longer it is ignored or tolerated, the less likely the relationship is to be repaired. A wilderness, like all efforts at reconciliation, seeks to repair and restore relationship, seeks to woo back the unfaithful partner and recover the lost love. When understood from a biblical perspective, a wilderness is a place of love, a place where God looks upon the unfaithfulness and subsequent distancing of the one he loves and passionately woos that person back into a heartfelt relationship. As C. S. Lewis wrote concerning God, "He cannot ravish. He can only woo."[8] A wilderness is often God's way of wooing his unfaithful beloved.

God's love is as persistent as it is passionate. He puts himself at risk to find a lost sheep.[9] He meticulously searches through closets and dresser drawers, sweeps under couches and beds, even sifts through week-old trash to find a lost coin.[10] He rises early every morning and stays up late every night, scanning the horizon in hopes of a prodigal's return.[11] And he does it all *"until he finds"*[12]—not until he grows tired or until day grows dark or until other matters call him away, but *"until he finds."* We may be content with our lostness, but God never is. Our longings for home and father may diminish, even disappear, but God's love for us persists and pursues. It is not the pursuit of a hunter for its prey, but of a lover for his beloved.

In the memoirs of his days as pastor of a small village church in Scotland, J. W. Stevenson wrote:

> I remember how Dr. Christopher had gone south to London from here many years ago to seek for the son who had dishonored

---

7. Mays, *Hosea*, 44–45.
8. Lewis, *Screwtape Letters*, 46.
9. Luke 15:3–7.
10. Luke 15:8–10.
11. Luke 15:11–24.
12. Luke 15:4, 8.

home and left father and mother in silence about what had become of him. There was no address to guide him. Only after many days was the name of the street discovered; and when the old minister, with his white hair, stood at the end of it he knew it was beyond him to go from door to door of its length. But a street musician came by just then and Dr. Christopher stopped him. Did he know an old air—one that had been a favourite in the manse when the children were young? Would he walk with him along the street as he played? And he told him why.

So they went slowly, the street musician and the old minister with his hat in his hand so that his face could be seen, taking this last slender chance to find where his son was who had no use for him, seeking him who had no understanding of the love in his father's heart.

He did not succeed that day; but he left us who came after . . . a memory which made us ask where he had learned that love which cannot be separated by anything at all from the one loved.[13]

When we are spiritually most in danger, with "no understanding of the love in (our) father's heart," God pursues us with "that love which cannot be separated by anything at all from the one loved."[14] Such pursuit, far from a threat, is a blessing—the stubborn, insistent search undertaken by pure love and longing. A wilderness is an extreme case of divine wooing, an extreme case of God pursuing the object of his heart. Upon finding us in our far-offness,[15] he proceeds with deep compassion to run to us, throw his arms around us, kiss us and love us all the way home.[16]

---

13. Stevenson, *God in My Unbelief*, 136–137.

14. See Rom 8:35–39.

15. Luke 15:20b.

16. Luke 15:20b-24. Years ago, I came across an isolated piece by Mother Teresa (source uncited) titled *"Christ's Compassion for the Suffering"* where she expounded on this truth in the following manner: "Suffering has to come because if you look at the cross, he has got his head bending down—he wants to kiss you—and he has both hands open wide—he wants to embrace you. He has his heart opened wide to receive you. Then when you feel miserable inside, look at the cross and you will know what is happening. Suffering, pain, sorrow, humiliation, feelings of loneliness are nothing but the kiss of Jesus, a sign that you have come so close that he can kiss you. Do you understand brothers, sisters, or whoever you may be? Suffering, pain, humiliation—this is the kiss of Jesus. At times you come so close to Jesus on the cross that he can kiss you. I once told this to a lady who was suffering very much. She answered, 'Tell Jesus not to kiss me—to stop kissing me.' That suffering has to come that came to in the life of Our Lady, that came in the life of Jesus—it has to come in our life also. Only never put on a long face. Suffering is a gift from God."

Sin damages our relationship with God and brings separation from him, but again in the words of Stevenson, "We are separated from Him, whose love will not allow him to be separated from us."[17] His love pursues, passionately and persistently, *"until he finds."* That sound we hear in a wilderness is not the west wind or a wild animal or approaching marauders, or any number of other things we may interpret as threats; it is, rather, the beat of our father's heart, footsteps of his longing that will never give up, the passionate pursuit of one who loves us more than life. In that sense, and contrary to popular opinion, God is not a gentleman.

Years ago, I worshiped with a church where a friend of mine pastored. As he concluded his sermon that day with an urgent appeal to heed God's invitation to follow his son Jesus, he said, "If you want to turn your back on God and walk away from him, God will let you go. After all, God is a gentleman—too much of a gentleman to chase after you should you turn and walk away; too much of a gentleman to pester you to change your mind, even though what you've decided is leading you into ruin, and even death. For good or bad, that is your decision, and as a Gentleman, God will honor it. He will leave you alone in your decision."

I had at times, in years past, preached a variation of those words, but that day as I listened to my friend, I realized that I did not believe that anymore. I think part of the reason was simply my being a father and a grandfather, and unable to imagine one of my children or grandchildren running away from home, becoming lost and in danger, and my not pursuing them and doing everything I could to find them and bring them safely home. It was not *just* that, though; maybe not even *mostly* that. It was more, I think, Jesus' understanding of his Father seeking *"until he finds"*—even though the sheep strayed from the fold on its own, even though the son wished his father dead and never to see him again—and the prophets' image of God pursuing and wooing those who had made a conscious decision to walk away from him and to seek other lovers who would ultimately destroy them.

That Sunday, listening to my friend preach, it abruptly dawned on me, for the first time really, that the God of the Bible is, in fact, no gentleman. Far from it. His lack of gentlemanly behavior is evident in his passionate pursuit of those who walk away from him, who forsake the only source of life and love in the universe to seek love and life where they cannot be found.[18] His lack of gentlemanly behavior is seen in his promiscuous[19] but persistent

17. Stevenson, *God in My Unbelief*, 138.

18. Jer 2:13.

19. See Barclay, *New Testament Words*, 235–36, where the author, in discussing what the apostle Peter wrote about God's grace in 1 Pet 4:10, points to the Greek adjective *poikiles* which describes that grace. The word originally referred to something

habit of going to all the wrong places and chasing after all the wrong people who are doing all the wrong things. Throwing caution to the wind and not caring a bit about what others might think, he keeps seeking in hope of finding, in hope of once more gathering into his arms the one he loves.

The God of the Wilderness is no gentleman; at least, not in the popular use of that word. Speaking personally, if he were a gentleman, he would never have come looking for me, because I have spent too much time in wrong places and doing wrong things—places no gentleman would go, things no gentleman would do. More times than I care to remember, I have been one of those people with whom no gentleman would dare associate. If God were a gentleman, I would long ago have been left alone in my far-offness and lostness, in my foolish decisions and blatant rebellion. Thankfully, God is no gentleman; certainly not if we let the wilderness narratives tell their story.

In fact, I would go so far as to say that a wilderness is a wilderness precisely because God is no gentleman. He refuses to honor our rebellion. He refuses to accept our far-offness. He refuses to acquiesce to our lostness. He refuses to leave us as we are, where we are. He rejects our rejection. His love will not allow him to be separated from us, though we have separated ourselves from him. Casting aside all gentlemanliness, like the spurned father in Jesus' parable who tucked in his robe at the waist and ran full-speed to welcome home his rebel-of-a-son, so God chases after us in love. That chase often takes the shape of a wilderness. A wilderness is a word of love spoken into the far-offness of our sin and rebellion, and reveals a God who goes to great lengths, unimaginable lengths, even at the cost of his own life, to bring us home.

Sometimes, though, God uses a wilderness less as an occasion of pursuit and more as an occasion to get reacquainted with a one-time lover. That

---

"cunningly made," then to "a person who is subtle . . . wily . . . to meet any occasion or emergency," and eventually described one who was overly "clever and subtle, a person full of tricks and stratagems to further his own ends and to get his own way." The word can even mean *promiscuous*. The promiscuous nature of both God's grace and love is evident in many Old Testament stories where God freely extends both to a seedy assortment of scallywags and scoundrels: Deceivers, seducers, prostitutes, adulterers and even murderers. It is seen in the New Testament portrait of Jesus, who was indiscriminate in his choice of company to keep—from conniving tax collectors to hated half-breeds to a wide spectrum of the sinful and immoral. The Pharisees, in particular, found Jesus' expression of God's grace and love far too promiscuous for their comfort. Jesus routinely went to places no gentleman would go, hanging with and loving on people with whom no gentleman would be caught dead. Jesus, of course, is the perfect expression of God (John 1:14–18; Heb 1:1–4) and reveals a promiscuous grace and love which repeatedly demonstrate that God will not wash his hands of us and leave us as and where we are, but will come to us as we are and where we are—regardless of what "gentlemen" might think—to bring us back into the fullness of his love.

is certainly true of his dealings with Israel in the early days after his people left Egypt. At the time of the Exodus, Israel's knowledge of God appears to have been limited to the oral traditions of its elders and the pagan religion of its captors. At best, Israel's belief system was a hodgepodge of Hebrew and hieroglyphics. As a result, some serious reprogramming was needed. Once leaving Egypt, God took his people to the desert where he essentially reintroduced himself to them.

The fact that the plagues which caused Pharaoh to relent and made the Exodus a reality were, in God's own words, *"judgment on all the gods of Egypt,"*[20] may have been as much for Israel's benefit as for Egypt's. In some ways, it was more important for God's long-enslaved people to learn, than it was for their pagan captors to learn, that Yahweh is the God of gods. It had been far too easy for Israel to lose its grip on that reality under the centuries-long secular and religious dominance of Egypt.

Just how deeply Israel was entrenched in Egyptian philosophy and religion may be seen by the fact that this long unheard-from and largely unknown God, when reintroducing himself to his suddenly-free people, used Egyptian imagery, which the Hebrews had absorbed through the osmosis of four hundred-plus years of enslavement. Well-known legends of Egyptian gods and goddesses suddenly became the domain of Yahweh, as Israel saw their God do in *fact* what Egyptian deities had done only in *story*. Ancient ballads about pillars of fire and cloud guarding against enemies, of the Red Sea parting for safe passage, and of stone tablets engraved with divine words carrying absolute authority were now the truth about *this* God who had called them out of slavery.

In a very real sense, at the time of the Exodus, Yahweh was someone Israel scarcely knew—familiar with him through story but not through experience. And, so, the pre-Jordan wilderness (the desert right out of Egypt) became the rendezvous where God and his people met to become reacquainted. A second honeymoon, we might say. A wilderness is not always a response to sin and rebellion. Sometimes it is necessary because we have, over time, grown numb to who God truly is or because the religion that has built up around or within us has crowded out a personal relationship with him. If we have the courage to be ruthlessly honest, we must own-up to the truth that there have been times—perhaps even now—when Yahweh has moved from a living, loving presence to a figure in oral tradition. He has become a stranger amid the familiarity of our religion. There are occasions when God leads us into a wilderness so that we can sit down with him and get reacquainted, spend time with him and fall in love all over again.

20. Exod 12:12.

In a wilderness, our memories of God are rekindled so that our passion for him might burn afresh; our history with God is recalled, so that we are restored to a proper view of who he is, what he does and what it all means. Otherwise, as with the Hebrews in Egypt, there is an ever-present danger of becoming like Pharaoh, who when told of God's command *"Let my people go,"*[21] replied, *"Who is the Lord, that I should obey him? . . . I do not know the Lord . . . ."*[22] In a wilderness, God reintroduces himself to us, enabling us to become reacquainted; God reaffirms his love for us, enabling our love for him to reawaken. In a wilderness, we are beckoned to know him better, beckoned to a more intimate and intense love relationship with our God. In a word, we are wooed.

A wilderness is a means God uses to alert us to the pervasive numbness that slowly but surely has turned cold our once fiery love for him. A wilderness is a means God uses to draw us close to his heart and into a deeper, more meaningful relationship. A wilderness is about falling in love all over again—not in some sentimental sense, but in the committed and covenantal sense. A wilderness is a word of love by which God woos us back into a proper love relationship with him.

But a wilderness is no cheap date. It is serious life-and-death business. In the days of Israel's wandering, as well as in Jesus' own day, a wilderness was a place where life itself was threatened. It was not hospitable to human habitation. People died in the wilderness, victims of elements or wild animals. As was the case with the scapegoat under the Old Testament law, to be dumped in a wilderness was do die. Even for a person with knowledge of its tracts and an adequate supply of provisions, the wilderness was still a treacherous place. It was the abode of bandits and wild animals, of poisonous vipers, mirages, quicksand, impassible gorges and deceptive distances. Not only that, but in the mind of most ancients, the desert was the abode of demons, a vast outpost of Satan's army. In other words, both physically and spiritually, the wilderness was a fight-to-the finish battleground.

The wilderness Israel knew for forty years was a fierce battleground where war was waged almost daily between righteousness and sin, between obedience and disobedience, and occasionally between God and his people. As with any battleground, of course, there were casualties, even corpses. Some died because of rebellion.[23] Others died from snakebites because they would not rush to the caduceus.[24] Nearly an entire generation was snuffed

---

21. Exod 5:1.
22. Exod 5:2.
23. Num 16:1–35.
24. Num 21:4–9.

out because of unbelief at the river's edge.[25] Every battleground has its casualties, and a wilderness is no exception.

The wages of a wilderness, like the wages of sin,[26] are death. Life lies only, but always, in God's free gift of love received. To spurn his overtures of love for grass we deem greener elsewhere, is to experience a fate worse than death. I choose that last phrase very carefully, for I believe that in his parable of the prodigal son, Jesus identified just such a fate.

When the wayfaring son was spied at a distance by his father, who was ever watching for him,[27] the old man ran to the boy, wrapped his arms around him, and in word and deed welcomed him home. Promptly, he ordered a celebration because, as he announced, *"My son was dead, and is alive again; he was lost, and is found."*[28] The order of the phrases may well indicate—I think, *does* indicate—that, at least in the father's mind, the son's state of *lostness* was a more terrible condition than his supposed state of *deadness*; that the boy being lost—cut off from father and home—was actually a fate worse than death.

Just to be sure the point was not lost on his hearers, Jesus repeated it—modified slightly for the sake of the older son in the story: *"Your brother was dead, and is alive; he was lost, and is found."*[29] As in the phrase used previously, the crescendo builds from the dramatic dead-and-alive to the climactic lost-and-found. Such a fate worse than death explains God's passionate *hounding* of us, his persistent seeking of us *"until he finds"*—for he will not, he cannot rest as long as we are cut off from father and family; he cannot abide our lostness. There is a deadness only a father knows in the lostness of his son; there is a death a father is willing to die if only his son is found. So it is that God's love is sometimes so urgent as to seem stern, so closely dogging our steps as to seem threatening. His is, after all, a wild and zealous wooing that refuses to allow us to ride rebellion and forgetfulness into lostness. Everything he does is so that we might fall in love again and find our way home again. He is ever on the hunt for us to bring us back into the embrace of his heart and home. Tough love is the hallmark of a wilderness.

In the imagery of Francis Thomson, *The Hound of Heaven* pursues us, not as a predator but as a lover—a lover who knows that true blessing can be found, experienced, and fully enjoyed by the pursued only when caught.

25. Num 26:63–65.
26. Rom 6:23.
27. Luke 15:20.
28. Luke 15:24.
29. Luke 15:32.

God's "hounding" is not to be feared but welcomed, not to be escaped, but embraced. When we turn from the one who chases after us in passionate pursuit, we ultimately turn on ourselves. No love can be found in driving him away. No life can be had in flight from the hounding pursuit of his perfect love.

PART V

TRUSTING GOD IN A WILDERNESS

"Our trust should never be in what God gives, but in the God who gives."[30]
BEN PATTERSON

---

30. Patterson, *Waiting*, 158.

TRUSTING GOD'S CHARACTER

God's character makes trust possible, even in a wilderness. Though circumstances may turn on a dime, as they did for Job and others mentioned in Scripture, God's character remains life's one constant, for he does *"not change like shifting shadows."*[1] Part of what it means for God's character to be constant, and for it to be constantly *holy*, is that God is not fickle or two-faced, he does not change his mind or go back on his word,[2] but is ever and only faithful in all respects, as regards his person, his words, and his deeds. Trust, in its biblical fullness, does not rest on *our faith*, which can and sometimes does weaken or wear thin over wilderness terrain, but rests rather on God's unfailing *faithfulness* in and through our wilderness.

The rural gravel and blacktop roads of my youth were dotted with one-lane bridges, most of which were decades old and in various stages of disrepair. Many bridges were rickety with sagging wooden planks and a history of not having collapsed . . . yet. Occasionally, motorists encountered a structure that looked unable to bear the load of a pedestrian, let alone a vehicle. On those occasions, if one genuinely had doubts about the possibility of a successful crossing, it was not helpful to sit in the vehicle and examine one's faith in the bridge. The smart and safe thing to do, the only way to be sure, was to exit the vehicle and examine the faithfulness, if you will—the trustworthiness, the dependability, the "character"— of the bridge. Once the bridge was deemed trustworthy, trust followed naturally.

That simple principle is at the heart of what is famously called the "faith chapter" of Christian Scripture—Hebrews 11. But that is really a misnomer, because the faith on display there does not exist on its own, magically floating in mid-air, but is grounded securely in the foundation of God's faithfulness. The author wrote of our father in the faith, *"By faith, Abraham, even though he was past age—and Sarah herself was barren—was*

---

1. Jas 1:17.
2. Lev 19:2; Num 23:19.

*enabled to become a father because he considered him faithful who had made the promise."*³ Abraham's faith was based on the faithfulness of God. In other words, it did not just come into existence on its own, standing there in lonely isolation. Rather, it resulted from something, flowed from something, was based on something. Abraham's faith was grounded securely in the faithfulness of God. God's faithfulness makes faith possible. God's character gives trust its foundation.

The Bible's great narratives of faith, like those on display in Hebrews 11, are not so much stories of human trust as they are stories of divine character. The individual stories in the Bible's faith chapter represent less a roll call of the faithful and more a reminder of God's faithfulness. What those specific men and women dared and did were dared and done because of who God is. His character made it possible for them to trust. His faithfulness made their faith possible.

In a wilderness, especially, we must not lose our grip on reality, we must not lose our grip on God—who he is and what he has done. God's faithfulness makes faith possible. God's character gives trust its foundation. If there is ever a time and place where faith and trust are crucial, it is in a wilderness.

As the people of Israel prepared to enter the Promised Land, Moses urged them to remember that the God who had called and led them was faithful:

> *The Lord did not set his affection on you and choose you because you were more numerous than other peoples. But it was because the Lord loved you and kept the oath he swore to your forefathers that he brought you out with a mighty hand and redeemed you from the land of slavery, from the power of Pharaoh king of Egypt. Know therefore that the Lord your God is God; he is the faithful God, keeping his covenant of love to a thousand generations of those who love him and keep his commands.*⁴

God's unchanging character and unfailing faithfulness are realities reiterated through Scripture, from the prophets[5] and psalmists[6] of the Old Testament to the apostles[7] and anonymous authors[8] of the New. His faithfulness

---

3. Heb 11:11.
4. Deut 7:7–9.
5. Isa 25:1; Lam 3:22–23.
6. Ps 40:10; 89:1–8, 33; 119:75, 86, 138.
7. 1 Cor 1:9; 10:13; 1 Thess 5:24; 2 Thess 3:3; 2 Tim 2:13; 1 John 1:9.
8. Heb 2:17; 10:23.

is *"perfect"* said Isaiah.[9] *"He cannot disown himself,"* wrote Paul.[10] *"Never will I be guilty of unfaithfulness"* declared Yahweh.[11] In desperate times of desert trekking, when menacing mirages render our senses untrustworthy and our faith fragile, there is a single concrete and unchanging certainty to which we must cling with utter trust: God's character. He is faithful always. He is faithful regardless.

"Committed faith holds to the promise," wrote William Lane, "even when the integrity of the promise is called into question by the evidence of harsh circumstances. Faith knows that the one who promised is himself faithful."[12] Always, the power of faith, the strength of trust lies not in the myriad of facts it does *not* know, but in the single fact it *does* know: God is faithful.

In a wilderness, certainty is not as valuable as we assume, while trust is the one truly invaluable commodity we possess. Speaking personally, the only thing more disheartening than my deserts has been my confusion in those deserts. That is also true of every wilderness pilgrim I have known. In a wilderness, certainty is the mirage while trust is the water. Trust is, therefore, a far more valuable commodity than certainty. Faithfulness—active trust in God's character—when we are certain of nothing or little else, keeps us alive.

Israel's entire exodus experience—from its miraculous release from Egypt to its successful journey to the Jordan; from God's miraculous provision of food and water to his miraculous preservation of clothes and sandals[13]—proved that God could be trusted, that his word was reliable, and that his character was constant.

There are times, of course, when God makes *conditional* covenants with his people[14]—if they do this, he will do that—but there are other times when he makes *pure promises* with no conditions attached.[15] Whereas God's fulfillment of his *conditional* covenants stands or falls, for the most part, on the response of his people, God's *pure promises* stand or fall, not on any human response at all, but solely on God's character. God *is* his promises; they are an extension of his person. There is no inconsistency between who God

---

9. Isa 25:1.

10. 2 Tim 2:13.

11. Ps 89:33.

12 Lane, *Call to Commitment*, 159.

13. Deut 29:5.

14. Exod 15:25b-26; 23:20—24:8; 34:10-28; Lev 26:1-46; Deut 4:1-40; 6:1-25; 8:1-20; 11:1-32; 26:16-19; 28:1—30:20.

15. Gen 8:21-22; 12:1-3; 15:1-21; 16:11-12; 18:1-10a; 25:23; Exod. 3:1-14; 6:6-8; Deut. 7:7-9.

is, what God promises, and what God does. In fact, God has "promises he intends to keep even when keeping them exacts a price"[16] because his character both demands and assures it. For God, to deny his promise is to deny himself. Trust is possible, even in a wilderness, because God cannot and will not deny himself. His *character* will not change with our circumstances. His faithfulness makes our faith possible.

Archimedes—the Greek mathematician and inventor who is credited with the first scientific description of a fulcrum, the solid support for a lever, which enabled people to lift enormous weight; all that was needed was a place to stand—was supposedly asked by the King of Syracuse (Sicily), "How much can you actually lift?" Archimedes replied, "If you give me a place to stand, I can lift the whole world." God's character gives us a place to stand—a solid point, a foundation from which we can bear the weight of even the most oppressive wilderness. Standing on God's unchanging character and unwavering faithfulness makes it possible for us to trust and obey, even when life tumbles in upon us.

At the practical level, God's character means that even if our circumstances change for the worse and an oasis abruptly transforms into a desert, God remains unchanged, ever himself and ever faithful. And should we never be delivered from a particular wilderness in this life, our faithfulness to God will still result in our good, in others' good and in God's glory; our faithful walk of trusting obedience, through long and even tortuous wilderness days, will make a significant difference for the kingdom of God. We have his word on it—a word that is trustworthy because God himself is.

I would like to be able to say at this point that if, as wilderness people, we remain faithful to our faithful God, he will lead us out of our particular desert and into the promised deliverance for which we so desperately long. If we mean by "promised deliverance" heaven itself, then I can say that confidently. One day God will lead us out of our temporal wilderness and welcome us into his forever home. If, on the other hand, we mean by "promised deliverance" this-world release from a wilderness and the subsequent fulfillment of all our earthly wishes, dreams and hopes, then I cannot say that. As much as I may want to say that, Scripture will not allow me to say that.

It is true that Joshua and Caleb led the children of Israel across the Jordan and into the land of Canaan. They exited the wilderness and entered the promise. But it is equally true that those they led into that new land were children of an entire generation that meandered in the desert for four decades and then died there without ever laying hands on the promise. Such

---

16. Smedes, "Power of Promises," 157

a scenario seems remarkably common in the Scripture. Remember these examples:

> *There were those who, under torture, refused to give in and go free, preferring something better: resurrection. Others braved abuse and whips, and, yes, chains and dungeons. We have stories of those who were stoned, sawed in two, murdered in cold blood; stories of vagrants wandering the earth in animal skins, homeless, friendless, powerless—the world didn't deserve them!—making their way as best they could on the cruel edges of the world.*
>
> *Not one of these people, even though their lives of faith were exemplary, got their hands on what was promised. God had a better plan for us: that their faith and our faith would come together to make one completed whole, their lives of faith not complete apart from ours.*[17]

The Bible calls for trusting faith that leans on the Lord and trusts his character through death or deliverance. It calls for the faith epitomized by an ex-American slave interviewed in the 1930s: "When asked, 'Are all your people dead?' Maria Jenkins replied, 'De whole nation dead . . . De whole nation dead—Peggy dead—Toby dead—all leaning on de Lord.'"[18] That is basically what the author of Hebrews 11 was saying: "De whole nation dead—all leaning on de Lord."[19] That is a key truth taught by the story of Israel's enslavement and exodus. More Hebrews died in Egypt than were delivered; but whether it was death or deliverance, they were called to be people "all leaning on de Lord."

What often makes it difficult for us to lean on the Lord for the duration of a wilderness is that we tend to have different ends in view than does God. We pray for his will but, in truth, want little more than his corroboration.[20] We see God's faithfulness and our faithfulness comprising a spiritualized mathematical equation where the two elements are added and the answer comes—our deliverance. God's track record, however—if we can speak of God, in fact, having a track record—is one of delivering some but not delivering others—and, most of the time, for no discernable rhyme or reason. Two righteous men, Peter and James, were imprisoned; one was freed,[21] the

17. Heb 11:35b-40, *Message*.
18. Roboteau, *Slave Religion*, 321.
19. Heb 11:35b-40.
20. See Morris, who imagines God writing in his diary concerning his children, "They ask for guidance but they really seek my corroboration." Morris, *God Kept a Diary*, 33.
21. Acts 12:3–17.

other executed.[22] Another righteous pair were stoned; one survived,[23] the other died.[24] Jesus endured a wilderness for forty days[25] before launching a three-year ministry; Moses spent the last forty years of his life in a wilderness before dying a few steps short of the Promised Land. Sometimes God delivers from a desert; sometimes he does not.

In truth, whether or not we are delivered from a desert is not our business, but God's. Who and when and even if he delivers is completely his business. Our business is simply to remain faithful. Scripture affirms that a person who remains faithful, even though a wilderness is delayed or denied, makes a significant difference—presently in the lives of those with whom life is shared, eventually in the lives of others yet-to-be impacted, and ultimately in a cosmic way that we cannot fully comprehend during our sojourn here.

Commenting on the faithfulness of a single wilderness traveler, the man Job, Philip Yancey wrote:

> The opening chapters of Job . . . reveal that God has much at stake in one man's wickedness or righteousness. Somehow, in a way the book only hints at and does not explain, one person's faith makes a difference. A tiny piece of the history of the universe was at stake.
>
> And that, to me, is the most powerful lesson from the book of Job. Like Job, we live in ignorance of what is going on "behind the curtains." Job teaches us that the little history of mankind on this earth—and, astonishingly, my own little history of faith—is enclosed within the drama of the large history of the universe. We are foot soldiers in a spiritual battle of cosmic significance.
>
> For Job, the battle ground of faith involved lost possessions, lost family members, lost health. We may face a different struggle. . . . Regardless, the message of this book calls for the hard-edged faith that believes, against all odds, that one person's response of obedience does make a difference.[26]

Carolyn Custis James condensed the same truth into a single succinct sentence: "You never know when some small everyday battle you are fighting may turn the tide for the kingdom in a big way."[27]

---

22. Acts 12:1–2.
23. Acts 14:19–20.
24. Acts 7:54–60.
25. Matt 4:1–11.
26. Yancey, "Facts Don't Add Up," 22.
27. James, *Gospel of Ruth*, 208.

Like Job, Joseph is an example of an imperfect individual who found the strength to walk faithfully through a wilderness with no promised deliverance in sight. In fact, in the end, unlike Job, Joseph never experienced this-world deliverance. Though he was earlier delivered from betrayal by his brothers, from the lies of his master's wife, and even from an Egyptian prison, Joseph eventually died having never tasted the promised fruits of the land God swore on oath to Abraham, Isaac and Jacob.[28] Yet, as is evident in his deathbed speech, Joseph came to the end of his life holding to the faith of his father—not having relinquished hope, still believing that God would somehow, some day get Israel's descendants safely to the land he had promised. He spoke his final words, as his father before him had, with unqualified trust in the faithfulness of God:

> *"I am about to die. But God will surely come to your aid and take you up out of this land to the land he promised on oath." And Joseph made the sons of Israel swear an oath and said, "God will surely come to your aid, and then you must carry my bones up from this place."*[29]

Centuries later, the author of the Hebrew epistle wrote that Joseph's end-of-his-life instructions about his bones were given *"by faith"*[30] God had promised a new land to his people and Joseph believed that the land-in-promise was as done a deal as the land-in-hand because his faithful God had spoken. At the end, Joseph's faith drank and refreshed itself from the well of God's spoken word and proven character. He had come a long way from those heady days under Pharaoh when Egypt needed Joseph and Joseph needed Egypt, when he had once left for Canaan only to return. As death approached, Joseph spoke, as had his father Israel, of his faith in the promise, of his faith in his father's God. At no time was Joseph given a timetable for the fulfillment of God promise. At no point was he told that he personally would set foot in the land of promise. But he had God's word that the People of Israel would one day enter in, and that is all faith ever needs.[31]

Joseph's faithfulness to the God who promised became the fuel that fired the faith of his descendants. As Israel carried those bones with them

---

28. Joseph, of course, did make his way to Canaan to bury his father, as he had promised, but quickly returned to Egypt where he eventually died and was buried, never truly knowing the Promised Land as his home, as the full blessing God intended it to be. See Gen 47:28–50:26.

29. Gen 50:24–25.

30. Heb 11:22.

31. "Our hope is in a promise heard, a promise trusted," wrote John Kirvan. "It is God saying, 'You have my word on it.'" Kirvan, *God Hunger*, 176.

wherever they went, they carried a visible reminder that God is faithful; that he will most certainly keep the promise he made. Regarding that promise, Joseph, in the end, like his father before him, could only welcome it from afar; but his faithfulness to the promise, and to the God who swore on oath, enabled those who came after him to grasp that promise with both hands and to one day know its fulfillment. One man's faithfulness—though he himself never tasted the delights of fulfillment—made a real and lasting difference in the lives of others. That faithfulness would one day welcome a promised Messiah, who welcomes us into the family of God. One person's faithfulness, even late in life, always makes a difference; God's character assures it.

God's people are called to *welcome* the promise in faith though they may never *see* the promise in flesh. As Scripture reveals, people seldom see, this side of heaven, the difference their faithfulness makes; yet such faithfulness always makes a difference. We have God's word on that, and God is faithful; his character guarantees his promise.

In his book *Loving God*, Charles Colson told of a Russian Jew named Boris Kornfeld, who lived and died in the wilderness of a *gulag*—a forced labor camp, especially for political dissidents, in the former Soviet Union. Kornfeld was imprisoned, though he was never told his crime. As a physician, he was put to work in the prison infirmary. One of his responsibilities was to sign medical release forms for fellow prisoners who were sentenced to *The Box*—a cramped cell which required a person to crouch for days or weeks on end. In the harsh Siberian winters, with insufficient heat and food, *The Box* became an execution chamber where death came slowly and agonizingly.

In time, Kornfeld learned from another prisoner about a man named Jesus. Like the Russian doctor, Jesus had been sentenced unfairly and suffered unjustly. Such similarities drew Kornfeld to Jesus. Eventually, he came to regard Jesus as the promised Messiah and soon committed his life to him as savior and Lord. Immediately, Kornfeld was a changed man. His new sense of faith and freedom altered his decisions and actions. He no longer signed forms sending men to their deaths in *The Box*. He no longer overlooked prison trustees stealing bread from starving or malnourished prisoners. In fact, the next time he saw a trustee stealing bread, he informed the prison authorities. Required to take some action, the powers-that-be sentenced the trustee to a token term in *The Box*. That meant that by the unwritten code of prison life, Kornfeld was now a dead man. The other trustees plotted to take the doctor's life.

One day, Boris Kornfeld was visiting a patient who was recovering from recent cancer surgery. The man had become his friend and the doctor had shared Jesus with him. As Kornfeld stepped into the hallway after their visit, he was attacked and beaten to death. "End of story," wrote Ben Patterson. "A man became a Christian, but it didn't get him out of jail. He waited and waited and then he died there. That's all that happened. Well, not quite. On the strength of Kornfeld's witness, the cancer patient became a Christian."[32]

Dr. Boris Kornfeld was never delivered from his wilderness. He lived and died in that brutal hellhole. In God's scheme of things, however, it did not ultimately matter. God's purpose could not be thwarted or stopped. One man stayed faithful in a horrible wilderness. Because of it, another man was saved. The angels in heaven rejoiced. God was once more proved faithful.

Though we may never live to see what God accomplishes through our faithfulness, he will most certainly accomplish something significant for his kingdom. His character guarantees it. Because God is God—even in a wilderness—"You never know when some small everyday battle you are fighting may turn the tide for the kingdom in a big way." That is why we trust. Even in a wilderness—*especially* in a wilderness—we trust.

---

32. Patterson, *Waiting*, 116–18.

TRUSTING GOD'S PRESENCE

A year-and-a-half into her battle with cancer, and a year before she died, I asked my dear friend Donna, "What is your most vivid memory through your entire ordeal with cancer?" "It was at the very beginning," she said, "when they were performing the biopsy on my breast to determine whether the engorged area was cancerous. They left me alone on the gurney in the hallway for a long time. As I waited, there were only two things I could do: Count the tiny holes in the ceiling tile or think about my situation. I laid there and thought. Then I turned my thoughts to prayer. The night before, at church, we had sung the song 'Precious Lord, Take My Hand.' Now I'm not one to hear voices, but as soon as I told God I was scared and asked him to hold my hand, he spoke to me. He said, 'Donna, I'm not just going to hold your hand; I'm going to carry you all the way through this.' Since that moment, I have never had any more fear. Since that moment, I have known his peace."

Three months later, I asked her, "What is the most valuable lesson you have learned through your wilderness journey?" "God answers prayer," she answered without hesitation and with a smile. "When he promises to be with you, he is. When he promises to walk with you, he does. When he promises to carry you in his arms and close to his heart that is where you find yourself. That is where I am right now." When she said that, I immediately thought of the prophet Isaiah's words:

> *He tends his flock like a shepherd:*
> *He gathers the lambs in his arms*
> *and carries them close to his heart;*
> *he gently leads those who have young.*[1]

Isaiah's words promptly led me to similar thoughts from the pen of a song writer named Asaph. When he crafted a ballad recounting Israel's

---

1 Isa 40:11.

wilderness journey and telling how God dealt with them those forty years—a song we know in Scripture as Psalm 78—he wrote:

> *Then he led his people out like sheep,*
> *took his flock safely through the wilderness.*
> *He took good care of them; they had nothing to fear.*[2]

God was lovingly present with his people as they traversed the desert, caring for them as a shepherd does his sheep. Moses spoke that same reality, minus the pastoral imagery, when he assured Israel, *"Do not be afraid . . . for the Lord your God goes with you; he will never leave you nor forsake you."*[3] It is important to remember that Moses did not pull out of thin air the promise of an ever-present God. In fact, he had met that God and heard that promise many years before.

> Stopped in his tracks by a flaming clump of chaparral that did not want to stop burning, Moses came to attention at the voice of an invisible, ineffable Someone calling him to lead his neglected people out of slavery.
>
> Moses was skeptical. "What is your name?" he asked the invisible Stranger. "The people need some identification." The name came from behind the flame; it came in a word of four cryptic Hebrew consonants that have defied confident translation. "I am who I am," the metaphysically bent scholars have rendered it. But Moses was not a metaphysician. He was a level-headed Hebrew who knew that everything depended on whether this Stranger God could be trusted.
>
> What Moses needed to know was whether he could depend on the Stranger. And what the Stranger God wanted to tell Moses was that he was a God who made promises and kept the promises he made. So the most likely translation of his name goes something like this: "I Am the One Who Will Be There With You." This is God's identity, this is who and what God is: a promise-maker and a promise-keeper.[4]

God promises to be present, to *"Be There With"* his people, in and through a wilderness. That is the promise of a God who is faithful through and through, and who is faithful through all the times of our lives, the bad as well as the good, the deserts as well as the oases. Whenever we must walk a wilderness, we never walk its terrain alone. God is present with us

---

2. Ps 78:52–53, *Message*.
3. Deut 31:6.
4. Smedes, "Power of Promises," 159.

as he promised he would be. God's presence is fundamentally related to his promise. His being-there-with-us is as solid and certain as his character.

William Lane insisted:

> God does not abandon his people. His word is the pledge of his continuing presence. The word announced by his Son is the word to which we must cling. We turn our backs upon its reality to our own peril. . . . The spoken word of God is the awesome reminder that God is with his people, even when they have an impression of his felt absence.[5]

God sometimes removes a *sense* of his presence to see if we will trust his word of promise.[6] Still, his promised presence is always with us. At other times, a sense of God's absence is due to hearts that are absent from him; but never because he is absent from us.[7] Our hearts can become numb to God, but God never becomes numb to us, never turns his heart from us. We must "never interpret our numbness as His absence. For amidst the fleeting promises of pleasure is the timeless promise of His presence."[8] Do not, however, confuse that *sure* fact with other *alleged* promises. Nowhere in Scripture, for example, does God promise a wilderness-free life.

How could the Bible, which recounts the trauma of Job's life, turn right around and promise *us* a tranquil life in an oasis? How could the Bible, which has at its center, at its core, a suffering savior and an executioner's cross, turn right around and promise *us* a divine detour around suffering and harsh seasons. If perhaps the most upright man under the old covenant was not exempt from wilderness calamity, and if the holiest heart that ever beat was not spared the wilderness of Calvary, how can we presume an exemption from wilderness seasons? God's promise is not that we will never find ourselves in a wilderness or, that if we do, we will not endure it for long. Rather, God's promise is that we will never know the experience of being *left alone* in a wilderness. He will never abandon us, but always walk with us. Nowhere in Scripture does God promise us a wilderness of short duration or of limited suffering simply because we are his people.

5. Lane, *Call To Commitment*, 41.

6. 2 Chr 32:31; Ps 22:31.

7. In the insightful words of my friend Kent Paris: "Adversity . . . and the crack-ups that sometimes go with it, are not the result of an absent God. God is very much with us. He became flesh and dwells among us. He is no stranger to the afflictions of the human condition, being himself the chief sufferer. No, adversity is not the result of an absent God, but rather of hearts that are absent from Him, and that refuse to appropriate the grace that He is always ready to give." Paris, *Nehemiah Ministries Magazine* (April 1991).

8. Lucado, *Eye Of The Storm*, 91.

There are, of course, biblical examples of brief stints in a wilderness: Paul and Silas in jail overnight;[9] Mary and Martha in mourning for three days;[10] and Abraham enduring a four-day nightmare with Isaac.[11] Yet the same Scripture that scrawls such short stories of relatively quick deliverance also spins thick volumes of prolonged and intense wilderness times. Think of Joseph, forced to sit in prison for two years;[12] Abraham and Sarah compelled to wait a quarter-century for their promised child;[13] or Moses bearing Midian's desert for forty years and Sinai's for forty more.[14] God did not promise that our time in a wilderness would be short or that it would be just slightly uncomfortable. Instead, he promised that whether our wilderness days are short or long, whether our experiences are mild or harsh, he will be with us the entire way. God did not even promise that we would ultimately be delivered from every wilderness we enter; merely that he would be present.

There are many stories in Scripture of miraculous deliverance: Peter from prison;[15] Daniel from a den of lions;[16] Elizabeth from the shame of barrenness;[17] and many from diseases.[18] But there are other not-so-glorious stories about people who were never delivered. Millions of God's children died in Egyptian bondage; Moses never crossed the Jordan into promise; Trophimus was left sick in Miletus;[19] and John the Baptist was executed from a prison cell.[20] God's promise to his wilderness-bound children is not one of *emancipation*, but one of *participation*. He will walk with us in and through every wilderness of our lives.

We should never allow the not-so-glorious stories of Scripture to discourage us, but it would be helpful if we did allow them to *dis-illusion* us. Illusions are false ideas or conceptions, beliefs or opinions not in accord with the facts. It is an illusion, for example, to think that we have an

9. Acts 16:16–40.
10. John 11:1–44.
11. Gen 22:1–18.
12. Gen 39:1—41:41.
13. Gen 12:1—21:5.
14. Exod 2:11–Deut 34:8.
15. Acts 12:1–17.
16. Dan 6:1–28.
17. Luke 1:5–25, 57–66.
18. Luke 4:38–44; 5:12–26; 7:1–10, 18–23; 8:26–48; 10:1–9; 13:10–17; 14:1–7; 17:11–21; 18:25–43 (to consider only Luke among the gospels); Acts 3:1–10; 8:4–8; 9:32–35; 10:38; 14:8–10; 19:1–20.
19. 2 Tim 4:20.
20. Mark 6:14–28.

ace-in-the-hole, a convenient "Get out of the Wilderness Free" card simply because we are God's people. That does not square with the biblical record. It is an illusion to think that if we ever find ourselves trudging through a desert, the journey is guaranteed to be short and the conditions mild because we are God's beloved. That is out of sync with Scripture's stories and teachings. It is never God's love that is the illusion, but the self-serving conclusions we sometimes draw from the fact of his love. The promise of God's presence is not in question, but the presumptions we make upon that promised presence are. The promise of God regarding any wilderness experience is that we will never walk that wilderness *alone*. He has promised to be present with us, and ever will be.

Often what we do *not* read in Scripture is as significant as what we *do* read.

David, for example, did *not* say, "I will walk *around* the valley of the shadow of death. David said:

> *Even though I walk*
> *through the valley of the shadow of*
> *death,*
> *I will fear no evil,*
> *for you are with me.*[21]

Isaiah did *not* say, "When high waters come, do not be afraid for you will walk *around* them; and when you face fire, do not be afraid, for you will walk *around* it." Isaiah said:

> *When you pass through the waters,*
> *I will be with you;*
> *and when you pass through the rivers,*
> *they will not sweep over you.*
> *When you walk through the fire,*
> *you will not be burned;*
> *the flames will not set you ablaze.*[22]

The apostle Paul did *not* say, "We will *avoid* all these things"—trouble, hardship, persecution, famine, danger, sword—rather, he said, *"in all these things we are more than conquerors through him who love us."*[23] Neither did Paul say, "God will *deliver* us from all trouble;" instead, he said that God *"comforts us in all our troubles."*[24]

21. Ps 23:4.
22. Isa 43:2.
23. Rom 8:37.
24. 2 Cor 1:4.

Jesus did *not* say, "Blessed are those who mourn, for they shall have their sorrow quickly *removed*." He said, *"Blessed are those who mourn, for they shall be comforted."*[25] Even Jesus' last recorded words in the gospel of Matthew were not a promise of deliverance, but a promise of his abiding and unfailing presence: *"Surely I am with you always."*[26]

The writer of Hebrews quoted God's promise to wilderness-weary Israel:

> *Never will I leave you;*
> *never will I forsake you.*[27]

Then, he added:

> *So we say with confidence,*
> *"The Lord is my helper; I will not be*
> *afraid.*
> *What can man to do me?"*[28]

In light of those verses, William Lane wrote:

> God identifies himself with his people and will never abandon them to their own limited resources. The emotions of fear, panic, discouragement, and despair would be appropriate if Christians were called to pilgrimage in the absence of God. The experience of his promised presence, however, justifies the confident affirmation, "The Lord is my helper; I will not be afraid! What can man do to me?"[29]

Why, then, do emotions such as fear, panic, discouragement and despair so often accompany God's people on wilderness journeys? For the same reason they dogged Israel through their desert days: A misplaced focus. Amid a wilderness, "the effort to keep the focus is always at risk."[30] When focus is taken from God and placed on circumstances, panic is sure to follow, just as it did with Israel.

> *As Pharaoh approached, the Israelites looked up, and there were the Egyptians, marching after them. They were terrified and cried out to the Lord. They said to Moses, "Was it because there were no graves in Egypt that you brought us to the desert to die? What*

25. Matt 5:4, *New American Standard Bible.*
26. Matt 28:20.
27. Heb 13:5 and Deut 31:6.
28. Heb 13:6 and Ps 118:6–7.
29. Lane, *Call To Commitment*, 175.
30. Peterson, *Reversed Thunder*, 189.

> have you done to us by bringing us out of Egypt? Didn't we say to you in Egypt, 'Leave us alone; let us serve the Egyptians'? It would have been better for us to serve the Egyptians than to die in the desert."[31]

A multitude of Hebrews, who had been promised the presence and protection of the God of the universe, cowered before the pursuing army of a world power, Egypt, from which that same God had just delivered them. Doubt and panic seized the day once Israel took its focus from God—forgetting his promise and presence—and placed its focus on the wall of water to one side and the war chariots of Egypt to the other. Whenever wilderness trekkers misplace their focus, panic ensues. In an instant, Moses directed Israel's focus back to God:

> Do not be afraid. Stand firm and you will see the deliverance the Lord will bring you today. The Egyptians you see today you will never see again. The Lord will fight for you; you need only be still.[32]

Once Israel returned its focus to God, panic withdrew and trust welled up within them. Long after that event, however, Israel continued to be stymied by misplaced focus. Like a bad story that kept repeating itself, Israel's focus would move from God to circumstances. Panic, doubt and, often, disobedience would quickly follow. God would call them back to proper focus, and Israel would look once more in trust to him. But it was never long before their focus strayed, and the scenario played out all over again.

Misplaced focus had even been the culprit as Israel balked on the banks of the Jordan when they were first ready to enter the Land of Promise. When the spies returned from scoping out the land and gave their assessment of what they had seen, the people's focus moved from God's promise to the majority report: "*We can't attack those people; they are stronger than we are.*"[33] In no time, panic swept through the camp and Israel returned to the wilderness until that entire generation had perished. The central mistake made by the people of God as they stood at the edge of promise was focusing on circumstances instead of on God.

The fact above all facts is God. As I heard someone say years ago—and found it then as I find it now to be biblically sound—"There is only one fact, and that is God; all other things are matters related to that fact." Wilderness travelers can never afford to ignore the one fact above all facts: God. He is

---

31. Exod 14:10–12.
32. Exod 14:13–14.
33. Num 13:31.

the eternal, immutable, omnipotent fact. To take our focus off the fact—off God—and to place it anywhere else is to become, like Israel, weaklings and whiners, recreants and rebels.

Near the end of 1856, David Livingstone received the Doctor of Laws degree from Glasgow University. Standing before an audience of scholars, students and dignitaries, he bore the marks of multiple struggles with the wild and his body testified to the toll taken by harsh conditions and many illnesses during his long and faithful service as a missionary and explorer in Africa. He was gaunt and haggard, all but broken from long bouts with fever and malaria. His left arm, crushed by a lion, hung helplessly at his side. Amid the reverential silence of the great hall, he announced his resolve to return to that dark continent:

> I return without misgiving and with great gladness. For would you like me to tell you what supported me through all the years? . . . It was this: "Lo, I am with you always." . . . On that pledge, He hazarded His all. And it did not fail Him. On that pledge, I hazard my all. And it will not fail me.[34]

The promise of his presence is, like all of God's promises, one he never fails to keep. It is a promise that has failed no one and will not fail us. "Oh never, never lose that sense of simple dependence on the presence of Jesus in your life," said Peter Storey, "because sometimes it is all that you will have."[35] But even if you have nothing else, you will always have that. His presence, like his promise, is sure.

In his sermon "The Power of a Promise," Lewis B. Smedes issued an important reminder for those who take God's word seriously:

> I want to say to you that if you have a ship you will not desert, if you have a people you will not forsake, if you have causes you will not abandon, then you are like God.
>
> What a marvelous thing a promise is! When a person makes a promise, she reaches out into an unpredictable future and makes one thing predictable: she will be there even when being there costs her more than she wants to pay. When a person makes a promise, he stretches himself out into circumstances that no one can control and controls at least one thing: he will be there no matter what the circumstances turn out to be. With one

---

34. The story is culled from many sources over many years, most notably from Myron J. Taylor's sermon "Lo, I Am With You Always," 87–92.

35. Storey, *God in the Crucible*, 97.

simple word of promise, a person creates an island of certainty in a sea of uncertainty.[36]

So it is with God's one simple word of promise: The promise of his presence. What a marvelous thing God's promise is.

I will never forget the first time I read *Night*, Elie Wiesel's poignant memoir from a Nazi death camp. One of the many lines to have stayed with me through the years was spoken to Wiesel by a fellow prisoner. "I've got more faith in Hitler than in anyone else," the man said. "He's the only one who's kept his promises, all his promises, to the Jewish people."[37] In the end, however, even Hitler was unable to keep his promise to exterminate every Jew.

There is only one who keeps all his promises. His name is Yahweh. He always has and always will keep all his promises. As the apostle Paul wrote, *"For no matter how many promises God has made, they are 'yes' in Christ. And so through him the 'Amen' is spoken by us to the glory of God."*[38]

The promise of God's presence never fails a wilderness trekker. Yahweh is always with us. That is why we trust. Even in a wilderness—*especially* in a wilderness—we trust.

---

36. Smedes, "The Power of Promises" in *A Chorus of Witnesses*, 156–57.
37. Weisel, *Night*, 77.
38. 2 Cor 1:20.

TRUSTING GOD'S PROVISION

A major theme of the last four books of the Torah[1] is that of a wilderness being Yahweh's blessing for his people. That blessing—as stake-your-life-on-it dependable as is God's character and presence—is a staple, but sometimes subtle gift, of the God of the Wilderness. Though we may not instinctively think of it in such terms, a wilderness is nonetheless among God's most remarkable provisions to assist his people on their spiritual journeys.

Blessing comes to us in spite of the demands of a wilderness; perhaps, because of them. God uses desert days to empty us so that he might fill us, to strip us of much that is incidental to our spiritual pilgrimage, dangerous to our spiritual health and vitality, so that we might become everything and possess everything that he desires. A wilderness forces us to break with those things that hold us too tightly or that we hold too tightly so that we might hold to God alone and steadfastly. For that reason, a wilderness can be viewed, at least in one sense, as a call of God.

The call to follow God has always involved making a break with those things we are attached to and that, if not released, might hinder or even halt our faithful following. As early as Noah, who was called to make a decisive break with a world spiraling into sin,[2] and later with Abram, who was called to leave his country, his family and his father's home to undertake a divine mission,[3] God's call to humankind has demanded a break, a release, a surrender.

The biographies of Jesus penned by Matthew, Mark and Luke ring out the same strong, clear note as Jesus called fishermen to abandon nets and boats, livelihood and families;[4] a tax collector to close up shop for

---

1. The first five books of the Hebrew text (Genesis–Deuteronomy).
2. Gen 6:5–7:5.
3. Gen 12:1.
4. Matt 4:18–22; Mark 1:14–20; Luke 5:1–11.

good;[5] a rich man to walk away from his wealth, giving his possessions to the poor;[6] would-be disciples to count the cost, make the break and follow;[7] and crowds of prospective followers to deny themselves, take up their crosses and follow him.[8] In the words of Karl Barth, "the call to discipleship makes a break"[9]—a reality evident in the responses of the earliest followers of Jesus and echoed in Peter's words to the Lord, *"We have left everything to follow you."*[10]

The reason that call—Old Testament or New—seems so decisive and divisive, so stern and uncompromising, is because, in the words of John Kirvan, "some part of us must die if we are to live. And the part of us that must go will not be some extra that we could easily and joyfully do without. It will certainly be something that we are clinging to with all our energy because we have come to believe that it is the source of our happiness, our lives."[11] For that reason primarily, a wilderness forces a break, a release, a surrender—we might even call it a death; in fact, it frequently feels like death—that we might recognize God alone as the source of our happiness, the wellspring of our living. There is a strip-and-shape aspect to every wilderness. God seeks to strip us of all those things—the unnecessary and cumbersome, the sinful and lethal—that hinder or halt our spiritual progress, and then seeks to shape us, through the time and trials of wilderness terrain, into the likeness of his son Jesus.

Understood in that way, a wilderness is a key provision for our spiritual progress. It is designed by God to move us from where we are to where we must be, and from who we are to who we must become, in order to fulfill his purpose for our lives. God often drives us where we would not go ourselves to give us what we could not get ourselves. A wilderness is, perhaps, God's most paradoxical yet indispensable provision. Within the larger provision of a wilderness, there lie numerous other provisions available to those who walk its expanse. Those provisions are most obvious in the story of Israel's journey to and through Sinai.

From the moment the freed Hebrew slaves left Egypt, God provided them with *guidance*, a crucial provision for wilderness survival, especially considering that the trip from Egypt to Sinai was fraught with danger, and

5. Matt 9:9; Mark 2:14; Luke 5:27–28.
6. Matt 19:16–26; Mark 10:17–27; Luke 18:18–25.
7. Matt 8:18–22; Luke 9:57–62.
8. Matt 10:37–39; Luke 9:23.
9. Barth, *Call to Discipleship*, 35.
10. Mark 10:28.
11. Kirvan, *God Hunger*, 118.

the still-to-come terrain and threats of a vast desert were unfamiliar to Israel. Joshua's command to God's people, as they prepared to follow the Ark across the Jordan an entire generation after their rebellion, to carefully heed God's directions because *"you have never been this way before"*[12] was equally imperative at the beginning of their journey. Without guidance, Israel would have been no match for the wild. The people would have perished.

God's guidance for his pilgrim people consisted of his sure presence and spoken word; the man Moses, who knew the ways and winding paths of the desert; and an angel sent ahead to lead them in the way.[13] Beyond those, there was the miraculous ministry of cloud and fire:

> *By day the Lord went ahead of them in a pillar of cloud to guide them on their way and by night in a pillar of fire to give them light, so that they could travel by day or night. Neither the pillar of cloud by day nor the pillar of fire by night left its place in front of the people.*[14]

Whenever the pillar lifted and moved on, Israel broke camp and followed.[15] Whenever the pillar stopped and settled, Israel bivouacked and bedded down.[16] Whether fire by night or cloud by day, the pillar was God's visible directive for his people to stay or to leave. It was an essential and unfailing means of guidance in a naturally disorienting place.

Obviously, not every wilderness pilgrim in Scripture had access to a leader who knew the lay of the land, an angel clearing the path ahead or, for that matter, a highly practical pillar of fire and cloud. At the same time, no wilderness trekker was ever left alone without God's guidance. The important matter in a wilderness—be it ancient or modern, physical or spiritual—is not *how* God guides but *that* God guides. God's guidance varies from desert to desert, as it does from person to person. Hence, Israel was directed along one route, Jesus along another. David was given one set of directions for his desert time, Paul a different set for his. Though the *how* of God's guidance varies from one time and place to another, from one person to the next, the *fact* of God's guidance does not. It is an ever-present provision for wilderness people.

It is true that guidance is not unique to a wilderness. God guides through oases as well, through good times as well as through bad.

---

12. Josh 3:4.
13. Exod 23:20–21.
14. Exod 13:21–22.
15. Num 9:17a (See 9:15–23 for fuller context).
16. Num 9:17b (See 9:15–23 for fuller context).

Interestingly, however, Israel did a better job hearing God's word, following his lead, and sticking close by his side when they were in a wilderness than when they were in an oasis. That probably had something to do with the distractions that attended an oasis, as well as with the dangers and life-and-death desperateness that was part and parcel of a wilderness. Even in our day and in our lives, it is in the crisis, not in the calm, that we are most prone to turn to God, look to God, hold to God, listen and obey.

Years ago, when my children were young, I was with my family at Six Flags over Missouri. It had been a long day, and my wife and daughter went in search of shade and refreshment. My boys and I opted to ride the Octopus. We excitedly got in the long line and waited for our chance to take a spin at the crack-the-whip end of one of the monster's tentacles. As we waited, we watched two complete cycles of the Monster. After each one, passengers unloaded, and the next group boarded.

During the first cycle, I noticed one compartment spinning wildly, seemingly out of control, its occupants a blur. As the ride slowed, I saw those occupants clearly—a now somewhat woozy college age couple. As soon they reached the bottom position and came to a complete stop, the door swung open, the young man jumped to the ground, zigzagged to his left and promptly vomited. With an easy laugh, I said to my boys, who were watching with me, "We'll probably get that compartment."

During the second cycle, I kept my eye on the man and his son who were loaded into that troubled compartment. The same in-air scenario played out, predictable blur and all. When the ride slowed, the man was hunched forward and the boy was shaking him, speaking urgently to him. I thought the man had suffered a heart attack. He had not; the ride had simply swept him into a swoon. As I watched the compartments unload and the passengers disembark, I quickly did the math, and said to my boys, this time attempting to hide my fear, "We are going to get that compartment." By that time, they were only half listening, their wide eyes staring at the crazy compartment. After it reached the unloading zone and man and boy exited, we watched the son lead his staggering father away from the monster. At that moment, we swallowed hard and braced ourselves for what was about to happen.

The attendant then motioned for us to get into *that* compartment—the blur box, the vomit chamber, the swoon cart. At that point, we made a major tactical error . . . we got in. What followed was one of the most physically disorienting experience I have ever known. After all were safely loaded and locked in, the motor hummed, and the ride began. As it rapidly picked up speed, my boys and I did our best imitation of little marbles sent into orbit on a roulette wheel. I quickly lost all sense of direction—up, down; left, right; in, out . . . none of it made sense anymore. I felt like the three of us were about to be thrown out of the compartment, and I frantically searched for some way to hold on to my boys while grabbing any part of the compartment so as to hold on to it. The best I can say is that we survived. We were also the last people allowed to ride in the compartment that day.

While whirling around madly, my boys were understandably scared. They sat as close to me as they could, held to me as tightly as they could, listened to my voice as carefully as they could, and did whatever I told them—without question, argument or hesitation. A harrowing ride will do that to you, and every wilderness trekker knows it. It is in the crisis, not in the calm that we are most prone to turn to God, look to God, hold to God, listen and obey. That fact alone makes a wilderness a priceless provision. The guidance, direction, instruction, words and wisdom we most need in the acute disorientation of a wilderness, are there for us unfailingly. It is the provision of an all-wise, all-loving God.

Another staple provision during Israel's four-decade journey through Sinai, as well as the journeys of many other wilderness trekkers mentioned in Scripture, was God's *practical care* for his people. Whether that care took the form of angels ministering to Jesus; ravens sent to Elijah and a companion provided for him; a rock miraculously affording water for Israel; the sky raining birds; or shoes and clothes not wearing out through long years of desert travel, each marked God's loving and care-full provision for his wilderness-strapped people. He saw to their needs.

Near the beginning of their desert trek, God said to his people, *"See, I am sending an angel ahead of you to guard you along the way."*[17] That marvelous provision, however, does not stand as the lone example of God caring for his people. The fingerprints of God's guardianship and practical care for Israel were all over that wilderness. The pillars of cloud and fire, for example, did not simply *lead* the Hebrews, but *protected* them as well. The cloud served as a massive umbrella raised against the fierce desert sun and the fire served as a furnace stoked against the cold desert nights. In addition, God provided abundant food and drink in a place where such life essentials were scarce at best.

God made certain that his people had all they needed for their wilderness journey—not necessarily all they wanted, but absolutely all they needed. The fact is that Israel longed for, even occasionally asked for, many things, particularly things they had enjoyed in Egypt, but God concerned himself only with life essentials. That seems to be the way of God in a wilderness.

---

17. Exod 23:20.

Should we be, like Israel millennia ago, stranded in a desert, wondering how we will possibly survive day-to-day, we may not receive all the provision we would like, not even all the provision we think we must have, but we will receive all the provision we truly need. God has higher purposes than coddling to our felt needs. And whereas God is committed to providing practical care for his people, he is not at all into pampering his people by indulging their wants and wishes. In God's economy, some things simply cannot be. In a creative vignette, *A Week in the Life of God: If God Kept a Diary*, Colin Morris pictured God writing in his diary entry one Friday:

> I cannot always give them what they ask for, not because they ask for too much but because they ask for what I do not possess. They cannot have square circles nor wet dryness nor curved straight lines. Nor can they have love without cost, life without pain, truth without effort. I cannot give them what I do not possess.[18]

Nor is God likely to give us maturity without a wilderness. A straightforward lesson of the Bible's desert stories is that God will provide all the practical care that wilderness people *legitimately* need to become everything and possess everything he desires.

Perhaps the most over-arching, all-inclusive wilderness provision, however, is *grace*—grace that is both saving and sustaining.

God's provision of grace is *saving* in that it is known to rescue, to free, to deliver those who are shackled by a wilderness. That is the grace Paul referenced when writing to the Corinthians: "God saved us from these great dangers of death, and he will continue to save us. We have put our hope in him, and he will save us again."[19] It is the grace to which Peter referred when he wrote, "The Lord knows how to save those who serve him when troubles come."[20] The evidence of Scripture, in both statement and story, is that God, by his grace, saves people from the wilderness, just as he ultimately saved Israel. Sometimes, however, he does not.

On occasion, we are stranded in a wilderness indefinitely, and sometimes, like Moses, for the rest of our lives. There is no honest way, biblically, to get around that. The hard fact of Scripture is that sometimes we are not rescued, freed or delivered; instead, we remain. When those moments come, and *saving* grace does not arrive, God provides his *sustaining* grace—grace that is sufficient and that sustains us in our wilderness. There are times, in Scripture as in our lives, when instead of saving us from our trials, God

---

18. Morris, *God Kept a Diary*, 15.
19. 2 Cor 1:10, *Youth Bible: New Century Version*.
20. 2 Pet 2:9, *Youth Bible: New Century Version*.

sustains us in them. Grace operates both ways, and which way it works in our lives, at any particular moment or point, is God's domain.

God's grace does not only save, but also sustains, providing staying power in periods of trial and tribulation. Paul had such grace in mind when he wrote:

> To keep me from becoming conceited because of these surpassingly great revelations, there was given me a thorn in my flesh, a messenger of Satan, to torment me. Three times I pleaded with the Lord to take it away from me. But he said to me, "My grace is sufficient for you, for my power is made perfect in weakness." Therefore, I will boast all the more gladly about my weaknesses, so that Christ's power may rest on me. That is why, for Christ's sake, I delight in weakness, in insults, in hardships, in persecutions, in difficulties. For when I am weak, then I am strong.[21]

As acceptable a translation as "thorn" is—*"there was given me a thorn in my flesh"*—it softens the harshness of Paul's words. "Thorn," like "splinter," is only a secondary meaning of the Greek word used. Despite the fact that most of us can easily relate to the image of a thorn, it falls short of capturing the sheer violence and viciousness, the sheer wilderness-like pain and trauma, of Paul's phrase.

The word Paul used—*skolops* in Greek—primarily means "stake" or "spike," "spear" or "peg."[22] I remember my grandfather pounding three-foot wooden stakes in the ground to mark off a house he was building. I remember my father driving pegs for our tent into the resistant soil of the Rockies and Tetons in the heart of a sunbaked summer. That is more what Paul had in mind—not a pricking, but a pounding; not a thorn or splinter, but a stake or peg; not something that pierced the flesh and was removed, but something which ripped the flesh and remained. That is far more than a bothersome inconvenience suggested by the word "thorn," and much more like a painful and prolonged wilderness.

Whatever were the specifics of Paul's pain (and Paul never says) it was like a stake driven into his flesh, like a peg pounded into his heart; it was a hurt that would not quit, a pain that would not go away; it was ongoing, constant, long-term; it went in, but it did not come out, and Paul struggled to go on. It was wilderness-like. It appears to have actually been a wilderness to Paul.

---

21. 2 Cor 12:7–10.
22. Arndt and Gingrich, *Greek-English Lexicon*, 348–51.

Repeatedly in 2 Corinthians 11–13, Paul referenced his *weakness*.[23] In the Gospels and Acts, that word was only used of physical illness and infirmity, usually describing a malady so debilitating that it sapped a person of strength, but Paul (who used the word in letters to half-a-dozen different churches) broadened the definition to include all those experiences and areas of our lives that are so difficult and enduring, so wilderness-like, that our strength is sapped and often fails. As a result, we feel weary, broken and vulnerable; frail and faint-hearted; frustrated by our limitations and inadequacies. Pick the word that best fits how you have felt or do feel in a wilderness—feeble, powerless, defenseless, ineffective, beaten, overpowered, crushed, defeated—all those things that can become true of us when a stake rips its way into our life and shreds our heart, all those things that are the experience of wilderness people. That is how Paul felt.

Through that which tore into his body like shrapnel on a battlefield, Paul learned that God's grace may not always deliver (it did not deliver Paul from his "thorn" or, for that matter, Jesus from the cross), but it will always sustain. Paul did not request a wilderness; instead, it was "given" to him, forced on him.[24] He did not immediately acquiesce to it; instead, he pleaded for deliverance from it.[25] Ultimately, however, Paul abandoned his prayer asking for saving grace and, instead, embraced the sustaining grace promised by Jesus,[26] having learned that life doesn't always give us what we want, but God's grace always gives us what we need.

Once Paul owned his weakness—his wilderness of perpetual pain—as a gift of God's grace, it became the very point at which God worked his transformation, enabling Paul to become everything and possess everything God desired. Once Paul owned his weakness—his personal, ongoing wilderness—as a gift of God's grace, he found grace where he had previously never seen it, and found a way, even in his intense and unyielding pain, to live in the wilderness for God's glory. It is a lesson all those in a wilderness are meant to learn.

The writer of Hebrews seems to have had God's sustaining grace in mind when penning the powerful promise, *"Let us approach the throne of grace with confidence, so that we may receive mercy and find grace to help us in our time of need."*[27] No matter how long we must endure a wilderness, God's grace sustains us in it. It is all-sufficient for all our needs. It is

---

23. 2 Cor 11:29–30; 12:5,9–10; 13:4,8.
24. 2 Cor 12:7.
25. 2 Cor 12:8.
26. 2 Cor 12:9–10.
27. Heb 4:16.

a provision that we will never exhaust no matter how long or severe is our wilderness journey.

God's grace never quits. God's grace never fails. It is part of God's priceless provision for us as we struggle in and through the deserts of our lives. As we own the wilderness and faithfully seek God's glory in it, we are able to persevere, to bring God glory, to be transformed, to become and possess everything he desires. That is why we trust. Even in a wilderness—*especially* in a wilderness—we trust.

TRUSTING GOD'S WISDOM

I have often wondered what the enslaved Hebrew people were praying—assuming they *were* praying—when Moses and Aaron had their initial audience with Pharaoh, determined to place before Egypt's king God's demand to *"Let my people go."*[1] Though we are not privy to the particulars of those prayers, my best guess is that the people were praying for the success of the venture, asking God to soften Pharaoh's heart so that he would relent and allow them to leave. That is almost certainly what I would have been praying: "God, please soften Pharaoh's heart that he might allow us to leave and offer sacrifices to you in the desert."[2] But had that been the slaves' prayer, they would have been asking God to do the opposite of what was his intent—at the very least, the opposite of what he did.

No less than twenty-one times between the arrival of Moses and Aaron in Egypt and Israel's crossing of the Red Sea to begin its journey to the Promised Land, we are told that God *hardened* Pharaoh's heart.[3] Not only that, but when God parted the Red Sea as a path for his people, he went so far as to harden *all* the Egyptians' hearts so that they would pursue Israel between the piled-up walls of water.[4] God, in his wisdom, knew—as he had previously explained to Moses—*"the King of Egypt will not let you go unless a mighty hand compels him."*[5] If Pharaoh was to release God's people, it would require, not the softening, but the hardening of his heart.

---

1. Exod 5:1.

2. The gist of Moses' request to Pharaoh was, according to Exod 3:18b, *"Let us take a three day journey into the wilderness to offer sacrifices to the Lord our God."*

3. Exod 4:21; 7:3,4,13,14,22,23; 8:15,19,32; 9:7,12,34–35; 10:1,20,27; 11:9–10; 14:4,8.

4. Exod 14:17.

5. Exod 3:19.

From a finite human perspective, God's wisdom is often counterintuitive. He does not think like we think; we do not know what he knows.[6] What seems best to us is often not best in God's scheme of things. King Saul once learned that, as he learned many things . . . the hard way.[7] With battle against the Philistines looming, he was told to wait until Samuel arrived to offer a sacrifice and blessing for the troops.[8] But Samuel was delayed and things at the front turned dicey. Saul's army grew tired of waiting, and the Commander-in-Chief saw his soldiers starting to disperse as the Philistines mustered.[9] Saul, the experienced warrior that he was, quickly assessed the situation and made the wise move—certainly wise from a military and leadership standpoint—galvanizing his men by offering the sacrifice in Samuel's stead. About that time, Samuel arrived.[10] Saul explained the wisdom of his move[11]—and again, humanly speaking, it *was* the wise move—but Samuel, speaking on God's behalf, called such wisdom foolishness.[12] Ultimately, reliance on his own wisdom rather than on God's cost Saul his kingship.[13]

In a wilderness, where odds are often stacked against us and where elements can come against us like an armed enemy, trusting what Eugene Peterson called "the seeming absurdity of God"[14] can seem exactly that—absurd. Yet, trusting God's foolishness is, in the end, the only wise move;[15] trusting our wisdom can prove foolish and end in ruin. In a wilderness, we must learn to trust God's wisdom. Trusting his wisdom makes our walk of obedience possible.

Often God's wisdom, because it transcends ours, leaves us scratching our heads, asking questions, seeking answers, lodging complaints and even toying with the possibility of abandoning faithfulness. In other words, thinking and living as Israel did through most of its wilderness journey. God's counterintuitive wisdom can leave us wondering if he really knows what he is doing. He does, of course. *We* are the ones who do not always know what he is doing. During those occasions of not knowing or, possibly, even thinking that we know better, we must trust his wisdom, trust that he

---

6. Isa 55:8–9.
7. 1 Sam 13:5–14.
8. 1 Sam 13:7b-9.
9. 1 Sam 13:5–8.
10. 1 Sam 13:8–10.
11. 1 Sam 13:11–12.
12. 1 Sam 13:13.
13. 1 Sam 13:13–14.
14. 1 Cor 1:25, *Message*..
15. 1 Cor 1:18–25.

knows best, trust that his move is the wise move. That is not an easy thing for us to do, considering that a divine wilderness is often, by its very nature, counterintuitive.

There come times in a wilderness when we fall victim to insidious and subtle suggestions that plant doubts about God in our minds, doubts similar to those faced by Adam and Eve in Eden,[16] causing us to wonder if what God is doing behind the scenes is somehow deceptively underhanded and to wonder if, were the truth uncovered, his motives would be revealed as ulterior. At times, because we do not know what God is up to behind the curtain, and because it hurts so badly out on the stage as we live-out our wilderness in real-time, sticking faithfully to God's script can be extremely difficult. In such periods of intense doubt and struggle, it would help us to remember a quartet of biblical principles.

We would do well to ask questions, but not accuse.

God has never turned away a sincere questioner. Scripture is saturated with examples of hurting women and men asking pointed and penetrating questions of God. Most of those questions are not in the form of polished prayers with carefully crafted words. They are, rather, real and rugged, often raw, voiced in moments of brutal honesty, fueled by panic or pain, the product of troubled minds, damaged emotions and burdened hearts. Such questions do not reveal people at their best, but at their most real. Whatever form those questions take—kicking the hardscrabble earth, screaming at the stars, or pleading angrily through tears—God's shoulders are broad enough and his heart is large enough to take what we dish out.

In his sermon, *Life is a Gift*, preached following the death of his daughter, John Claypool advised his listeners:

> There is more honest faith in an act of questioning than in the act of silent submission, for implicit in the very asking is the faith that some light can be given....
>
> I do not believe God wants me to hold in these questions that burn in my heart and soul—questions like: "Why is there leukemia? Why are children of promise cut down at the age of ten? Why did you let Laura Lue suffer so excruciatingly and then let her die?" I am really honoring God when I come clean and say, "You owe me an explanation." For, you see, I believe he will be able to give such an accounting when all the facts are in, and until then, it is valid to ask.[17]

---

16. Gen 2:1–7.
17. Claypool, "Life is a Gift," 125.

It is not, however, valid to accuse. To sincerely question "why?" is one thing, a proper thing, but to accuse God of neglect or lack of love or latent sadism is quite another. God may well "owe" us answers, in the sense Claypool suggests, but he does not deserve our accusations.

David Wilkerson, in his sermon *Accusing God of Child Neglect*, raised an issue I had never before considered, but an issue which I was forced to face, and which needs to be honestly faced by every wilderness pilgrim:

> In recent weeks, as I sought the Lord for this message, another question popped into my heart. The Lord asked me this:
>
> "David, do you accuse me of child neglect?"
>
> I was astounded at the very thought! Then the Spirit whispered to my soul:
>
> "You are my child—I am your Father. Yet do you doubt me? Do you accuse Me in your mind of neglecting you, of not hearing your sincere cries?"
>
> Again I had to search my heart before answering. And the Lord quickly brought up a number of other questions—all of them dealing with accusing God of neglect!
>
> Now, we Christians rarely verbalize our doubts and unbelief. We never say to others that the Lord has neglected us—that He has been silent to our cries, He has not heard our prayers, He has not been working in our behalf.
>
> But the fact remains—we do think such thoughts! These questions and doubts exist deep within us. They are things we feel when God seems to be absent from our lives.
>
> I believe God gave me this message because the Spirit wants to deal with each of us about trusting him fully. Our glorious worship in church, our heart-felt praise, our daily Christian walk—all are in vain if we think for a moment that God has neglected us in any area of our lives![18]

We may freely and fearlessly take our questions to a God who loves us—hard questions from hurting hearts—for every wilderness trekker has them and God is willing to hear them. Let us not, however, accuse God, whose ways are higher than ours,[19] of child neglect.

We would do well to expect answers, but not all the answers.

The God of the Wilderness provides all the answers we *need*, though perhaps not all the answers we *want*. There is, of course, coming a time when we will have all our answers, when we will fully understand the purpose of

---

18. David Wilkerson, "Accusing God of Child Neglect!" (Sermon delivered June 21, 1993).

19. Isa 55:8–9.

desert days, but that time is not now. At this moment, in our particular wilderness, we must walk by faith with what few answers we have, trusting that we do not need answers nearly as much as we need presence, we do not need an explanation nearly as much as we need God.

Imagine a two-year-old child who, with seemingly every breath, asks "why?" standing on a chair beside its mother at the sink, and the patient mother answering the chain of questions with half-an-ear but with a whole heart while washing dishes. At last, she says, "That's enough for now, get down and go play." That temporary end of questions-and-answers never in the least leads the child to suspect the mother is less than one hundred percent loving and wise. Even her occasional I-don't-knows never erode the child's utter faith in her. Similarly, God may not answer all the questions we ask of him, but he remains all-loving and all-wise, and he still provides all the answers we truly need . . . for now.

We would do well to offer praise, but not complaints.

God is working his will for us, weaving it through our lives with every wilderness step we take. If we could step behind the curtain to see and grasp what God is doing, I think we also would choose the way he has chosen for us. In fact, I am confident of that. The more I read Scripture, the more deserts I traverse, the more firmly convinced I am that if God laid out all the options before me so that I could see them in their entirety, from beginning to end, and know the final result, I would choose what God has already chosen. As John Newton wrote, "If it were possible for me to alter any part of his plan I could only spoil it."[20] Even in the most debilitating wilderness, God is working his perfect will for our lives. That calls for praise, not complaint.

Decades ago, when I was in the clutches of an intense and tenacious wilderness, I was blessed to be part of a prayer-and-accountability group that kept me sane and saw me through the most difficult of those desert days. My prayers, like my wilderness, were extreme as I asked God for things I so desperately needed and asked my friends to join me in those prayers. In retrospect, most of my shared prayer requests in that group were, at the time, thinly veiled complaints. I did not know that then, but I do now. One day, about two or three months before I left for a new pastorate, a good friend, the worship pastor with a church in town, looked me in the eye right before our group prayed and said, "I believe God has given me a message for you." I asked him what that message was. He replied, "I believe God wants you to spend the next thirty days without asking him for a single thing. All you are to do for the next month is to praise him." I took that as a word from God and obeyed.

---

20. Newton, *Works of John Newton*, 623–24.

Years later, having returned to that community, I saw my worship pastor friend at an area-wide Thanksgiving service. I asked him if he remembered that word God had given him for me. He told me he did not. I rehearsed the story for him that night and told him how that simple word from God he shared with me had not only transformed my wilderness but had also forever changed my life in fundamental ways. For me, as I struggled my way through that prolonged and painful wilderness, it was truly revolutionary to replace asking with praising.

There is certainly nothing wrong with asking God for what we need—there are abundant Scripture texts and examples to back it up—but we must be careful not to merely disguise our complaints as requests. Offering praise in lieu of complaints is more than merely good advice; it often proves to be lifesaving and life changing, especially in a wilderness.

We would do well to stay faithful and not abandon God's ways.

A truly intense wilderness hurts like nothing else in life. Job and Jesus, as well as countless others before and since, have borne the extreme hurt of a severe wilderness. Job and Jesus most notably stand as examples of remaining faithful to God and to his word through the toughest of times. Job steadied himself and stayed on course by remaining true to the word and the will of God:

> *My feet have closely followed his steps;*
> *I have kept to his way without turning aside.*
> *I have not departed from the commands of his lips;*
> *I have treasured the words of his mouth more than*
> *my daily bread.*[21]

Jesus, as well, kept to the path laid out by God's wisdom and will. Even amid the excruciating agony of Gethsemane, he prayed, *"Not as I will, but as you will."*[22]

Jumping ship in a storm is a sure way to drown. We are far safer with God in a hurricane of hurt than in the fairest weather without him. To trust God's wisdom means to stay faithful, to keep to the path, to not abandon his ways. When the going gets tough, the tough do not get going; instead, they stay close, they cling in trust to God. They may hang on barely, perhaps by their fingernails, but they hang on—not to thin air, however, but to the solid, reliable and unfailing word of God. Trusting God's wisdom makes such hanging-on faith possible. "If only you knew the outcome," Thomas a Kempis is credited with saying, "you would hang on to the end."

---

21. Job 23:11–12.
22. Matt 26:39.

When the pain of a wilderness is real and unrelenting, and our prayers are many and urgent, it is difficult to grasp why God sometimes seems so nonchalant about our dilemma, so silent in the face of our cries for help, so incapable of rescuing us, or—worse yet—so uncaring. Sometimes we are called to trust God when all our natural instincts tell us he cannot be trusted. Ben Patterson helps us understand:

> Often God will say no to our specific requests so that he might say yes to the hope that lies behind the requests, and give us something far better. As Luther phrased it, "We pray for silver, but God often gives us gold instead." The Puritan Richard Sibbes wrote that God will sometimes heal us not by healing, but by leaving "infirmities to cure enormities." The prayer that wrestles with the living God has the faith to believe in the end that even the apparent silence of God is the silence of his higher thoughts and that his no is spoken that he might give us a more resounding yes.[23]

Those are words worth remembering, definitely in a desert, as is Patterson's additional reminder that "everything that comes to us comes by (God's) hand and through his heart."[24] The hand of a God with a heart like ours can be trusted to give only and always what is best.

God's will is of greater importance than our desert deliverance. God's accomplishing in our lives what he wants accomplished is of greater importance than what *we* may want God to do in our lives at any given, painful moment. There are times when his will means our deliverance, but not always. Perhaps not even often. God's will led Jesus through Gethsemane, to the cross and then laid him on a cold slab in a borrowed tomb. The outcome of that wilderness journey was of infinitely greater importance than was Jesus' deliverance from the sufferings that surrounded the cross or his deliverance from death on the cross. The grace of God is a terrifying thing—slaying his son to save sinners—but always works in conjunction with his perfect will. And his will is always of greater importance than our deliverance. Sometimes grace is only grace when deliverance is denied.

God's will is also of greater importance than our understanding what God is doing. There are times when God's will is clear, his wisdom known, but not always; perhaps not even often. God's will, revealed in a bizarre vision, left Daniel confused and with his head spinning. He was, in his own words, *"exhausted and lay ill for several days."*[25] *"I was appalled by the vision,"*

---

23. Patterson, *Waiting*, 147.
24. Patterson, *Waiting*, 168.
25. Dan 8:27.

Daniel explained, *"it was beyond understanding."*[26] Later, of another vision, Daniel confessed, *"I heard, but I did not understand."*[27] At that point, he asked, *"My Lord, what will the outcome of all this be?"*[28] Pay careful attention God's answer:

> He replied, "Go your way, Daniel, because the words are closed up and sealed until the time of the end. . . .
> As for you, go your way till the end. You will rest, and then at the end of the days you will rise to receive your allotted inheritance."[29]

God's answer was not an answer at all. In fact, his words remind me of Jesus' reply when the disciples asked him, *"Lord, are you at this time going to restore the kingdom to Israel?"*[30] Jesus completely ignored their question, saying to them simply, *"It is not for you to know the times or dates that the Father has set by his own authority."*[31] In like manner, God tells Daniel, "It is not for you to know."

Often, it is not necessary to understand the specifics of God's will; it is only necessary to obey. To say it another way, it is not for us to know but to obey. In Hebrews 11, the author's remarkable phrase about Abraham— *"when called to go to a place he would later receive as an inheritance, obeyed and went, even though he did not know where he was going"*[32]—reveals that, in the words of William L. Lane, "the details were unclear to Abraham, but the fact of God's direction was an indelible impression."[33] So much so that "Abraham's experience with God demonstrated that God is faithful, that his words are reliable, and that he stands behind his promises."[34] In the not-knowing that can be so prevalent in a wilderness, it is important to remember that Abraham nonetheless obeyed, and set an example to be followed by all wilderness travelers who come after him. Our particular wilderness journey may be without the understanding we seek, may even be without the deliverance we crave, but if it is a walk of trusting-obedience, it will honor

---

26. Dan 8:27.
27. Dan 12:8.
28. Dan 12:8.
29. Dan 12:9, 13.
30. Acts 1:6.
31. Acts 1:7.
32. Heb 11:8.
33. Lane, *Call to Commitment*, 152.
34. Lane, *Call to Commitment*, 100.

God and bless us, it will bring us to the point where we become everything and possess everything God desires.

In C. S. Lewis' *Screwtape Letters*, Screwtape wrote to Wormwood:

> He (God) wants them to learn to walk and must therefore take away his hand; and if only the will to walk is really there He is pleased even with their stumbles. Do not be deceived, Wormwood. Our cause is never more in danger than when a human, no longer desiring, but still intending, to do our Enemy's will, looks round upon a universe from which every trace of Him seems to have vanished, and asks why he has been forsaken, and still obeys.[35]

When it is all a wilderness walker can do just to drag one foot behind the other and press on, "and still obeys," God will have the victory and the glory.

Elisabeth Elliot Leitch told of spending time in the mountains of North Wales with her friends John and Mari Jones. John was a shepherd, and Mrs. Leitch loved to watch the daily ritual of John on horseback, herding the sheep, and Mack, a champion Scottish collie, keeping the sheep in formation.

One day, John and Mack led the sheep into a special pen. When the animals were securely locked in, John began grabbing them by the horns, one by one, and forcing them into a dipping trough filled with antiseptic, completely immersing them for a few seconds. "When the rams had been dipped," said Mrs. Leitch:

> John rode out again on his horse to herd the ewes which were in a different pasture. Again I watched with Mari as John and Mack went to work, the one in charge, the other obedient. Sometimes, tearing at top speed around the flock, Mack would jam on four-wheeled brakes, his eyes blazing but still on the sheep, his body tense and quivering, but obedient to the command to stop. What the shepherd saw the dog could not see—the weak ewe that lagged behind, the one caught in a bush, the danger that lay ahead for the flock.
>
>> "Do the sheep have any idea what's happening?" I asked Mari.
>> "Not a clue!" she said.
>> "And how about Mack?" I can't forget Mari's answer.
>> "The dog doesn't understand the pattern—only obedience."[36]

---

35. Lewis, *Screwtape Letters*, 47.
36. Leitch, "Glory of God's Will," 129–30.

The story of Mack is meant to be the story of every wilderness pilgrim: Obedience flowing from trust in the shepherd's wisdom. Will we understand the pattern of a God whose thoughts and ways are infinitely above ours? Not always. Perhaps not often. Maybe never. The fact remains, however, that we need not understand the pattern—only obedience.

Viktor Frankl, after three gruesome years at Auschwitz and other Nazi prison camps, spoke and wrote often of the mindset of Holocaust survivors by quoting the succinct but extraordinary statement of Friedrich Nietzsche: "He who has a why to live can bear with almost any how." But what if we cannot discern a *why*? What then? Scripture's message goes radically beyond that of Nietzsche's. The message of Scripture is: he who knows the *Who* can bear with any *what*, even though he might never know the *why*.

The apostle Paul's confidence, shared with his dear friend Timothy, was not "I've got God figured out." Paul knew better than to think he could grasp God to that degree. Paul did not even say, "I know what's going on." Instead, Paul confessed, *"I know whom I have believed"*[37] . . . *"whom."* If, in a wilderness, the *whom* does not trump the *why*, we are in trouble.

The attitude "When I know my master's specific purpose, in clear and complete detail, I will obey" will drive us to despair in a wilderness, for we may *never* know our master's specific purpose with any degree of confidence. By contrast, the attitude that brings us to hope and an awareness of a future is this: "Because I know my master, I will trust . . . I will obey." The difference between those two attitudes is the difference between possibly dying in the desert and coming forth as gold.

Dietrich Bonhoeffer prayed from Tegel Prison:

> "Thy ways are past understanding, but
> Thou knowest the way for me."[38]

We lack the wisdom to know God's ways—they are indeed, as Bonhoeffer stated, and as Scripture affirms, *"past understanding"*—yet we can still rest confidently in what is more than a line of poetry from prison, but is in fact a biblical reality about God: "Thou knowest the way for me." Trusting his wisdom in our ignorance is what gets us through even the most disorienting deserts.

The posture of King Jehoshaphat is worth noting and emulating. As the Moabites and Ammonites threatened war against God's people,[39] he prayed, *". . . we have no power to face this vast army that is attacking us. We*

---

37. 2 Tim 1:12.
38. Metaxas, *Bonhoeffer*, 449.
39. 2 Chr 20:1–4.

do not know what to do, but our eyes are upon you."[40] That is a remarkable affirmation of trust. In our ignorance (*"We do not know what to do"*), we trust God's wisdom (*"but our eyes are upon you"*) because we have come to believe that his heart beats for us and he knows the way for us.

Trust begins where knowing ends. In the words of Joan Chittister, "the irony of the struggle"—or, we might say the irony of the wilderness—"is that this unknowing is, in the end, what faith is all about."[41]

If God is who he says he is, as his written word describes him, then he has only our best interests at heart. His specific will in a specific wilderness—though seldom shared with those who travel its terrain—seeks always and only the best for us, and always and only directs us along his perfect path for us. In his will is our ultimate blessing. That is a vital truth about the wilderness. That is why we trust. Even in a wilderness—*especially* in a wilderness—we trust.

---

40. 2 Chr 20:12.
41. Chittister, *Gift of Years*, 213.

PART VI

WILDERNESS WORDS

"I like good strong words that mean something."
Louisa Mae Alcott

COMMUNITY

*"But hasn't our life together meant more . . .
than either of us could have meant on our own?"*

LEAH PRICE NGEMBA[1]

Community is a good strong word that means something. It is good and strong and means something always, but it is a particularly powerful ally in a wilderness.

Dr. John Brantner advised that "everything is intensified by isolation and relieved by sharing."[2] That observation from a professor of clinical psychology at the University of Minnesota was spoken at a 1972 symposium on death and dying. The statement, though dated, still rings true of facing death. It also rings true of walking a wilderness—a reality that the modern church, particularly in America, no longer buys into beyond superficial head-nodding.

Stanley Hauerwas and William H. Willimon were accurate in their assessment that "American Christians have fallen into the bad habit of acting as if the church really does not matter as we go about trying to live like Christians."[3] In the modern Western world's in-practice version of Christianity, community is routinely considered *valuable*, but rarely *invaluable*. It is *optional* rather than *essential*. It is accepted, even embraced, in the context of church things on church days, but is given little thought in our workaday

---

1. Leah Price Ngemba is a major character in Barbara Kingsolver's book *The Poisonwood Bible*. The quote is found on page 473.
2. Brantner, *Death and Attitudes*, 42.
3. Hauerwas and Willimon, *Resident Aliens*, 69.

world, whether that world is, at any given moment, an oasis or a wilderness. Community is not what it once was, not as Scripture describes.

The importance of not isolating oneself from a community of believers, especially in a wilderness, is stressed by the writer of Hebrews, who had more to say about Israel's desert days than any other New Testament author. Near the end of that letter, he wrote:

> Let's keep walking with a pure motive and an abundance of faith. Let's cleanse our hearts from any unworthy feeling and let's bathe our group in clean water. Let us hang on with tooth and toenail to our promising commitment for he who maps our strategy can be completely trusted. And let's think up ways to provoke everybody into "fits of love and kindness." Don't fail to meet together . . . as some are beginning to do. Rather, keep everybody on his toes . . . .[4]

Note the corporate words and images: *"Let's keep walking;" "Let's cleanse our hearts;" "Let's bathe our group;" "Let us hang on;" "Let's think up ways;" "Don't fail to meet together;" "Keep everybody on his toes."* The writer is not addressing individual pilgrims, but "the wandering people of God."[5] When it comes to desert days, we must remember *that* because we must remember *this*: The very nature of a wilderness demands that we make the journey together or, chances are, we do not make it successfully. A wilderness "needs to be shared if it is to be endured."[6]

The pain and confusion of desert days intensify whenever we isolate ourselves from our Christian community. To survive a wilderness and emerge as gold,[7] it is imperative that we draw on the shared lives and loving support of our sisters and brothers in Jesus. Living in community means that we need not walk a wilderness alone, as an isolated pilgrim, but as part of a vital and intimate spiritual family.[8] That does not mean community is easy, only that it is essential. As Henri Nouwen observed:

---

4. Heb 10:21–25, *Cotton Patch Version of Hebrews and the General Epistles.*
5. Kasemann, *Wandering People of God.*
6. Holmes III, *Ministry and Imagination*, 212.
7. Job 23:10; 1 Pet 1:7.
8. This is not meant to imply that we are never meant to walk a wilderness alone. There is no solid biblical basis for making such a claim. Job, Jacob, Joseph and Jesus (others as well) walked their wildernesses, for the most part, as isolated individuals, without the support of true community. We, too, may find ourselves alone in a desert. Many, if not most of our wilderness wanderings, however, take place while we have access to the support and strength of vital Christian fellowship. Not to avail ourselves of that provision when it is available is foolish and dangerous, possibly deadly.

> Nothing is sweet or easy about community. Community is a fellowship of people who do not hide their joys and sorrows but make them visible to each other in a gesture of hope. In community we say: "Life is full of gains and losses, joys and sorrows, ups and downs—but we do not have to live it alone. We want to drink our cup together and thus celebrate the truth that the wounds of our individual lives, which seem intolerable when lived alone, become sources of healing when we live them as part of a fellowship of mutual care."[9]

Private Christianity is a concept foreign to Scripture and a practice potentially deadly for those who find themselves in a wilderness.

I vividly remember an experience one day during my early weeks in first-year Greek class at what was then Lincoln (Illinois) Christian College. Our professor, Dr. Heine, was pointing out that the word "you" in Greek can be, as it is in English, either singular or plural. In the row behind me and to my right was a girl from Kentucky, and she immediately took issue with the statement. "Dr. Heine, 'you' is not plural; it is only singular." He once more pointed out that it could be either and she once more objected. Finally, Dr. Heine asked her, "If I am talking to you individually, what word do I use?" She replied, "You." He nodded approvingly and continued, "And if I am talking to the entire class, what word do I use?" She answered, "Y'all" . . . and she was completely serious. All of us Yankees erupted in laughter.

The modern church largely views the Christian life in terms of the singular "you," while Scripture largely views the Christian life in terms of the Kentucky plural—"y'all." That is, at least, the gist of Jack Levison's words, if I understand them. Writing about the modern Church's obsession with the Christian life as an exercise in individuality, Levison pointed out that in the apostle Paul's question from 1 Corinthian 6:19—*"Do you not know that your body is a temple of the Holy Spirit, who is in you, whom you have received from God. . . . "* —the word "you" is plural in the original language. He then added, "Christians are a spirit-filled temple—not one spirit-filled room in the temple, and certainly not just individual, spirit-filled priests in an empty temple. Driven to distraction, (Paul) asks, 'Don't y'all know that y'all are God's temple and that God's Spirit dwells in y'all?'"[10] The Christian life, like the Church, is communal by nature.

When we withdraw from the community that God has provided for us, we run the risk of ruin, of a possible falling away. That, Ernst Käsemann pointed out, is the unmistakable teaching of the book of Hebrews:

---

9. Nouwen, *Can You Drink the Cup?*, 57.
10. Levison, *Fresh Air*, 137–38.

> With a certain naivete, Hebrews seems to explain Christian existence by way of . . . fellowship. Only in union with Christ's companions is there life, faith, and progress on the individual's way of wandering. As soon as a person is no longer fully conscious of membership and begins to be isolated from the people of God, that person must also have left the promise behind and abandoned the goal.[11]

I freely confess that I would have left the promise behind and abandoned the goal during my most difficult desert days had it not been for that gift of God's grace called the Body of Christ. Without the ministry in my life of prayer-and-accountability partners, intimate prayer groups, and loving church family—people who shared with me their lives and their wisdom, and who refused to let me walk my wilderness alone—I would have lost my way, quite possibly my faith. God never intended for us to be isolated from and independent of spiritual community. His purpose was not that each of us live as an individual "you," but that all of us live as a corporate "y'all." Hauerwas and Willimon nailed it: "There is no substitute for living around other Christians."[12] That is certainly true if we are to become and possess everything God desires for us. It takes a village—the community of Christ—to make that happen.

God did not lead Israel through the wilderness one by one, as isolated individuals, but in community, as a people. They were not even "a gathering of individuals who happened to be going the same direction,"[13] but a pilgrim people traveling the wilderness en masse, as one. They were the people of God.

Through Moses, God promised Israel, *as a whole*, that they would be his people:

> *I am the Lord, and I will bring you out from under the yoke of the Egyptians. I will free you from being slaves to them, and I will redeem you with an outstretched arm and with mighty acts of judgment. I will take you as my own people, and I will be your God.*[14]

---

11. Kaseman, *Wandering People of God*, 21.
12. Hauerwas and Willimon, *Resident Aliens*, 102.
13. Foster, *Celebration of Discipline*, 151.
14. Exod 6:6–7.

Later, following Israel's deliverance from Egypt, God once more spoke the promise through Moses: *"I will walk among you and be your God, and you will be my people."*[15]

The theme of Israel as the people of God was picked up by the apostle Paul, who applied it to the church, which he viewed as the new Israel, the true Israel of God.[16] Peter, harkening back to rich Old Testament imagery,[17] like a dog doubling back to pick up the scent or trail again, informed his readers: *"But you are a chosen people, a royal priesthood, a people belonging to God."*[18]

The importance of viewing the church as the people of God, of seeing it as a true spiritual community, cannot be overstated. That is particularly true in an age that is becoming increasingly more individualistic, making it progressively more difficult to think, let alone to live, in corporate terms. Yet, "the church is no mere collection of isolated individuals," Howard Snyder reminded us, "but . . . it has a corporate or communal nature which is absolutely essential to its true being."[19] In fact, "authentic Christian living is life in Christian community."[20]

The modern prevalent emphasis on "Jesus and me" is certainly biblical, but just as certainly incomplete, unbalanced, one-sided. Theology is like pizza in that it is a mighty thin slice that has only one side. "Jesus and me" is a true but one-sided statement. Our being Jesus-followers who truly live in and as community, who truly see ourselves, not as isolated pilgrims but as the people of God on pilgrimage together is clearly God's intent. The church functions as community or it does not function properly.[21] As part of that church, we have literally been remade in Jesus to function as part of and to need the ministry of a community of believers.[22] Put simply, there are truths we cannot know, growth we cannot experience, and blessings we cannot receive without the give-and-take of church life, without the mutual ministry of God's redeemed community. Again, in the words of Hauerwas

---

15. Lev 26:12.

16. See Rom 9:1–33 and Gal 6:16.

17. Exod 6:6–8; 19:1–6; Lev 26:9–12; Deut 4:12–14; Ps 135; Isa 43:20–21; Hos 2:21–23.

18. 1 Pet 2:9.

19. Snyder, *Community of the King*, 58.

20. Snyder, *Community of the King*, 75.

21. Eph 4:11–16.

22. Eph 4:11–16; 1 Cor 12:12–27.

and Willimon, "The church enables us to be better people than we could have been if left to our own devices."[23]

Wilderness travelers desperately need community, whether they recognize that or not. Without true spiritual community—*"left to our own devices"*—a wilderness trek can prove deadly for a solitary traveler. That may explain why God was so quick to get wilderness-weary Elijah out of isolation and back into meaningful fellowship. *"Go back,"*[24] he told the tattered, discouraged prophet, sending him promptly into the support of a new prophet, Elisha,[25] who was but one of *"seven thousand in Israel . . . whose knees have not bowed down to Baal."*[26] That may also explain Jesus' urgent request to Peter, James and John as he led them deeper into Gethsemane's garden: *"This sorrow is crushing my life out. Stay here and keep vigil with me,"*[27] as well as his passionate question when finding them asleep: *"Can't you stick it out with me for a single hour?"*[28] The one thing above all others that Jesus needed as he agonized in that wilderness called Gethsemane was the one thing he did not get: spiritual support from his spiritual community.

It amazes me that with no one around to help shoulder his load, Jesus still walked victoriously through his final wilderness, perhaps life's ultimate wilderness. By contrast, the disciples' walk through that same Gethsemane was anything but victorious; it was, in fact, an ignominious defeat for all concerned as, to a man, *"everyone deserted (Jesus) and fled."*[29] The reason that is important to remember is quite simple: We are not nearly as much like Jesus as we are like Peter, James and John. Absence of community is likely to do us in when we walk a wilderness, as it did in that trio of disciples.

Jesus was not the only one who failed to get community support in Gethsemane's wilderness. The same rang true of the three friends he took with him there. They were sound asleep instead of supporting each other, and the wilderness of Jesus' passion snuck up on them and sucked them into itself like a black hole.[30] Ultimately, it took the power of Jesus' resurrection and Pentecost to finally pull them free.

23. Hauerwas and Willimon, *Resident Aliens*, 81.
24. 1 Kgs 19:15.
25. 1 Kgs 19:15–21.
26. 1 Kgs 19:18.
27. Matt 23:38, *Message*.
28. Matt 26:40, *Message*.
29. Mark 14:50.
30. See Thomas More, where referencing Matt 26:40–41 and Mark 14:37–38, he wrote, "And He said to Peter, 'Simon are you sleeping? Could you not stay awake one hour with me? Stay awake and pray that you may not enter into temptation. For the spirit is indeed willing, but the flesh is weak.'" More suggested that Jesus purposely

The ministry of other Christians is an invaluable resource in our wilderness struggles. We should rejoice that God has placed others in community with us to walk alongside us and to pastor us through difficult times and places. Ultimately, however, we are meant to be resources to other wilderness wanderers, to move beyond only *using* community resources to *becoming* community resources. Moses, Joshua, Caleb, and others were just such resources—"pastors," if you will—to Israel. Whereas they might have been more comfortable receiving ministry, they became effective ministers to God's people. The community-in-transit did not need just another travel companion, but a pastor who could help them without needing them in the same way they needed her or him.[31] A pastor is always a pilgrim, but never *only* a pilgrim.

The wandering community needs a pastor, not in the professional sense, but in the spiritual sense. "The pastor is a pilgrim who has returned with the light"[32] and is now able to lead others in and through their journey. The strength and wisdom of such a pastor are borrowed from God and lent freely to the community.[33] The cry of Christians in community is for

---

referred to Peter as "Simon" ("listening," "obedient") rather than "Cephas" ("rock"), adding a marvelous summarizing soliloquy: "Simon, no longer Cephas, are you sleeping? For how do you deserve to be called Cephas, that is, rock? I singled you out by that name because of your firmness, but now you show yourself to be so infirm that you cannot hold out even for an hour against the inroads of sleep. As for that old name of yours, 'Simon,' certainly you live up to that remarkably well: can you be called listening when you are sleeping this way. Or can you be called obedient when in spite of my instructions to stay awake, I am no sooner gone than you relax and doze and fall asleep? I always made much of you, Simon, and yet Simon are you sleeping? I paid you many high honors, and yet, Simon, are you sleeping? A few moments ago you boasted that you would die with me, and now, Simon, are you sleeping? Now I am pursued to the death by the Jews and the gentiles and by one worse than either of them, Judas; and Simon, are you sleeping? Indeed, Satan is busily seeking to sift all of you like wheat, and Simon, are you sleeping? What can I expect from the others, when in such great and pressing danger, not only to me but also to all of you, I find that you, Simon, even you are sleeping." More, *Sadness of Christ*, 26–27. Sleeping kept Peter, as well as the two other disciples, from the mutual ministry of community which Jesus saw as spiritually essential for surviving the wilderness. The result was that they not only failed Jesus in his hour of greatest need, but also knew personal failure from which they could have easily never recovered.

31. For this concept, I am indebted to Henri J. M. Nouwen and his insightful writing on "Becoming the Father" in his book *The Return of the Prodigal Son*: "My people, whether handicapped or not, are not looking for another peer, another playmate, nor even for another brother. They seek a father who can bless and forgive without needing them in the way they need him. I see clearly the truth of my vocation to be the father . . ." Nouwen, *Return of the Prodigal Son*, 138.

32. Dobson, *Pastoral Call* (unpublished monograph).

33. See Eric Metaxas, *Bonhoeffer*, where it is said of Bonhoeffer ". . . *his strength was*

women and men who will be resources to them for their wilderness journey. One of our greatest resources and blessings through weary wilderness days is that even though we may have a long way yet to go, we do not walk that way alone.[34] We walk a wilderness as it is meant to be walked, in and as community, being resources to one another.

But the community of Christ needs even more than resources.

As sisters and brothers in Jesus, we are with each other on the way in order to help each other along the way. We are, in fact, our brother's—and our sister's—keeper.[35] More to the point, perhaps, we are our brother's and our sister's "helper."[36] That Hebrew word (*'ezer*) deserves a better fate than the generic translation it routinely receives. "Helper" is too flat and familiar a translation for such a forceful and formidable word. Of the two dozen occurrences of *'ezer* in the Old Testament, a full two-thirds are descriptions of God. The word itself is military in nature, and could be translated variously as "champion," "hero," "elite warrior" or, perhaps best, "protector." Gilbert Bilezikian prefers the word "rescuer"[37]—the way it is used most to describe God. As such, an *'ezer* is not someone who is conveniently close at hand if and when we need them—there merely to help or assist occasionally, as needed—but, more fully, someone who is actually essential for our survival,[38] someone who makes it possible for us to reach our intended potential, to fulfill our God-given purpose.[39]

Among other things, that understanding of *'ezer* provides a fresh way to look at Eve's role as "helper" for Adam. Why did the Serpent in Eden attack Eve *first*? Was it because she was the weaker of the two and, therefore, an easy mark, or was it because she was Adam's *'ezer*—Adam's "protector"— and with his "protector" out of the way, with no "rescuer" to intervene, Adam was now an easy mark? Regardless, Eve failed to be Adam's "protector" much as Cain failed to be Abel's "keeper."

When Eve, then Adam, ate the fruit, the garden of Eden, once an oasis, became a wilderness to history's first couple. Not merely their innocence

---

borrowed from God and lent to others."

34. Kirvan, *God Hunger*, 191: "You have a long way to go. But you are not alone."

35. Gen 4:9. Implicit in God's question to Cain (verse 9a), as well as in his reply to Cain's question (verses 10–12), is the expectation that Cain is indeed to be his brother's keeper.

36. The Hebrew word is *'ezer* and first appears in Gen 2:18 where God announces his intent to make a "helper" for the man he has created. God fashioned from man a woman and brought her to Adam to be his *'ezer* (Gen 2:19–24).

37. Bilezikian, *Community 101*, 21.

38. Bilezikian, *Community 101*, 21.

39. Bilezikian, *Community 101*, 21.

was lost, but so was their chance of becoming everything and possessing everything God desired for them. As early as Eden we learn that we need each other to become who we are meant to be and to possess what we are meant to have. We are each meant to be an *'ezer* for the other—not just to *be* alongside our brothers and sisters, but to *fight* alongside our brothers and sisters, to protect and serve so that together, as community, we become everything and possess everything God desires for us.

In the end, a wilderness is about, not simply our *individual* becoming, but also our *shared* becoming. We are, after all, not individual appendages functioning on our own, apart from the whole, but are collectively part of the Body of Christ. Whereas we are each meant to mature, to grow individually into the likeness of Jesus,[40] "God's intention is not the fashioning merely of mature individuals but of mature communities as well. The Christian community does not exist just as a means to individual ends . . .."[41] That is why community is essential in order for the people of God to become everything and possess everything God desires. In a sentence, wilderness or no wilderness, we need community and community needs us. There is no possessing or becoming without that shared life, without each being an *'ezer* for the other.

There is a word that must not be forgotten in a wilderness—we forget it to our own peril—and that word is community.

---

40. Rom 8:29; 2 Cor 3:18; Eph 4:11–16; Col 1:28.
41. Banks, *Paul's Idea of Community*, 67.

WAIT

"I realized that the deepest spiritual lessons are not learned by His letting us have our way in the end, but by His making us wait, bearing with us in love and patience until we are able to honestly pray what He taught his disciples to pray: Thy will be done."

ELISABETH ELLIOTT

Wait is a good strong word that means something. It is good and strong and means something always, but it is a particularly powerful ally in a wilderness.

In Jesus' story of the prodigal son,[1] the boy leaves father and home with his inheritance in hand and searching for a better life, sacrificing the only meaningful inheritance and the only real life he ever had. As Middle Eastern scholar Kenneth E. Bailey pointed out, when the prodigal leaves home:

> A relationship is broken, not a law. Deuteronomy 21:17 states that the younger son's portion is one third. The law does not specifically say that the son must wait for his father's death. The son has not broken the law. Rather he has broken his father's heart....
> He cuts himself off from his roots as he seizes his share of the wealth and in the process breaks fellowship with his father. Thereby he cuts himself off from his real inheritance.[2]

---

1. Luke 15:11–32.

2. Bailey, *Cross and the Prodigal*, 42–43. Bailey goes on to point out that "the very inheritance he refused to ask for he has now forfeited. A man's security in the village is his family. This is as precious to him as life itself. His family is his social security, his

The subsequent wasting of the young man's wealth was merely an extension of the wasting of his life. As Robert Farrar Capon explained in a parenthetical statement from his book *The Parables of Grace*:

> One word about the words for "life" in this parable. The "living" the father divided was "ton bion," one of the Greek words for "life." The "goods" that the son requested, and that he wanted immediately, were "ten ousian," which is the Greek for "substance" or "being." In any case, what the father gave away and what the son wasted was not just some stuff that belonged to them; it was their whole existence, their very being, their lives.[3]

Such a heartless demand on the part of the son[4] and the cavalier attitude with which he so carelessly threw away an invaluable treasure[5] wounded the father in a way and at a level the son could never guess, let alone experience. The wounds of the lover are always deeper than the wounds of the loved. As the father suffers, the son celebrates, at least until his decisions bring him to a devastating dead-end he somehow never envisioned.

In time, though Jesus provides no hint of how much time elapsed, the prodigal's downward spiral empties into a wilderness on the far fringe of his worst nightmare. One day, in what appears to be a moment of either desperateness or despair, perhaps both, he thinks of his father who, unbeknownst to him, has been walking daily to the end of the road, scanning the horizon, wondering if his son will ever return, ready to welcome him with open arms if he does. Kenneth E. Bailey described the father as one who "waits day after day, staring down the crowded village street to the road in the distance along which the son disappeared with arrogance and high hopes."[6] That is the heart of the story—as the son wanders, the father waits. Helmut Thielicke called the story, not the parable of the prodigal son, but the parable of the waiting father.[7]

Jesus began his story of that young wilderness wanderer where such a story—where *all* our stories—must begin: with the father. As Thielicke pointed out, "(Jesus) first shows us the Father and points to the heart of all things. Then from there the things themselves gain their meaning. . . . The

---

inheritance, his old-age pension, his assurance of marriage, his physical and emotional well-being; in short, it is everything. The tie to the land and to the 'house of so-and-so' is a profound one," 43.

3. Capon, *Parables of Grace*, 138.
4. *"Father, give me my share of the estate"* (Luke 15:12).
5. "... *the younger son . . . squandered his wealth in wild living*" (Luke 15:13).
6. Bailey, *Jacob and the Prodigal*, 107.
7. Thielicke, *Waiting Father*.

heart of all things discloses the things themselves."[8] At the heart of any wilderness is the waiting father.

Ultimately, God wants his wilderness children to return home, to come back where they belong. Ultimately, he wants us becoming everything and possessing everything he desires for us—all that cannot be had in *"a distant country,"*[9] away from home, apart from the father. For that reason, God never just cools his heels, waiting for *waiting's* sake, but always he waits for *coming's* sake and for *becoming's* sake, for our coming to *where* we are meant to be and our becoming *who* we are meant to be. God does not wait in the powerless, passive, helpless or frustrated sense that we sometimes do—like we might wait in an insufferably long line at a government office or fight barely moving bumper-to-bumper traffic during rush hour—but he waits actively, dynamically, hopefully and expectantly. He is not idle while he waits but works while he waits.

"God, to me, is a verb," said Buckminster Fuller, "not a noun." The more I read Scripture, the more I realize the truth of that observation. I think the thing that would most strike me about the God of the Bible if I encountered him in Scripture for the first time is his very active involvement with the creation and creatures he had made. Even his silence is less absence and more presence-in-hiding, and he is never so much passive as he is poised. God's silence is often the sign of his higher thoughts and ways. God's passivity is often the sign of his active working behind the scenes, beneath the surface, off stage, working subtly but surely. When God waits, he waits *for*, he waits *on*, he waits *until*; he never just *waits*, but always waits intentionally, deliberately, purposefully, and strategically.

It seems that a wilderness—at least those barren and hostile times and places so often mentioned in Scripture—is all about waiting. Whether desert days drag on for forty days or forty years, whether it is Jesus or Israel being tested and tried, waiting is always part of the wilderness equation. Whether or not, as Simone Weil suggests, "all of life is a waiting for God,"[10] it is true that most, if not all of a wilderness is. But it is only secondarily about *our* waiting; primarily, it is about *God's* waiting, and that on which God is waiting—*us*.

A wilderness can easily breed the mistaken notion that *we* are the ones waiting on God, wasting away while he decides whether or not to act on our behalf. In truth, however, it is the *father* who waits on us. A wilderness

---

8. Thielicke, *Waiting Father*, 12.
9. Luke 15:13.
10. Wiederkehr, *Tree Full of Angels*, 98.

is always more about the waiting father than it is the wandering child. Ben Patterson sees it as a marvelous mystery:

> Herein lies the greatest mystery of our waitings. Through them all it is really God who is doing all the waiting! We think we are the ones waiting for him, but in reality it is he who waits for us.... It makes no difference to God—a day or a thousand years, a thousand years or a day; it's all the same. However long it takes, he can wait until we open our eyes. If we wait it is because God is waiting for us to become the people he wants us to be.[11]

Whether our walk is through a desert of sin, sovereignty or systemic evil; whether we are wanderers or sojourners, God is the one who most bears the burden of wilderness waiting.

If we are in a wilderness of sin, God is waiting for us to *"come to our senses,"*[12] repent and return home, where we will find our father doing what he has been doing since we left—waiting.[13] The father in Jesus' story did not set out on a search and rescue mission to reclaim his in-danger son—though in that string of parables from Luke 15, the God-figures (a shepherd seeking a lost sheep, a housewife seeking a lost coin) are on the hunt to rescue and reclaim[14]—but chose instead to wait until the wilderness ran its course.[15] God is infinitely dimensional, rescuing or waiting almost in the same breath, but seeking all the time. There is, either way, a great deal of waiting that is endured. Neither the shepherd nor the housewife recovered what they sought in the blink of an eye, but were committed to search as long as it took—searching *until they find* is the way that Jesus put it.[16] "We do not know how long they searched," noted Kenneth E. Bailey. "But any Lebanese or Palestinian peasant can tell you that it may take a day or more

---

11. Patterson, *Waiting*, 111–12.

12. Luke 15:17.

13. The only time in the story when the father does not wait is near the end when he sees his son *"still a long way off"* (verse 20), runs to him, receives him with open arms, and refuses to even let him finish his confession. He does not wait to welcome this weary wanderer—who had wished him dead and broken his heart—as *"this son of mine"* (verse 24), nor does he wait to start the no-holds-barred celebration (verses 22–24). But from the time father watches his son walk away from home until the time he sees his son in the distance trudging heavily home, the father waits.

14. Luke 15:1–32.

15. Concerning God's work in a wilderness, Stevenson (*God in My Unbelief*) wrote, "He allows me to go . . . in my own way till I am willing to go his," 137.

16. Of the shepherd, Jesus asked, *"Does he not leave the ninety-nine in the open country and go after the lost sheep until he finds it?"* (Luke 15:4), and of the housewife, Jesus asked, *"Does she not light a lamp, sweep the house and search carefully until she finds it?"* (Luke 15:8).

of climbing over rugged wilderness terrain to find a lost sheep."[17] Again, regardless of the actual length of time, both shepherd and housewife search *"until they find."*

A question worth considering is: "What would happen to us if God, doing his best Navy Seal imitation, rescued and delivered us at the onset of every wilderness we entered?" It seems to me that if God rescued us immediately every time that we sinned ourselves into a desert, we would probably never turn loose of sin—briefly and partially, perhaps, but not long-term and completely; momentarily, perhaps, but not with constancy. We are probably familiar enough with ourselves to admit that is true. It was certainly true of Israel. What good would it have done, for example, for God to have quickly delivered repetitively rebellious Israel from Sinai's expanse and have taken them directly to the Promised Land? Had he done that, his people would never have learned to close their hearts to sin and open them to God's sanctifying work. They would never have *possessed*, never have *become* everything God desired for them. That is why God waited. That is also why, in God's waiting, the Hebrew children waited. Deserts represent a waiting game, to be sure, but the real burden of that waiting is borne by God.

God is dealing with much higher stakes than we imagine. He is not so much interested in the penny ante game of "Deliverance from the Desert" as he is the high stakes game of "Deliverance from Sin." The former solves a temporary dilemma; the latter gets to the root of the problem between us and God. The former solves the problem from an impatient human perspective; the latter solves the problem from a patient divine perspective. If God does not wait long enough to make certain our sin is pulled up by its roots, the very work he is trying to do within us is choked out. If he does not wait long enough to make certain all cancer is eradicated, the very surgery he performs on us is wasted. That is why God waits—and why, in *his* waiting, *we* must wait.

If our current terrain is not a wilderness of sin, but one of sovereignty, God is waiting for us to become the person he desires us to be. Ben Patterson calls us to "Remember: from God's reckoning, at least as important as the thing we wait for is what we become as we wait. Faith and character are forged in delay."[18] What we become as we wait is *the* issue to God, it is his primary interest and investment in a sovereign wilderness.

---

17. Bailey, *Cross and the Prodigal*, 31. Concerning the peasants's comments about searching for lost sheep, Bailey adds a footnote which reads, "I have discussed this matter with many of them. After two days the animal is presumed to be stolen or killed and eaten by wild animals."

18. Patterson, *Waiting*, 122.

As the record of Scripture reads, no one *becomes* without a wilderness. For that reason, God waits on our becoming and we wait to become, sometimes foolishly fighting against the very process that makes our becoming possible, failing to realize that God's finest wilderness work often involves his waiting and, along with it, our waiting as well.

There are in the story of the wandering people of God, certainly in the story of the drifting and rootless prodigal son, two perspectives on waiting. Both involve suffering. For the boy in Jesus' story, it had to be an agonizing wait. In fact, as Jesus' story delves more deeply into the young man's mind and heart, the son's pain progressively intensifies[19] until his only options are to die like a pig in a foreign field or to drag himself home to the father he had wished dead—a fate, perhaps, worse than death. If we have ever found ourselves stranded in an unrelenting and seemingly unending desert with no end or hope in sight, we know, at least in part, the suffering involved in the prodigal's experience.[20]

But there is more to Jesus' story than the suffering of the son. There is the suffering of the father as well, a suffering felt more deeply and profoundly by the father than by the son—a reality any loving parent with a prodigal child understands. His heart already broken by his youngest son, the father drags himself into each new day with diminishing hope, somehow summoning the strength to walk to the end of the farm lane or to the edge of town, thinking this might be the day his son returns, endlessly repeating the process but always returning home empty-handed and heavy-hearted.

It is the nature of love to suffer for the sake of the one it loves. All that patient waiting done by the father is prolonged suffering. "Patience," wrote Gerard Wegemer, "comes from the same root as 'passion,' both meaning 'to suffer.'"[21] So it is that in all God's long waiting there is great suffering. Because God never simply waits, but always loves and hopes in his waiting, he suffers.

Why wait, then?

My best guess is that sometimes God waits because if he acts too early, we are rescued before the lesson is learned, the insight gained, and the faith

---

19. He " . . . *squandered his wealth*" . . . "*he began to be in need*" . . . "*he went and hired himself out*" . . . "*he longed to fill his stomach with the pods the pigs were eating*" . . . "*but no one gave him anything*" . . . "*so he got up and went to his father.*" (Luke 15:13–16).

20. A wilderness, of course, need not be lengthy to be painful, or prolonged to involve great suffering. A great deal of grief can be, and often is, compressed into a short span of time. When Alice asked Wonderland's White Rabbit, "How long is forever?" the hare replied, "Sometimes, just one second." Even a short wait can mean great pain and intense suffering. A wait of any length is a hard thing.

21. More, *Sadness of Christ*, vii (Introduction)

birthed—leaving us short of the real and lasting change he is after. I have often wondered concerning the story of Jesus stilling the storm on Galilee[22] what might have happened had Jesus, who was asleep in the boat, abruptly awakened at the initial drop of rain or first clap of thunder and immediately quieted the elements and calmed the gathering storm. Rather than doing that, Jesus slept on until the storm was raging, the ship was reeling and the disciples were desperate, fearing for their lives, pleading with Jesus to save them.[23] It was Jesus speaking, not at the *start* of the storm but into its *teeth*, into its fury, and finding nature obedient, that brought to the frightened fisherman the awareness that altered their thinking about that man in the boat: *"Who is this? He commands even the winds and the water, and they obey him!"*[24]

Similarly, in the story of the prodigal, had the father immediately gone after his son to bring him home, the young man might never have become aware of the nature of his sin. That sin had only been *manifested* in the demand for his portion of the inheritance. Its roots ran much deeper. Until the son came to terms with the roots of his sin, he might conceivably go home, but there would be no real return. Kenneth E. Bailey sees in the boy's hiring on to slop pigs and, later, of his planned and carefully phrased request to be made a servant on his father's estate, an attempt to earn enough money to pay back to his father the money he had wasted, thereby mending the fences.

> Sadly, the prodigal does not yet understand the nature of his sin. He thinks the issue is the lost money. It isn't! It is the father's broken heart. The problem is not the broken law but the broken relationship. If he is a servant, he can get a job, earn the money and pay his debts. But if he is a son of the house, such a solution will not satisfy his father. As yet he understands none of this. Hence the nature of his proposed "confession."
>
> The prodigal . . . does not yet understand what he has done and what it really means. In the far country the job training proposal seems like an excellent plan. He has not faced the fact that he broke his father's heart. Thus the problem of the healing of that broken heart does not occur to him. If he can return the money, he imagines that all will be well.[25]

---

22. Matt 8:23–27; Mark 4:35–41; Luke 8:22–25.
23. Mark 4:35–41.
24. Luke 8:25.
25. Bailey, *Cross and the Prodigal*, 59, 61.

But, of course, all will not be well. The fences will not be mended. Despite the son's best-laid plans, the root of the problem remains unreached, the heart issue remains unresolved.

Wilderness time is essential to get us in touch with the root of the problem, the heart of the issue, to force us to deal with the core of the matter rather than incessantly nipping at its corners. That doesn't happen overnight. It takes time. Even Jesus' resurrection did not happen instantaneously on the heels of his death, and the prodigal's death-to-life transformation[26]—his own death, burial and resurrection of sorts—took a lot of waiting . . . *for* and *on* and *until*.

It had to be an agonizing wait for the boy, but even more so for the father, who not only *worked* while he waited, but also *suffered*. Looking back on Israel's wilderness wandering, the prophet Isaiah reminded God's people that they were not alone in their affliction and suffering, but that God shared in all of it at a profoundly personal level: *"In all their distress he too was distressed."*[27] That is the other thing that might have gone unseen by the son. Had the father refused his son the inheritance he demanded or, after thinking better of having handed it over, quickly and physically dragged the prodigal back home with the money, the son might never have known the *heart* of his father. The boy might never have seen the intense suffering borne by the waiting father.

When I think of certain systemic wildernesses, where people made in their father's image and loved by him more than they could ever imagine are treated like worthless, disposable junk and are ruthlessly disenfranchised or even slaughtered wholesale, my mind is not large enough to wrap around the father's intense pain and unending suffering. And where is the *coming* and *becoming* in such a scenario? What does all the waiting mean in such a wilderness? I throw up my hands in ignorance. Maybe Peter Storey gets us as close as we can get to the truth: "If you want to know where God is alive, don't go to the places of comfort and ease. Inquire rather in those places where the fire of testing burns most fiercely. Living in the furnace of apartheid forges a unique experience of God. It melts away cheap piety, until all that is left is something you know is real–someone you know is real. You discover that with you in the furnace is another, 'whose form is like that of the Son of God.'"[28] Maybe that is where we have to leave it—with Jesus, like with the father, suffering in the furnace of affliction with us, still working toward an end our eyes cannot see, our minds cannot fathom.

26. Luke 15:24.
27. Isa 63:9.
28. Storey, *God in the Crucible*, 66.

The God who works and suffers in his waiting never waits merely to wait, but always waits for our *coming* and *becoming*, that we might *become* everything and *possess* everything he desires. Gregory Boyle's words are directly on point:

> "Teilhard de Chardin wrote that we must 'trust in the slow work of God.' Ours is a God who waits. Who are we not to? It takes what it takes for the great turnaround. Wait for it."[29]

But *living* that advice is far from easy. As Anne Lamott confessed, "Believing isn't the hard part; waiting on God is."[30] It is difficult to "trust in the slow work of God" because such trust demands a great deal of drawn-out waiting, which is never purely waiting, but is many times waiting while suffering, but always in hope. Ben Patterson wrote, "To wait in hope is not just to pass the time until the wait is over. It is to see the time passing as part of the process God is using to make us into the people he created us to be. Job emerges from his wait dazzled and transformed. Abram becomes Abraham and Sarai becomes Sarah."[31] In our waiting, we also become who we are meant to be. That is why we wait. Though we may suffer, we wait in hope of our *becoming*.

There is a word that must not be forgotten in a wilderness—we forget it to our own peril—and that word is wait.

---

29. Boyle, *Tattoos on the Heart*, 113

30. Lamott, *Grace (Eventually)*, 56. In an imaginative work, Collin Morris pictured God making the following diary entry regarding his people: "They must learn to wait. That is what fervent believers find hardest to do. It is easier for them to engage in strenuous effort or costly sacrifice or heroic discipleship for my sake that it is for them to wait. Their inability to wait is not just human impatience, it is also a false perception. They feel no need to wait for me because they imagine they already have me imprisoned within a doctrine or pressed between the leaves of a holy book or enclosed within an ecclesiastical structure. They must learn to wait." Morris, *God Kept a Diary*, 69.

31. Patterson, *Waiting*, 169.

PRAISE

"This is not the time to panic, this is the time to praise."
Cynthia Patterson, *It Had to Happen*

Praise is a good strong word that means something. It is good and strong and means something always, but it is a particularly powerful ally in a wilderness.

Perhaps the best biblical example of praise offered in an ongoing wilderness of pain and suffering is that of Job, who in one unparalleled day of disaster was financially wiped out, losing entire herds of oxen and donkeys, of sheep and camels, as well as the servants who cared for them;[1] and, later the same day, received news that all ten of his children had been killed when a powerful storm struck and destroyed the house in which they were partying.[2] *"At this,"* we are told, *"Job got up, tore his robe and shaved his head"*—all signs of intense grief and lament—*"and worshiped."*[3] That worship shaped itself into prayer, perhaps into song, doubtless into an affirmation of faith. But whatever the specific form, its content was praise:

> Naked I came from my mother's womb,
>   and naked I will depart.
> The Lord gave and the Lord has taken away;
>   may the name of the Lord be praised.[4]

On yet another day, Job lost his health. He was afflicted *"with painful sores from the soles of his feet to the top of his head. Then Job took a piece of*

---

1. Job 1:13–17.
2. Job 1:18–19.
3. Job 1:20.
4. Job 1:21.

pottery and scraped himself with it"—probably in an effort to find momentary relief—*"as he sat among the ashes."*[5] When his wife, who had also suffered through the ordeal, suggested seriously to her husband that he *"curse God and die,"*[6] or sarcastically that he *"bless God and die"* (the Hebrew word can mean either), Job quickly corrected her and called for a response of praise: *"You are talking like a foolish woman. Shall we accept good from God, and not trouble?"*[7]

Somehow, in the smoldering rubble of a ruined life, Job was able to see God "mysteriously at work in the mess"[8] and to offer genuine praise to God "even when . . . looking at him from ground zero."[9] *Praise in the midst of*—a lesson God's wilderness-weary children, generations later, struggled mightily to learn.

A song went up in camp the day Yahweh safely delivered Israel from Egypt through the parted Red Sea[10]—and rightfully so. It was a triumphal shout of praise from people who had just witnessed *"the great power of the Lord displayed against the Egyptians."*[11] But as right as Israel was to praise God in a moment of victory, they were wrong *not* to praise him in the time of testing. Unlike Job, who poured out praise in the heavy agony of the test itself, Israel praised God after the fact, *only* when the test was finished and they finally saw divine deliverance.[12]

In Psalm 106, David sang of God saving Israel in spite of its sins and doing it for his name's sake. There he listed God's marvelous, miraculous acts on their behalf:

> He rebuked the Red Sea, and dried it up;
>   he led them through the depths as through
>   a desert.
> He saved them from the hand of the foe;
>   from the hand of the enemy he redeemed them.
> The waters covered their adversaries;
>   not one of them survived.[13]

Then David added this telling phrase:

5. Job 2:7–8.
6. Job 2:9.
7. Job 2:10.
8. James, *Gospel of Ruth*, 51.
9. James, *Gospel of Ruth*, 123.
10. Exod 15:1–21.
11. Exod 14:31.
12. Exod 14:31.
13. Ps 106:8–11.

> *Then they believed his promises*
> *and sang his praise.*[14]

It was only *then*—*after* deliverance, *after* crossing over to the east side of the sea—that Israel sang praises. On the west side, there had been no praises; only panic.[15] Without question, it was proper for the nation to sing praises after such a deliverance. A God who delivers is certainly worthy of praise, and not to thank him is unthinkable. The point is, however, that praise should have been lifted to God *before* the deliverance, while still on the west side of the sea. Anyone can sing songs after a safe arrival home, but:

> *How can we sing the songs of the Lord*
> *while in a foreign land?*[16]

Yet that is precisely where such songs must be sung, precisely where Job sang his remarkable song of praise. By contrast, Israel tended to grumble and complain one moment, flat-out panic the next, postponing praise until the crisis had passed and all was once more well with their world—a habit which testified to Israel's limited understanding of praise and its utter disregard for God's purpose in a wilderness.[17]

God's people are meant to voice praise *in the midst of* pain and sing songs *in the midst of* suffering. Often, however, in the grip of that pain and suffering, or in a moment of crisis, God's people panic or complain—sometimes both—choosing to praise only if and when deliverance comes. But God longs to be known and praised by his people in the dark nights of their souls as the one *"who gives songs in the night."*[18] And through all history,

---

14. Ps 106:12.
15. Exod 14:10–12.
16. Ps 137:4.
17. Songs from an oasis and songs from a wilderness are in different keys with different rhythm and cadence. The best songs, however, like many Psalms penned by David, begin in pain but rise above it to praise. The prime examples may be Lam 3:19–24 and Ps 22, which both begin with a painful minor key, then transition to a joyous major key on the chorus. Pain is real and is unashamedly voiced in such places as the songs of David and the laments of Jeremiah and Job, yet even those songs of great hurt and heartache ultimately transition into praise, though the pain remains and deliverance has not yet arrived. Israel, as a whole, struggled to grasp that. The truth was grasped more quickly by individuals like David, Jeremiah, Job, and others who were able to sing on the pain side of their lives, prior to any relief or deliverance. If a wilderness truly is for our good and God's glory, if its purpose is to enable us to become everything and possess everything that God desires for us, then we must not withhold praise until deliverance arrives. Praise, not *in place of* pain but *in the midst of* it, is the only appropriate response to a wilderness.
18. Job 35:10.

women and men of faith have been those who sang songs of praise through long and oppressive wilderness nights.

David sang from such depths in Psalm after Psalm. Jehoshaphat, with the odds stacked against him in the form of a vast approaching army, was alarmed,[19] but turned his heart to God and gave him praise.[20] Paul and Silas lifted songs of praise to God from the inner cell of a prison with their feet in stocks.[21] Even Israel eventually learned to sing praises while still enduring a wilderness.[22] And do not forget Jeremiah's astounding song of praise voiced at, perhaps, the lowest moment of his life:

> *I remember my afflictions and my*
> > *wandering,*
> *I well remember them,*
> > *and my soul is downcast within me.*
> *Yet this I call to mind*
> > *and therefore I have hope:*
>
> *Because of the Lord's great love we are not consumed,*
> > *for his compassions never fail.*
> *They are new every morning;*
> > *great is your faithfulness.*
> *I say to myself, "The Lord is my portion;*
> > *therefore, I will wait for him."*[23]

Of that glorious burst of praise, Edith Schaeffer wrote:

> Next time you lustily sing this hymn in church or conference—"Great is Thy faithfulness, Great is Thy faithfulness, Morning by morning new mercies I see"—remember that it was what Jeremiah said to the Lord, right after he had been expressing his despair and depression, and while he was still in the same unchanging affliction. We are apt to sing that hymn and think of fresh dew on the morning grass or rose garden (or even of beautiful food spread on a snowy-white linen cloth), without remembering that Jeremiah gave the Lord this praise after he had just been talking about being desolate and being the laughingstock of the people as they tortured him. It was both the memory of the past and the hope for the future that made Jeremiah able to say those lifting

---

19. 2 Chr 20:1–3.
20. 2 Chr 20:5–10 (note especially verses 5, 6 and 22).
21. Acts 16:24–25.
22. Deut 32:1–43.
23. Lam 3:19–24.

words of praise to the Lord. It was trust in the Lord, kindled by rethinking who He is, and faith in the ultimate victory of the Lord that enabled Jeremiah to break into song. . . .[24]

Sometimes, it seems, we must endure a wilderness until we learn to siphon praise from our pain. We are able to praise when we realize that, often, the finest work God will ever do in our lives will be his wilderness work. That is why even in the pain of our desert days, we voice our praise.

Since the early 1980s, I have maintained a weekly one-on-one prayer-and-accountability relationship with three different individuals. My current iron-sharpening-iron partner has been my spiritual companion since the summer of 2000. From time to time, I have also been part of prayer and accountability groups of five to fifteen people, mostly but not exclusively pastors. Such prayer partners and groups represent safe places where each trusts the other at a deep spiritual level. Those individuals and groups have been my salvation, in more ways than one and more often than once.

I mentioned previously that in one of those groups, I was called by God, through a friend, to reshape my heavy-on-asking prayers into pure praise for a solid month. For maybe the first week, that was one of the hardest things I have ever done, one of the most difficult burdens I have ever borne. It was excruciatingly difficult for me to craft songs and sing them on the west side of the sea, trapped between the water and my pursuers. Prior to that experience, my habit had always been to panic and plead. When my need was desperate, I cried to God for an answer, for help, for deliverance. But now I had vowed to silence all pleas. Still, I needed God's help, desperately. I needed it now, not later. In fact, I needed it just to get through most days. But I did not ask for a single thing; I simply praised him. It was an almost unbearable burden. After that first week, however, an amazing thing happened. The burden transformed into one of the greatest blessings of my life.

At the end of thirty days, one of my prayer group family asked, "So, how is your situation and how are you?" I remember well my response. I answered, "My situation has not improved, but Pat Heston has changed radically and is doing remarkably well, thank you."

I had found close kinship with Jeremiah, whose situation had also not changed:

> *I'll never forget the trouble, the utter lostness,*
> *the taste of ashes, the poison I've swallowed.*
> *I remember it all—oh, how well I remember—*
> *the feeling of hitting the bottom.*[25]—

24. Schaeffer, *Affliction*, 97.
25. Lam 3:19–20, *Message*.

though he himself had been renewed:

> *But there's one thing I remember,*
> *   and remembering, I keep a grip on hope.*
>
> *God's love couldn't have run out,*
> *   his merciful love couldn't have dried up.*
> *They're created new every morning.*
> *   How great is your faithfulness!*
> *I'm sticking with God (I say it over and over).*
> *   He's all I've got left.*[26]

What a difference it makes when we learn to sing on the west side of deliverance. What a difference praise makes, if not in our situation, then most assuredly in us. That difference *in us* is what God is after in any wilderness.

There is a word that must not be forgotten in a wilderness—we forget it to our own peril—and that word is praise.

---

26. Lam 3:21–24, *Message*.

OBEY

"The great test of life is to see whether we will hearken to and obey God's commands in the midst of the storms of life."

Henry B. Eyring

Obey is a good strong word that means something. It is good and strong and means something always, but it is a particularly powerful ally in a wilderness.

In a small midwestern farming community, when combines and harvesters were raising walls of dust while stripping fields bare, a man who owned a large farm was laid-up, recuperating from surgery. As was the community's custom, area farmers came together one weekend to ingather the man's crops. At the end of one very long day, a man atop a tractor was backing a large wagon into a barn. A teenager was standing just inside the doorway. Somehow, the youngster did not hear the machinery, and the adult on the tractor did not see the boy. Before anyone knew what was happening, the wagon ran over the boy, crushing him. He was rushed to the nearest hospital where a doctor in the emergency room pronounced him dead.

The young man's parents, who at the time were proverbial pillars in one of the many country churches that dotted the rural landscape, promptly blamed God for the tragedy. They withdrew from church attendance and involvement, withdrew from fellowship with believers, and decided that they had no further use for God. So far as I know, they never again darkened the doors of that church building and never made their peace with God.

In a major midwestern city, a pastor—the guest speaker at a local church—was invited home for Sunday dinner with one of the leading families in the congregation. As the wife busied herself in the kitchen with meal preparation, the husband and pastor retired to the living room. Soon, the young daughter bounded downstairs and asked permission to ride her bike before dinner. The parents told her she could, but to remember that she was to stay on the sidewalk in front of the house and not cross an intersection. She promised, and out the door she went. In short order, those in the house heard from outside the screech of tires and crash of metal. Knowing instinctively what had happened, the parents rushed outside while the pastor phoned for an ambulance. It arrived too late. After the paramedics announced sorrowfully, "We're sorry, but there's nothing we can do," the weeping parents asked the pastor to kneel with them before the body of their only child and offer a prayer of thanks for the gift of years they had with their daughter.

The last I knew, all these decades later, the parents of that precious child—though never throwing off the burden and heartache of their loss—remain faithful, contributing members of their church and are loving God and following Jesus with all their hearts.

Why the different endings to that pair of scenarios? Being somewhat familiar with both events, I suggest that the difference finds its source in the *reason* those two sets of parents obeyed God. The first couple obeyed because of what God does or does not do. The second couple obeyed because of who God is.

To obey God because of what he does or does not do—because he answers our prayers, because he does not allow harm to come to us— is fraught with danger always, but particularly in a wilderness. To obey God *if* (his will and ours coincide), *only when* (he answers our prayer), or *because* (he rescues us or delivers a loved one) is a recipe for a spiritual train wreck. Sooner or later, the crash will occur. Clearly, as Israel learned during its desert days, God *is* to be praised for what he does; not to praise him when he acts and answers is an untenable decision. What Israel failed to learn, however, until very late was that God is to be obeyed *even if* he does not answer or act the way we think he should.

Our grasping of that truth might well be the reason the book of Job is in our Bibles. In that emotional, heart-wrenching story of an intense wilderness and its lonely sufferer, a story that left no area of life or grief untouched, Job's wife personifies Israel as it was, while Job illustrates Israel as it was meant to be. *"Are you still holding on to your integrity?"*[1] asked this mother of ten, all of whom had been killed in a great storm. *"Curse God and die!"*[2] To which Job replied, *"You are talking like a foolish woman. Shall we accept*

---

1. Job 2:9a.
2. Job 2:9b.

*good from God, and not trouble?"*³ That is the same broken man who earlier, in the fresh rawness of their shared grief, confessed:

> *Naked I came from my mother's womb,*
> *and naked I will depart.*
> *The Lord gave and the Lord has taken*
> *away;*
> *may the name of the Lord be praised.*⁴

The question of *why* Job served God is a major issue in the book that bears his name, and the issue surfaces quickly. As early as the fifth paragraph of the narrative, God seems to be bragging on Job, saying to Satan, *"Have you considered my servant Job? There is no one on earth like him; he is blameless and upright, a man who fears God and shuns evil."*⁵ Translation: "You haven't been able to get your grimy little paws on Job, have you?" Satan is quick to reply, and with a sting in his words: *"Does Job fear God for nothing?"*⁶

Other translations are more creative than the NIV. "So, do you think Job does all that out of the sheer goodness of his heart?" (*The Message*). "'Job fears his God,' the Enemy answered, 'and loses nothing by it'" (Knox). "'Why shouldn't he when you pay him so well?' Satan scoffed." (*The Living Bible*). Translation: "Okay, Job may well serve you, but he doesn't serve you for *nothing*; he serves you for *something*—for everything he gets out of it." Then Satan lays out the evidence: *"Have you not put a hedge around him and his household and everything he has? You have blessed the work of his hands, so that his flocks and herds are spread throughout the land,"*⁷ followed by the challenge: *"But stretch out your hand and strike everything he has, and he will surely curse you to your face."*⁸ Translation: "For crying out loud, God, even I could obey you if you were that good to me, but just strand Job in a wilderness and see what will happen. I'll tell you what will happen: So long obedience!"

In Satan's opinion, Job's obedience had ulterior motives or was, at best, suspect. I can see why Satan might have thought that. I can see why I might have thought that had I been a contemporary of Job's. When we simply tote-up the amount of material possessions the man had—*"he owned seven thousand sheep, three thousand camels, five thousand yoke of oxen and*

3. Job 2:10.
4. Job 1:21.
5. Job 1:8.
6. Job 1:9.
7. Job 1:10.
8. Job 1:11.

five hundred donkeys, and had a large number of servants"[9]—we see how deserved was his title *"the greatest man among all the peoples of the East."*[10] There is, as well, something else we might notice after doing the math: Everything the man touched turned to gold. No wonder he was so good. It is easy to see, if nothing else, at least the logic of Satan's position. He presents a solid argument.

It certainly seemed clear to Satan that Job obeyed God because of what God did or did not do. Hence, the challenge: "Dump him in a desert and see what happens to that obedience. With all those things you've done for him, all those blessings you've given him—material wealth,[11] close-knit family,[12] devoted friends,[13] a good marriage and excellent health—how faithful would Job be if you hadn't done or given *any* of those things? Take it to the next level, God. What would happen if you took away *everything* from him? He wouldn't obey you . . . I know that much."

To Satan's surprise, I think—and possibly to ours—Job proved worthy of God's bragging. Though Job struggled to come to terms with what was happening to him and dumped a load of plaguing questions and personal pain on God, he nonetheless remained obedient. As Satan learned by watching, and as we learn by reading, Job did not obey God because of what God did or did not do, but because of who God is. Even though Job's circumstances changed suddenly and drastically—his nothing-short-of-perfect oasis abruptly became an all-but-unbearable wilderness—he knew that God was God over both blessing and tragedy, that God remained God, unchanging and faithful, even though nothing else in his life was certain.

Job may have *praised* God because of all the blessings the giver *"of every good and perfect gift"*[14] had poured into his life, but Job *obeyed* God and *served* God because of who God is.

Likewise, Jesus did not obey because of what his father did or did not do—God, after all, refused his request in Gethsemane,[15] did not deliver him from death on a cross,[16] and, in fact, at least from Jesus' perspective, even

---

9. Job 1:3a.
10. Job 1:3b.
11. Job 1:3.
12. Job 1:2, 4–5.
13. Job 2:11–13.
14. Jas 1:17, *"Every good and perfect gift is from above, coming down from the Father of the heavenly lights, who does not change like shifting shadows."*
15. Mark 14:36.
16. Matt. 27:50.

forsook him at Calvary[17]—but he obeyed because of who God is. That is evident from Jesus' repeated prayer in the garden, *"not as I will, but as you will."*[18]

As he had with Job, Satan misjudged Jesus' reason for obeying God, and he misjudged it from the very beginning. On the cusp of the commencement of Jesus' public ministry, Satan squared off with the Son of God in a wilderness. The Enemy seems from the beginning to have questioned Jesus' *reason* for obedience—"How can you obey when God is giving you no food in your hunger,[19] when he may or may not come through for you with your life on the line,[20] when he's offering only pain and privation when you deserve better?"[21] Jesus' answers to Satan reveal an obedience centered on who God is, not on what God does or does not do: *"Man does not live on bread alone, but on every word that comes from the mouth of God"*[22] . . . *"Do not put the Lord your God to the test"*[23] . . . *"Worship the Lord your God and serve him only."*[24] Eventually, Satan walked away defeated.[25]

No train wreck there.

What happens to our obedience when a wilderness hits; when God, who has always poured out blessings, suddenly withholds them; when all the hurtful things God refused to let touch us are now allowed to touch and tear at our lives? Do we think such things could never happen to us, that such a wilderness could never be ours? Maybe not. But what if?

Abraham's life had been an oasis when one day, quite unexpectedly, he found himself in an unimaginable wilderness: *"Take your son, your only son, Isaac, whom you love, and go to the region of Moriah. Sacrifice him there on one of the mountains I will tell you about."*[26] Do we think an Abraham moment could never come to us? Do we think Abraham ever thought it could come to him? The important question is: What happens when such a wilderness comes?

Ezekiel's life had been blessed when one day, just like that, he was forced into the most painful wilderness of his life: *"Son of Man, with one blow I am*

---

17. Matt 27:46.
18. Matt 26:39, 42, 44; Mark 14:36, 39; Luke 22:42.
19. Matt 4:1–4; Luke 4:1–4.
20. Matt 4:5–7; Luke 4:9–13.
21. Matt 4:8–11; Luke 4:5–8.
22. Matt 4:4.
23. Matt 4:7.
24. Matt 4:10.
25. Matt 4:11.
26. Gen 22:2.

about to take away the delight of your eyes."[27] In a shockingly matter-of-fact statement, the prophet explained: *"So I spoke to the people in the morning, and in the evening my wife died."*[28] Do we think an Ezekiel moment could never come to us? Do we think Ezekiel ever thought it could come to him? The important question is: What happens when such a wilderness comes?

I once heard the late Dr. Fred Craddock tell of a missionary in China who, along with his wife, served faithfully on that field for years. The pair built a church there and began raising a family there. One day, without warning and for no apparent reason, Communist officials came to the man and said, "You and your family must leave China tomorrow. We'll be back in twenty-four hours to escort you to your ship. You and your wife may take two hundred pounds with you." That was that. Well, two hundred pounds—how much, or how little, is that? It might sound like a lot until you stop to consider how little of a lifetime together of *stuff* that really is? The husband and wife began debating what was essential and what was not, then began weighing this item, that item, and totaling the amounts. Finally, they had it on the nose—two hundred pounds.

The next day, as promised, the Communist officials returned and asked, "Are you ready to go?" "Yes," replied the missionaries. "Did you weigh everything?" "Yes, we did. We have exactly two hundred pounds." "Did you weight the kids?" Stunned silence followed. Finally, the man said, "No, of course not. We didn't weigh the kids." An official shot back, "Weigh the kids." Suddenly, yesterday's oasis became today's wilderness.

Whoever expects a wilderness like that? Did a family serving happily in China expect one? Did Ezekiel? Did Abraham? I somehow doubt it. In those cases, the wilderness came anyway, unexpectedly and uninvited, like most wildernesses do come. What about us? Will such a wilderness come? The *real* question for our consideration is, rather, what happens *when* such a wilderness comes? The answer will, in all probability, be determined by our reason for obeying God. Do we obey God because of what he does or does not do, or do we obey him because of who he is? The former can easily cause us to abandon obedience in a wilderness. Only the latter will sustain obedience in a wilderness. Ultimately, that makes the difference between a train wreck and a successful journey to becoming everything and possessing everything God desires.

There is a word that must not be forgotten in a wilderness—we forget it to our own peril—and that word is obey.

---

27. Ezek 24:15.
28. Ezek 24:18.

HOPE

"We must accept finite disappointment, but never lose infinite hope."
MARTIN LUTHER KING, JR.

Hope is a good strong word that means something. It is good and strong and means something always, but it is a particularly powerful ally in a wilderness.

In her magnificent work *The Gospel of Ruth: Loving God Enough to Break the Rules*, Carolyn Custis James issued an important reminder that "the Bible doesn't teach us that God is working from some divine balance sheet and will eventually even up accounts so that we will recover our losses and our sacrifices are repaid."[1] James went on to point out that such a view trivializes both the sufferings we endure and the lessons God teaches.[2]

God's purpose has never been to *fix* everything in this life. He did not, for example, fix everything for his own son, who kept—even in his resurrected body—the wounds and scars of crucifixion.[3] God's purpose has never been to *balance* this life with equal portions of painful deserts and pleasing oases. He did not do that for Moses, who spent the last two-thirds of his life in a wilderness. An honest read of Scripture, a read which gives both Old

---

1. James, *Gospel of Ruth*, 197. She continued, "It's obvious to anyone who has experienced a significant loss that the sorrows of this world and the wounds they inflict in our souls cannot be compensated no matter how much good fortune and prosperity come our way. Many holocaust survivors ended up wealthy, raised beautiful families, and enjoyed the good things in life. But they never stopped hurting or felt their suffering evened out. That's just how life works."

2. James, *Gospel of Ruth*, 197: "To suggest that everything is balanced out in the end for Naomi is to trivialize both her sufferings and also what God is trying to teach us throughout her story."

3. John 20:24–29.

and New Testaments their weighty say, reveals a God who seems largely unconcerned about this-world compensation, about everything balancing out in the end. That seems to be a human, rather than divine pre-occupation. God, in fact, seems at ease with life not balancing out here and now.

When I was a still-wet-behind-the-ears preacher, in my late teens, I spoke at a church gathering one Sunday night about Job—a difficult character to tackle even for a seasoned preacher, let alone for a novice. In retrospect, I did relatively well until I came near the end of the message and talked about God *compensating* Job for his losses. That may not have been the exact word I used, probably was not, but it was definitely the idea I was communicating. I said something like, "Yes, Job lost his ten children. But God made up for that loss by giving him ten new children." The first easily discernable fact from that statement is that, at the time, I had no children. How could I have had children and made a statement like that? Any parent knows that children are not interchangeable. When you lose one, you do not just go out and get another one, like you are replacing a screwdriver or flashlight batteries, so that everything is better and everyone is happy. There is no this-world compensation for the loss of a child.

Somewhere in literature there is the story of parents who lost their only child, a daughter named Elizabeth. The couple quickly decided to have another child. Soon the woman was pregnant and, in the customary nine months, the baby was born— a girl, whom they named Elizabeth, believing that would make up for the loss of their first child. It did not. There is no this-world compensation for the loss of a child. The fact is there is no this-world compensation for most things.

In *this* world, at least, God does not appear to be in the compensation business or much concerned with balancing books. He does not, for example, replace all our losses with gains, nor does he become a surrogate for what we lose. Whereas it is true that God will always *"be there for us"* in and through our losses, it is important that we understand *how* God will and will not *"be there for us."* John Kirvan encouraged us to keep in mind that "God will be there, not as a replacement for what we have lost or surrendered, but as that for which there is no substitute and who alone is enough."[4] Along that same line, God does not promise to be there to replace every this-world loss which we incur; merely to be there *in* our losses, to be there *with* us.

It helps to remember that God's work in this world is not to compensate us for our losses or to balance the bad with equal portions of good so that the two columns cancel out each other. "Our world is not tidy," wrote

---

4. Kirvan, *Raw Faith*, 118.

Kirvan, "and the role of faith is not to tidy it up."[5] Neither is that the role of God, not in this life anyway. Instead, God takes the hard and hurtful things of our lives—our losses, bad experiences, painful circumstances, wildernesses journeys—and transforms them into occasions of grace which serve our good and his glory.

In a poignant memoir, Carlo Carretto wrote:

> Thirty years have passed . . . since my dream went wrong. Now here I am . . . and you have your dreams too, or have had them. And I can tell you something. That mistaken injection that paralyzed my leg was not a stroke of bad luck. It was a grace. Let's be precise. There's no point in pious platitudes. It was bad luck, yes. It was a misfortune. But God turned it into a grace. I had a useless leg. I could not climb. So I got a jeep and became a meteorologist. Through no wish of my own, there I was where I belonged: in the desert. Instead of trudging through the snow I trudged through the sand. Instead of mountain passes I came to know caravan routes. Instead of chamois I saw gazelles. Life suddenly appeared to me as it was, an immense personal exodus. Now I saw the desert as an extraordinary environment of silence and prayer. My crippled leg helped me to 'stand firm' (Jas 1:12). I the runner—now stood firm. I who'd always tried to do two things at once—now I stood firm. No doubt about it, it was a plus.
>
> Deep down inside I began to understand that I hadn't been cheated. Misfortune had thrust me upon new paths. Brothers and sisters before me with your misfortunes, I testify to you of one thing only. Today, thirty years after the incident that paralyzed my leg, I don't say it wasn't a misfortune. I only say that God was able to transform it into a grace. I have experienced in my flesh what Augustine says: "God permits evil, so as to transform it into a greater good." . . . God loves his children, and when he sees that someone or something has hurt them, what imagination he has—to transform the evil into good, inactivity into contemplation, the cry of pain into a prayer, grief into an act of love![6]

In one of the great stories from Hebrew Scripture, what was done to Joseph by his brothers was transformed by God into a grace, which Joseph—in retrospect—privately recognized and then confessed to his siblings: *"You intended to harm me, but God intended it for good to accomplish what is*

---

5. Kirvan, *Raw Faith*, 28.
6. Carretto, *Why O Lord?*, 6–7.

now being done, the saving of many lives."[7] I do not know what Joseph's expectations were as a youngster, but if the dreams he shared with his family were any indication, those expectations did not include being sold to a band of slave traders and doing a two-year stint in an Egyptian prison. But somewhere along the line—perhaps from his prison cell or maybe later in Pharaoh's palace—Joseph exchanged his expectations *of* God for hope *in* God, which brought him to the realization, as it did Carlo Carretto many centuries later, that he hadn't been cheated, but merely thrust on a new path of God's making and for God's glory. Joseph ultimately put his hope in the God who forged that path.

It is important for God's people to maintain a clear distinction between personal expectations and biblical hope. John Kirvan pointed out, "Nothing proves to be a greater stumbling block than our own expectations."[8] That is important to always keep in mind, but especially in our wilderness times where personal expectations will only drive us deeper into despair while biblical hope alone will sustain us and see us successfully through long desert days. Our wilderness expectations tend to be finite and subject to disappointment, whereas hope is infinite and will in no way ever disappoint. As God promised through the prophet Isaiah, *"those who hope in me will not be disappointed."*[9]

My years of traveling wilderness trails, alone or with others, has convinced me that the vast majority of wilderness expectations are self-focused and temporal, breeding disappointment. By contrast, hope is God-focused and eternal, bringing satisfaction. It is the nature of wilderness expectations to presume deliverance; it is the nature of hope to calmly endure, even though deliverance is delayed or denied, knowing that the finished product God is fashioning is of ultimate importance. Saying it another way, we should hold *eternal* hope *tightly*; after all, we are holding to something God has *promised*; but we should hold *temporal* hope *loosely*; after all, we are holding to something God *can* and *might* do but has nowhere *promised*.

In a wilderness, we live with *expectation*, but not of *temporal* things like this-life release from pain and suffering, or here-and-now deliverance into the place of our dreams. Quite honestly, scripturally, those blessings may never be ours. We have no promise guaranteeing them. Rather, especially in a wilderness, we live with *expectation* of *eternal* realities, of those things grounded firmly in the promises of God—things like transformation into Christlikeness, or God bringing *ultimate* release from sin and death,

---

7. Gen 50:20.
8. Kirvan, *Raw Faith*, 187.
9. Isa 49:23.

or his bringing us to that Land of Promise we call heaven. We could say that regarding *temporal* things, we are meant to live with *expectancy*—open to those things that God can and might do, without holding him to them (*expectation*)[10]—while confident that if we remain faithful in and through a wilderness, we will become everything and possess everything God desires for us. "The note we end on is and must be the note of the inexhaustible possibility of hope."[11]

In the end, deliverance from any wilderness in life is only temporary. Should God save us from a desert of physical suffering or financial ruin today, our circumstances could easily change tomorrow and leave us once more in the throes of yet another wasteland. Should God grant miraculous healing from terminal disease, it would not prevent death, but merely postpone it. As a matter of fact, each of us will die—those who never knew healing as well as those who were miraculously healed—unless the Lord returns first. Neither the deed of deliverance nor the denial of deliverance is *ultimately* significant.

What *is* ultimately significant is our relationship with God-in-Jesus. Our walk in a wilderness is temporary, and there we serve God's purpose. Our life in heaven is eternal, and there we share God's glory. How can we realistically compare the two? As Paul wrote, *"I consider that our present sufferings are not worth comparing with the glory that will be revealed in us."*[12] For that reason, our wilderness walk becomes "a confident wandering"[13] because glory waits for us just around the corner.[14]

I will never forget the first time I saw Sydney, Australia. The first two-thirds of my coast-to-coast trip by rail had been across that continent's vast and barren wasteland, the dirt-choked Nullarbor Plain. The last leg of the journey, however, cut through the pot-marked sandstone and thick, lush bush land of the Blue Mountains. As we snaked our way downward toward the sea, Australia's largest city came into view, pristine and sparkling in the awakening sun. The humpbacked Harbour Bridge and the white pinnacled

---

10. Expectation and expectancy describe two ways of living when we do not have a personal promise from God. When we live with *expectations* of God, we hold him to our personal list of things he is to do, even though nothing on that list is ours by actual promise. By contrast, when we live with *expectancy* of God, there is no list to which we hold him. Instead, we expect *that* he will act—true to his character, always for our good and his glory—without holding him to *how* or *when* he must act in our specific case. The Bible's great figures of faith were, to a person, those who lived with *expectations* when possessing a promise but with *expectancy* without a promise.

11. Kirvan, *God Hunger*, 182.

12. Rom 8:18.

13. Käsemann, *Wandering People of God*, 44.

14. A phrase used by Eugene Peterson in *The Message* translation of 1 Pet 4:13.

Opera House dominated the spectacular skyline. At the time, I thought Sydney was the most beautiful city I had ever seen. But a week later, it took a back seat to St. Louis, Missouri.

I had spent a month preaching, teaching and training disciples in Southeast Asia and Australia. The engagements were many, the demands heavy and the pace grueling. The last week was a veritable wilderness for me, for I had grown weary of sitting in airports and living from suitcases. More than that, I was lonely and longed to see my wife and children.

My responsibilities ended on a Sunday, and the next afternoon I left Sydney for St. Louis, via Los Angeles. St. Louis was home, and as we began the long-awaited, early evening descent to Lambert Field, the city beneath me looked like a picture from a children's story book. A soft sapphire glow blanketed the neighborhoods, and the riverfront arch shone in the October moonlight. But the most beautiful thing about that descent was simply that I had, at long last, arrived home.

When the jolt and screech announced that the tires had found the runway, I was suddenly unburdened, released from the cramped restrictions of the airplane, free of the weariness of travel. As the plane taxied to a stop, the burdensome demands and hectic pace of the previous month became utterly insignificant. As I walked into the airport and embraced my wife and children, only joy remained.

As God's people, we are going home. We are waiting to be embraced by and to embrace the perfect object of our love. That is our hope. For us, there is coming a day of ultimate freedom and joy, a day when hope is realized, our homecoming a fact and our victory final and full. Then all weariness will end, all suffering will cease, all tears will be wiped away;[15] *"there will be no more death or mourning or crying or pain, for the old order of things has passed away."*[16] That is our ultimate hope, the truth put to music by the old Freedman's hymn from the antebellum South:

> Shout the glad tidings o'er Egypt's dark sea
> Jehovah has triumphed, his people are free![17]

Glory waits for wilderness wanderers just around the corner. Though we cannot be certain of deliverance here and now, we can be certain of glory then and there. Until we are home, we are bound to walk some wilderness terrain. For the remainder of our journey here, no matter how short or long that journey is, there will be pain and tears, heartache and heartbreak,

---

15. Rev 21:4a.
16. Rev 21:4b.
17. Raboteau, *Slave Religion*, 319.

suffering, disease and death. This is, after all, a broken world and we are broken people. But we hope for more than this brokenness. We hope for the perfect unbrokenness that will one day and forever be ours.

As God's people, we are sojourners on this earth.[18] We do not wander aimlessly as some do. We do not become settlers here. We are *in* but not *of* the world.[19] We do not sink our roots too deeply here.[20] We do not give our hearts to this world.[21] This land, this country is not our own. We admit *"that (we are) aliens and strangers on earth."*[22] We admit that we are *"longing for a better country—a heavenly one."*[23] We are simply passing through this world, whether the terrain is an oasis or a desert. Our sights, like our hearts are set elsewhere.

The apostle Paul approached life as a sojourner, not as a settler or wanderer. Though he lived, worked and ministered in the world, he did not belong to the world. He was on a long journey—a foreigner, stranger and alien here. He was, as it were, abroad, in a place far from his native land, longing to return home one day. When writing to the church in Corinth, Greece, he seems to have grown almost nostalgic, perhaps even homesick, using words and images that were, in his time and place, used to describe sojourners far from the land they loved: *"As long as we are at home in the body, we are away from the Lord;"*[24] then adding, *"We . . . would prefer to be away from the body and be at home with the Lord."*[25] Put simply, Paul was weary of being "away from home."[26] Hence, "my preference is to be done with my sojourn here and to be back home where I belong." Meanwhile, as long as he was sojourning, Paul's aim was to please the Lord in all things.[27]

Whether in a wilderness or an oasis, Paul was content:

> *. . . I have learned to be content whatever the circumstances. I know what it is to be in need, and I know what it is to have plenty. I have learned the secret of being content in any and every*

18. 1 Pet 2:1, 11. See also 1 Chr 29:15; Ps 119:19; Phil 3:20; Col 1:12-13; Heb 11:13-16.
19. John 17:15-16. See also Rom 12:1-2 and 1 John 2:15-17.
20. Rom 12:1-2; Phil 3:20; Col 1:12-13.
21. 1 John 2:15-17.
22. Heb 11:13b.
23. Heb 11:16a.
24. 2 Cor 5:6.
25. 2 Cor 5:8.
26. The Greek phrase is *ek demountes apo tou kyriou*—away from the people and place he belongs, where the Lord is.
27. 2 Cor 5:9, *"So we make it our goal to please him, whether we are at home in the body, or away from it."*

situation, whether well fed or hungry, whether living in plenty or in want. I can do everything through him who gives me strength.[28]

Paul, like Abraham before him, found contentment without becoming a settler. In fact, after Sarah's death, Abraham identified himself to the Hittites by saying, *"I am an alien and a stranger among you."*[29] The Hebrew phrase (*ger v'toshav*) tells us much about the man. Quite literally, it describes "a passing through resident." A *ger v'toshav*— which both Abraham and Paul were—neither releases life nor clings to it, always holds things lightly yet passionately as gifts from God, fully engages life without being entrapped by it, and has eyes wide open to this visible, physical world, while seeing, even focusing on, the invisible.[30] A sojourner lives life fully while longing for the promise yet to come. That is why there is always a self-imposed distance between where a sojourner pitches his tent and where he places his heart.[31] The land God has promised, and the God who promised it, are always the goals. That is why, as Paul wrote, we live in the visible but see the invisible:

> *For our light and momentary troubles are achieving for us an eternal glory that far outweighs them all. So we fix our eyes not on what is seen, but on what is unseen. For what is seen is temporary, but what is unseen is eternal.*
>
> *Now we know that if the earthly tent we live in is destroyed, we have a building from God, an eternal house in heaven, not built by human hands. Meanwhile we groan, longing to be clothed with our heavenly dwelling, because when we are clothed, we will not be found naked. For while we are in this tent, we groan and are burdened, because we do not wish to be unclothed but to be clothed with our heavenly dwelling, so that what is mortal may be swallowed up by life. Now it is God who has made us for this very purpose and has given us the Spirit as a deposit, guaranteeing what is to come.*[32]

The promise is guaranteed. Pain is temporary; heaven is forever. Even the worst wilderness experience will end in our father's embrace. That is our

---

28. Phil 4:11–13.
29. Gen 23:4.
30. 2 Cor 4:18.
31. The Hebrew word *"ger"*—*"stranger"*—refers literally to *"one who is estranged."* For those the apostle Peter calls aliens and strangers in this world—sojourners—there is always an element of estrangement with this world, for it is not where we belong and it cannot answer the true longing of our hearts.
32. 2 Cor 4:17—5:5.

hope. That is the invisible we see, the reality we cling to and live by because of the Jesus of the gospels.

Philip D. Jamieson urged us not to forget how the gospel story ends:

> The final chapter is not the lonely suffering of the young man on a hill but rather it is the early morning discovery of an empty tomb. The individual tragedies . . . are all too real. They burn their victims, inflicting terrible emotional pain. But, in the light of the Great Narrative, they are not allowed to have the final word. They hurt, but not forever.[33]

That is our hope. Even in the deepest wilderness where God's face is not seen, his voice is not heard, his presence is not felt, and his work in this world seems to have shut down, boarded up windows and doors, and left town, that remains our unwavering hope. "I am a man of hope," said Leon Joseph Cardinal Suenens, "not for human reasons nor from any natural optimism, but because I believe the Holy Spirit is at work in the church and in the world, even when his name remains unheard."[34] The God of the Wilderness is our hope—our one sure hope both now and forever.

God "does not allow our affliction to be wasted,"[35] nor does he allow Satan, sin and death to have the final word.

Months after my mother died, I was at her graveside. I lingered, reminisced, conversed—all those things you do at the graveside of a loved one whose life ran out before your love for them did. As I prepared to leave, I said, "I'll love you forever, mom." No sooner had I spoken those words than words were spoken to me—clearly, unmistakably, but silently. I heard them in my mind and felt them in my heart. I am convinced, though I did not hear an audible voice, that God spoke to me in that moment. The words I heard, on the heels of my own, were these: "Yes, but you will not *miss* her forever."

The hurt is not forever. The missing is not forever. The wilderness is not forever. Even death does not have the final word. God-in-Jesus has the final word. Always. Remember: "The final chapter . . . is the early morning discovery of an empty tomb." God "does not allow our affliction to be wasted." There is coming a promised day, a promised land. Its coming is certain as the character of the God of the Wilderness.

That is our hope.

---

33. Phillip D. Jamieson, *Young Men and Fire*, 107.

34. Gomes, *Scandalous Gospel of Jesus*, 209.

35. Schaeffer, *Affliction*, 160: *"As we turn to Him in our affliction and ask for help, He does not allow our affliction to be wasted."*

The apostle Peter left behind perhaps the best advice, the most hopeful assurance for weary wilderness travelers:

> *Friends, when life gets really difficult, don't jump to the conclusion that God isn't on the job. Instead, be glad that you are in the very thick of what Christ experienced. This is a spiritual refining process, with glory just around the corner.*[36]

There is an element of great courage needed in a wilderness; that is the courage to live by hope.

There is a word that must not be forgotten in a wilderness—we forget it to our own peril—and that word is hope.

---

36. 1 Pet 4:12, 13, *Message*.

EPILOGUE

HAGAR'S PRAYER

(Genesis 16)

God Who Sees Me—
On the run,
Between where
I have come from
And where
I am going,
Between what
I have known
And what
Remains unknown,
Between what
I have done
And what was done to me,
Between the from
Of my yesterday
And the to
Of tomorrow—
As I stop
And rest
And hurt
And cry
And fear
And wonder

And worry
And weep
At this refreshing
Though momentary
Spring of worship,
I realize
That while I know you
At a distance,
You know me
With a closeness
That both
Frightens and calms
Me,
That both
Stalks and saves
Me.
Over the screams
Of my past
And the angry voices
Of my present,
The changelessness
Of what is
And the inevitability
Of the yet to be,
Your presence invades—
Calling my name,
Knowing my life,
Speaking my future,
Assuring me that
I can face the fear
I had fled,
Though now
And no longer
Alone.
And with your presence
A promise,
A hope,
A future,
A confidence
That for now
And now on,

For ever and ever,
You are
Unchangingly,
Unwaveringly,
Unendingly
The God Who Sees Me.
And so my heart
Cries out
Amen!
And amen!
And for ever and ever
Amen![1]

---

1. Original poem/prayer by author.

BIBLIOGRAPHY

Joanna Adams, *The Only Question in A Chorus of Witnesses*. Edited by Thomas G. Long, and Cornelius Plantinga, Jr. Grand Rapids: Eerdman's, 1994.
Albom, Mitch. *Tuesdays With Morrie: An Old Man, a Young Man, and Life's Greatest Lessons*. New York: Doubleday, 1991,
American Missionary 6.2 (February 1862) 33.
Arndt, William F., and F. Wilbur Gingrich, eds. *A Greek-English Lexicon of the New Testament and Other Early Christian Literature*. Chicago: The University of Chicago Press, 1957.
Bailey, Kenneth E. *Jacob and the Prodigal: How Jesus Retold Israel's Story*. Downers Grove, IL: IVP Academic, 2003.
———. *The Cross and the Prodigal: Luke 15 Through the Eyes of Middle Eastern Peasants*. Downers Grove, IL: InterVarsity, 2005.
Banks, Robert J. *Paul's Idea of Community*. Peabody, MA: Hendrickson, 1994.
Barclay, William. *New Testament Words*. London: SCM, 1964.
Barth, Carl. *The Call to Discipleship*. Minneapolis: Fortress, 2003.
Barth, Marcus. *Ephesians* in the *Anchor Bible Series*. New York: Doubleday, 1974.
Bilezikian, Gilbert. *Community 101: Reclaiming the Local Church as Community of Oneness*. Grand Rapids: Zondervan, 1997.
Bonhoeffer, Dietrich. *Life Together: A Discussion of Christian Fellowship*. New York: Harper & Row, 1954.
———. *The Cost of Discipleship*. New York: McMillan Company, 1959.
Boyle, Gregory. *Tattoos on the Heart: The Power of Boundless Compassion*. New York: Free, 2010.
Brantner, Dr. John. "Death and Attitudes Toward Death." Edited by Stacy B. Day. Minneapolis: University of Minnesota Medical School, 1972.
Brown, Colin, ed. *The New International Dictionary of New Testament Theology*. Grand Rapids: Zondervan, 1976.
Bunyan, John. *The Pilgrim's Progress*. Edited by Roger Sharrock. London: Penguin, 1965.
Cameron, Julia. *The Artist's Way: A Spiritual Path to Higher Creativity*. NY: Putnam, 2002.
Capon, Robert Farrar. *The Parables of Grace*. Grand Rapids: Eerdmans, 1989.
Card, Michael. *In the Wilderness* from *In The Beginning*. Chatsworth, CA: The Sparrow Corporation, 1989.
Chittister, Joan. *The Gift of Years: Growing Older Gracefully*. Katonah, NY: BlueBridge, 2008.

Claypool, John. "Life is a Gift." In *A Chorus of Witnesses*, edited by Thomas G. Long, and Cornelius Plantinga, Jr, 120–30. Grand Rapids: Eerdmans, 1994.

Dillard, Annie. *Pilgrim at Tinker Creek*. San Francisco: HarperCollins, 1998.

Delton, Judy. *The 29 Most Common Writing Mistakes (And How to Avoid Them)*. Cincinnati: Writer's Digest, 1985.

Dobson, Dr. Kenneth. *The Pastoral Call: A Theological Evaluation of the Psychodynamics of Religious Experience*. Self-published, 1989.

Dunbar, Paul Lawrence. "The Debt." In *The Book of American Negro Poets*, edited by James Weldon Johnson. Ann Arbor, MI: University of Michigan Library, 1922.

Foster, Richard J. *Celebration of Discipline*. New York: Harper and Row, 1978.

———. *Life With God: Reading the Bible for Spiritual Transformation*. San Francisco: HarperOne, 2008.

Foster, Thomas C. *How to Read Literature Like a Professor*. New York: Harper, 2003.

Franzmann, Martin H. *Follow Me: Discipleship According to Saint Matthew*. St. Louis: Concordia, 1961.

Gomes, Peter J. *The Scandalous Gospel of Jesus: What's So Good About the Good News?* San Francisco: HarperOne, 2007.

Hahn, Scott. *Lord, Have Mercy*. New York: Doubleday, 2003.

Harris, Mark. *Companions for Your Spiritual Journey: Discovering the Disciplines of the Saints*. Downers Grove, IL: InterVarsity, 1999.

Hauerwas, Stanley, and Willimon, William H. *Resident Aliens*. Nashville: Abingdon, 1989.

Hendricks, Jr., Obery M. *The Politics of Jesus: Rediscovering the True Revolutionary Nature of Jesus' Teachings and How They Have Been Corrupted*. New York: Doubleday, 2006.

Holmes, Urban T. *Ministry and Imagination*. New York: Seabury, 1976.

James, Carolyn Custis. *The Gospel of Ruth: Loving God Enough to Break the Rules*. Grand Rapids: Zondervan, 2008.

Jamieson, Phillip D. "Young Men and Fie: Norman Maclean and the Pastoral Vocation," *Theology Today* (April 1995).

Käsemann, Ernst. *The Wandering People of God*. Minneapolis: Augsburg, 1984.

Kass, Leon R. *The Beginning of Wisdom: Reading Genesis*. Chicago: University of Chicago Press, 2003.

Kessler, Jay. *Growing Places*. Old Tappan, NJ: Fleming H. Revell, 1978.

Kidd, Sue Monk. *When The Heart Waits*. New York: Harper and Row, 1991.

Kierkegaard, Søren. *Either/Or*, 2 vols. Garden City, NJ: Doubleday, 1959.

Kingsolver, Barbara. *The Poisonwood Bible*. New York: Harper Perennial, 2002.

Kirvan, John. *God Hunger: Discovering the Mystic in All of Us*. Notre Dame: Sorin, 1999.

———. *Raw Faith: Nurturing the Believer in All of Us*. Notre Dame: Sorin, 2000.

Korda, Michael. *Hero: The Life and Legend of Lawrence of Arabia*. New York: HarperCollins, 2010.

Krutza, William J. ed. *Knee Exercises: Studies in the Meaning and Practice of Prayer*. Grand Rapids: Baker, 1979.

Lamott, Anne. *Grace (Eventually): Thoughts on Faith*. New York: Penguin, 2007.

Lane, William L. *A Call to Commitment*. Peabody, 1988.

Leitch, Elizabeth Elliott. "The Glory of God's Will." In *Declare His Glory*, edited by David M. Howard. Downers Grove, IL: InterVarsity, 1977.

Levison, John R. *Fresh Air: The Holy Spirit for an Inspired Life*. Brewster, MA: Paraclete, 2012.
Lewis, C. S. *Mere Christianity*. New York: Macmillan, 1960.
———. *The Screwtape Letters*. New York: Macmillan, 1961.
Lucado, Max. *In The Eye of the Storm*. Dallas: Word, 1991.
Mays, James Luther. *Hosea*. Philadelphia: Westminster, 1969.
Metaxas, Eric. *Bonhoeffer: Pastor, Martyr, Prophet, Spy. A Righteous Gentile vs. The Third Reich*. Nashville: Thomas Nelson, 2010.
More, Thomas. *The Sadness of Christ*. Princeton, NJ: Scepter, 1993.
Morris, Collin. *A Week in the Life of God: If God Kept a Diary*. London: Epworth, 1986.
Newton, John. *The Words of John Newton*. Edinburgh: Banner of Truth, 1955.
Nouwen, Henri J. M. *Can You Drink the Cup?* Notre Dame: Ave Maria, 1996.
———. *The Return of the Prodigal Son*. New York: Doubleday, 1992.
Paris, Kent. "Adversity." *Nehemiah Ministries Newsletter*, April 1991.
Paton, Alan. *Cry, the Beloved Country*. New York: Charles Scribner's Sons, 1948.
Patterson, Ben. *Waiting: Finding Hope When God Seems Silent*. Downers Grove, IL: InterVarsity, 1989.
Perrin, Nicholas. *The Exodus Revealed: Israel's Journey from Slavery to the Promised Land*. New York: Faith Words, 2014.
Peterson, Eugene. *A Long Obedience in the Same Direction: Discipleship in an Instant Society*. Downers Grove, IL: InterVarsity, 2000.
———. *Reversed Thunder: The Revelation of John and the Praying Imagination*. San Francisco: Harper and Row, 1988.
Plummer, Alfred. *A Critical and Exegetical Commentary on the Second Epistle of Paul to the Corinthians*. Edinburgh: T & T Clark, 1966.
Reardon, Patrick Henry. *The Jesus We Missed*. Nashville: Thomas Nelson, 2012.
Roboteau, Albert J. *Slave Religion: The "Invisible Institution" in the Antebellum South*. New York: Oxford University Press, 1978.
Schaeffer, Edith. *Affliction*. Old Tappan, NJ: Fleming H. Revell, 1973.
Smedes, Lewis B. "The Power of Promises." In *A Chorus of Witnesses*, edited by Thomas G. Long, and Cornelius Plantinga, Jr, 156–62. Grand Rapids: Eerdmans, 1994.
Snyder, Howard A. *The Community of the King*. Downers Grove, IL: InterVarsity, 1977.
Speare, M. E. *The Pocket Book of Verse*. New York: Washington Square, 1967.
Stevenson, J. W. *God in My Unbelief*. New York: Harper and Row, 1960.
Storey, Peter. *With God in the Crucible: Preaching Costly Discipleship*. Nashville: Abingdon, 2002.
Stockett, Kathryn. *The Help*. New York: Penguin, 2009.
Taylor, Barbara Brown. *Leaving Church: A Memoir of Faith*. San Francisco: HarperCollins, 2006.
Taylor, Myron J. "Lo, I Am With You Always." In *My Best Missionary Sermons*, edited by William McGilvery. Kempton, IN: Mission Services, 1980.
Thielicke, Helmut. *The Waiting Father*. New York: Harper and Row, 1959.
Thomas a Kempis. *The Imitation of Christ*. Edited by Claire L. Fitzpatrick. New York: Catholic Book, 1977.
Tozer, A.W. *Keys to the Deeper Life*. Grand Rapids: Zondervan, 1979.
Waite, Terry. *Taken on Trust*. London: Hodder and Stoughton, 2010.
Elie Wiesel. *Messengers of God: Biblical Portraits and Legends*. New York: Touchstone, 1976.

———. *Night.* New York: Bantam, 1982.
Weatherhead, Leslie. *The Will of God.* Nashville: Abingdon, 1974.
Wiederkehr, Macrina. *A Tree Full of Angels: Seeing the Holy in the Ordinary.* San Francisco: HarperCollins, 1990.
Wilkerson, David. "Accusing God of Child Neglect!" Sermon preached June 21, 1993.
Wolterstorff, Nicholas. *Lament for a Son.* Grand Rapids: Eerdmans, 1987.
Yancey, Philip. "When the Facts Don't Add Up." *Christianity Today,* June 13, 1986.
———. *Where is God When it Hurts?* Grand Rapids: Zondervan, 1996.

Subject Index

Aaron, 20, 29
Abraham
    Beersheba and, 10n1, 98n8
    binding Isaac to the wood, 32
    called by God, 113n16, 115, 189
    chose the wilderness as his place of growing flocks and family, 116–17
    effect of the wilderness on, 124
    enduring a four-day nightmare with Isaac, 11, 183
    experienced problems in settlements (cities), 20n12
    faith of, 172
    found contentment without becoming a settler, 248
    God demonstrated faithfulness to, 205
    God tested, 31
    learned the wilderness way, 35
    life changed to a wilderness in one day, 239
    not wavering in unbelief, 153–54
    obedience of, 205
    passed off his wife as his sister in Egypt, 99
    sharing clarity and purposefulness, 117
    as a sojourner, 112
    steered clear of Egypt, 99
    waiting a quarter-century for his promised child, 183
Abram, becoming Abraham, 228
Absalom, 35, 112

absence, sense of God's, 182
absurdity of God, trusting, 199
accusations, of God as not valid, 201
Accusing God of Child Neglect (Wilkerson), 201
Achan, 62
Ada Price, 32n6
Adam, 103n32
Adam and Eve, 200
Adams, Joanna, 139
affliction, God afflicted in all our, 156
agony, of Job, 126
AIDS virus, from an emergency room patient, 5
"alien stranger," permeating the Hebrew Bible, 82n13
altar, wilderness as, 33
angels, 193
anti-Christian cultures, 82
apartheid, 82
Apollo 8 astronauts, 46
appetites, driven by, 27n7
Archimedes, 174
Asaph, 180–81
assaying gold, gold, 34
attitude, of trusting in God, 207
Augustine, on God permitting evil, 243
author
    diagnosed with rectal cancer, 143–46
    loving his mother forever, 249
    too much time in wrong places, 163
    wilderness experience of, 4
"away from home," Paul weary of, 247

SUBJECT INDEX

Babylonians, as a universal symbol of evil, 82
Bailey, Kenneth E., 220, 221, 223–24, 226
Barclay, William, 121n1
barren women, of Scripture, 11n3
Bartchy, S. Scott, 51n4
Barth, Karl, 190
Barth, Marcus, 138
Bathsheba, 35
battleground, casualties of, 165–66
battles, everyday, 179
becoming, God waiting on our, 225
Beersheba, 10n1, 98n8
Begin, Menachem, 92
being-there-with-us, of God, 182
belief system, of Israel at the time of the Exodus, 164
believers, not isolating oneself from a community of, 212
Bible
    assuming testing, 33
    calling for trusting faith, 175
biblical hope, sustaining us, 244
Biko, Steven, 37n1
Bilezikian, Gilbert, 218
binocular vision, 13
blame, assigning in a sovereign wilderness, 61
blessing, coming in spite of a wilderness, 189
blessing-in-disguise nature, of discontent, 22
blindness, resulting in an opportunity for God to be glorified, 138
Body of Christ (church), 214, 219
boldness, true measure of, 93
Bonhoeffer, Dietrich
    on Christians sharing in Christ's large-heartedness, 91
    on confession versus resistance, 87
    on doing the will of God, 95
    on encountering biblical stories, 8n15
    on God knowing the way, 207
    price paid by, 89
The Box, prisoners sentenced to, 178
Boyle, Gregory, 228
Brantner, John, 211
bread, metaphorical meaning of, 25–26
bridges, examining the "character" of, 171
bringing out theme, of God, 148–49
broken heart, of the prodigal son's father, 226
broken world, fault lines inescapable in, 62
brokenness, 29
Brueggemann, Walter, 28
Buechner, Frederick, 7
Bunyan, John, 4
burnt offering, 31, 32
Busingye, Rose, 96

Cain, 114, 218
Caleb, 38, 71, 130, 174
call of God, 94, 118, 189
Cameron, Julia, 156
Canaan, Moses never crossing into, 17
cancer. *See also* leukemia
    author diagnosed with rectal, 143–46
    Cheryl died of, 23–24
    Donna's experience during, 134–35, 180
    patient recovering from, 178–79
    Phil lost his wife to, 155
    as systemic evil, 79
Capon, Robert Farrar, 221
captivity, being determined in, 132
Carol, suicide attempt failed, 139
Carretto, Carlo, 21–22, 243
cause-and-effect, examining, 81
"Cephas," meaning "rock," 217n30
certainty, 65, 173
change-agents, in the world here and now, 142n24
character, 50, 171–79
Cheryl, died of cancer at the age of nine, 23–24
chess, 49
child of God, never journeying or suffering alone, 148
children of Israel, 110, 112
China, Christians converted because of one man, 137
Chittister, Joan, 208

SUBJECT INDEX   261

choosing
    to step in alongside others, 97
    what God has already chosen, 202
chop shop theology, 33
Christian community, not a means to individual ends, 219
Christian husband and father, diagnosed with rectal cancer, 143–46
Christians
    called to sympathy and action, 91
    compelled to step in alongside, 92, 93, 94, 97
    as spirit-filled, 213
Christlikeness, as the intent of a wilderness, 50–51
"Christ's Compassion for the Suffering" (Mother Teresa), 161n16
church, viewing as the people of God, 215
church life, give-and-take of as necessary, 215–16
circumstantial will, of God, 63–64, 63n12
city, in contrast to the wilderness, 10n1
civil disobedience, 83, 84, 86
clarity, 118
class identity, Hebrew as, 82n13
Claypool, John and Laura Lue, 200
cloud and fire, miraculous ministry of, 191
Coffin, William Sloane, 88
Colson, Charles, 178
commitment, *hesed* driven by, 93
Communist officials, told a missionary to leave China in one day, 240
community, as a powerful ally in a wilderness, 211–19
community-in-transit, needing pastors, 217
complaints, as requests, 202, 203
conditional covenants, of God, 173
confession, 87
constancy, of God's character, 171
contentment, 20, 21, 22
corporate exercise in discipline, wilderness as, 44
counterintuitive wisdom, of God, 199

courage, to live by hope needed in a wilderness, 250
course correction, as essential for Elijah, 46
covenants, God making conditional, 173
Craddock, Fred, 240
crisis, turning to God in, 192
Cry the Beloved Country (Paton), 132, 149n22
cup, as full of pain, 154

Daniel, confused by a vision of God's will, 204–5
David
    effect of the wilderness on, 124
    on his own state as one of wandering, 113n13
    learned the wilderness way, 35
    paying long-term interest, 70
    sang of God saving Israel in spite of its sins, 230–31
    song of the wilderness endured by God's people, 54–55
    walking through the valley of the shadow of death, 184
    as a wanderer, 112
    wilderness period for, 4n5
death
    of a dear friend for God's glory, 139
    a father willing to suffer if only his son is found, 166
    wilderness forcing, 190
    wilderness of as meant for God's glory, 140
"deathright," demanded by Jacob, 107
death-to-life transformation, of the prodigal, 227
deconstruction, 33n10
delay, faith and character forged in, 224
deliverance
    from any wilderness as only temporary, 245
    crying to God for, 233
    God leading us into, 174
    God's will and, 204
    Israel sang praises after, 231
    Joseph never experienced, 177
    as not our business, but God's, 176

deliverance (continued)
    people in Scripture never experiencing, 183
    wilderness expectations presuming, 244
Delton, Judy, 74
demons, 47, 165
dependency, wilderness humbling us away from, 26
desert days
    drove the author to Scripture's wilderness narratives, xvi
    God using to empty us so that he might fill us, 189
    hard to see a pattern in, 66
    pain and confusion of intensifying, 212
    teaching us that to have God as enough, 23
desert pressure, purging and purifying our minds and hearts, 72–73
desert stories, as invaluable reminders, 70
deserts
    being compelled to enter, 90
    as a divine refusal to allow us to sin, 160
    doing saving and sanctifying work within us, xv
    as ever God's domain, 136
    God's understanding of, 147
    not having definable boundaries, 11
    of our lives as not part of God's original plan, 59
    persecution and imprisonment as, 131
    pinning backs against walls, 129
    redeeming even the most harrowing and hopeless, 132
    seeming totally devoid of grace, 151
    as a waiting game, 224
desire, possessing God's for us, 49–55
despondency, of Job, 126
detours, 62, 63
Dillard, Annie, 53, 74–75
disciples, 46–47, 216
discipline, in a wilderness, 43–48

discontentment, in the wilderness, 17–24
disenfranchised minorities, 82
disobedience, wandering tied to, 114
disorienting place, wilderness as, 5
distant country, apart from the father, 222
distractions, attending an oasis, 192
divine purpose, wilderness time always serving, 53
divine wilderness, as counterintuitive, 200
divine wooing, wilderness as an extreme case of, 161
DNA, of a cell as its knowledge, 79
doctor, treated Donna through her cancer, 135
domino flicker, working as, 80–81
Donna
    cancer ordeal, 134–35, 180
    on suffering as a gift of grace, 155–56
double postcards, comparing our lives to, 13
doubts, falling victim to in a wilderness, 200
drama, playing our part in God's, 89
drunk friend, fell from a highway overpass, 59
Dunbar, Paul Lawrence, 69–70
duration, of stints in a wilderness, 183
dying, 41, 42, 141

earthly attachments, turning away from, 27n7
Egypt
    ambiguity of fueling wariness, 102n27
    assimilating its own, 104, 110
    cultural antagonism toward Israel, 104n36
    history of Abraham and his descendants with, 99
    Israel preserving identity and independence in, 98
    Israel yearning for, 20
    as the Land of Pharaoh, not of promise, 111

SUBJECT INDEX 263

as an oasis, 17, 102–3, 104
people known collectively as, 80n10
preserving identity and
  independence in, 102
producing wariness, 102
as a saving oasis or a lethal
  wilderness, 103
as synonymous with all that is
  opposed to God, 102n27
systemic evil running the show, 80
as systemic wilderness, 83
Egyptian imagery, used by God, 164
Egyptian life, systemic evil in, 80
Egyptians
  God hardening all hearts of, 198
  as much more discerning, 130–31
  of Old Testament history, 82
  understood more than Israel, 131
Elijah, 45–46, 112, 216
Elim, an oasis, 20
Elisha, 216
emotions, negative, 185
empires, as paradigms of systemic
  evil, 82
endgame
  God always having in view, 123
  keeping in view, 49
  as paramount to God, 50
  as seeking and saving the lost, 50n2
  of wilderness as soul-making, 53
enemy, God appearing to be, 7, 7n9
energy, wilderness running on its own,
  82
environment, God adapting to his,
  63–64
Ephraim, 104
eternal impact, of a walk through a
  wilderness, 135
eternal realities, living with
  expectation of, 244
eternal salvation, Jesus as the source
  of, 48
ethnic cleansing, Pharaoh's attempt
  at, 83
Eve, 103n32, 200, 218
evil, constantly refueling itself, 80
execution chamber, *The Box* as, 178
exodus

as the distinctive grace event, 149
of Israel proved that God could be
  trusted, 173
from a systemic wilderness, 86
expectancy, 245, 245n10
expectations, 244, 245n10
Ezekiel, 160, 239–40
'ezer, Eve's role as "helper" for Adam,
  218
Ezra, xiv

fact
  God above all, 186–87
  of God's guidance not varying, 191
faith
  of Abraham, 172
  battle ground of for Job, 176
  Bible's great narratives of, 172
  encountering troubles, 4
  Jesus stretching his disciples,' 139
  lives of not complete apart from
    ours, 175
  not tidying up this world, 243
  taking us safely through all the
    storms of life, 140
  trusting God's grace, 152, 155
  walking by, 202
"faith chapter," of Christian Scripture,
  171–72
faithful suffering, enduring a systemic
  wilderness, 88
faithfulness
  carrying across the years, 134
  as crucial, 68
  glorifying God, 137
  of God, 171, 172
  to God resulting in good, 174
  of Joseph, 177–78
  making a difference, 178
  testimony of changing lives, 140
  wildernesses demanding, 67
  as a witness to those who watch,
    131
fallen world, 61
family, as security in the village, 220n2
family blessing of Jacob, carried on
  through Joseph's sons, 105
far-offness, God refusing to accept, 163

SUBJECT INDEX

father
- prodigal breaking fellowship with, 220
- running to his son, 223n13
- suffering more deeply than his prodigal son, 225
- waiting, 222–23

fault, assigning for a wilderness, 61
fear, 77, 93
fellowship, prodigal breaking with his father, 220
fighting, alongside our brothers and sisters as community, 219
final destination, as the Promised Land, 49–50
flicking, toppling thousands of living dominos, 81
flooding, of the home of the author's youngest son, 117
focus, 185, 186
formative discipline, in a wilderness, 45
forty years, in the wilderness suffering for sins, 11n6
Foster, Richard J., 8, 155
Frankl, Viktor, 207
freed slaves, options of, 37
freedom, 37, 111
friendship, with the world making an enemy of God, 7n9
frozen shoulder, requiring surgery, 122
fruitfulness, promises of to Abraham and Isaac, 103n32
fulfillment, 26, 27, 27–28n9
Fuller, Buckminster, 222
funeral, Carol's words for her, 140
future, open-ended for Abraham, 12
future promise of God, grace as, 149

Gandhi, Mahatma, 88, 89
generation, of Hebrew children died in the wilderness, 71
gensetai, meaning "to taste or to partake of," 147n3
gentleman, God as not, 162
ger v'toshav ("a passing through resident"), 248
"ger"-"stranger," referring literally to "one who is estranged," 248n31

"Get out of the Wilderness Free" card, as God's people, 184
gift from God, suffering as, 161n16
glory
- God gaining from wilderness encounters, 137
- for God's, 136–46
- just around the corner, 250
- waiting for us just around the corner, 245
- waiting for wilderness wanderers, 246–47

God. *See also* Yahweh
- allowing to be glorified, 141
- answering prayer, 180
- bragging on Job to Satan, 237
- called Hosea to love his unfaithful wife still, 158
- caring for his people like a shepherd, 181
- carrying Donna through her ordeal, 180
- coming to us as we are and where we are, 163n19
- compensating Job for his losses, 242
- confronting us in a wilderness, 136
- countering every detour with a reroute, 64
- delivering his people by grace, 148
- delivering some but not delivering others, 175
- depending upon for survival, 25
- desiring a people who will praise him, 138
- driving us where we would not go ourselves, 190
- as ever-present in our lives, 66
- forgetting about us, 125
- found in places of faithful suffering, 88–89
- getting his people off the deadly diet in Egypt, 44
- getting reacquainted with, 164
- giving Naomi a key role, 67
- hardened Pharaoh's heart, 198
- having only our best interests at heart, 208

having the power to do what he promised, 154
humbled the people of God in the wilderness, 18
as the key player, 136
known and praised by his people in the dark nights of their souls, 231–32
led the Israelites around by the desert road, 3
making himself known, 129
as the master therapist using a wilderness, 122
as never aloof in our wilderness experiences, 147
as no gentleman, 162–63
not allowing affliction to be wasted, 249
not always making sense, 5
not answering Daniel at all, 205
not fixing everything in this life, 241
not forcing his will, 60
not isolating us from spiritual community, 214
not leading Israel one by one, 214
not promising a wilderness-free life, 182
not promising to be there to replace every this-world loss, 242
obeying because of what he does or does not do, 236
as one who confronts and stands against, 7n9
as our true source of life, 26
perspective on hearts turning back to Egypt, 39
promises of, 98–99, 130, 181, 214, 244–45
providing all the answers we need, 201–2
pursuing us with love, 158, 160, 161
recognizing as the giver, 27
remaining unchanged, 174
reminding to keep the endgame in view, 49
removing sin, 76
saving people by his grace, 194
seeming lightyears away in a wilderness season, xv
sharing our suffering, 7
speaking truth, 131
tasting a wilderness, 147–48
telling Abraham to sacrifice Isaac "as a holocaust," 32
testing the heart, 35
transforming hard and hurtful things into occasions of grace, 243
trusting, 12, 14, 39
turning to in a crisis, 193
unconcerned about this-world compensation, 242
using a wilderness to pry open our clenched fists, 28
views of, 119
waiting, 222, 223, 224, 225, 228
walking with us, 182
welcoming hitches and glitches, 60
of the wilderness, 3–8, 35, 60
"working for the good of those who love him," 13
"God stories," Donna famous for, 135
God-figures, on the hunt to rescue and reclaim, 223
God-in-flesh, Jesus as, 96
God's chosen people, wilderness narratives of, 8
God's people
    called to welcome the promise in faith, 178
    Hebrew text accusing of unfaithfulness, 158
    not immune to trials, 4
    others watching their travels, 129
    waiting to be embraced by God, 246
God's perspective, viewing our lives in tandem with, 13
God's purpose, wilderness always serving, 124
God's sovereignty, wilderness as, 5
God's word, wilderness as, 134
gold, testing the purity of, 34
Gomer, Israel paralleled to, 159
good of others, enduring a wilderness for, 129–35

SUBJECT INDEX

good people, bad things happening to, 6
gospel, power of unleashed by God's people, 92
The Gospel of Ruth: Loving God Enough to Break the Rules (James), 241
grace
    described, 36n26
    failure to discern, 149
    fitting into the same space with suffering, 154
    God slaying his son to save sinners as, 204
    as grace when deliverance is denied, 204
    groping to find even a flicker of, 152
    as harsh as the desert itself or noticeably gentle, 155
    never failing, 197
    oasis as a gift of, 27
    providing staying power in, 195
    provision of, 194
    regularly in tandem with suffering, 154
    seeking in a wasteland, 156
    in a sin wilderness leaving us transformed, 77
    sustaining, 196
    trumping sorrow, 152
    in the wasteland to Israel, 148
    wilderness as, 36, 148
    in a wilderness of great suffering, 151
    wilderness seeming devoid of, 149
"Great is Thy faithfulness..." hymn, 232–33
grief, compressed into a short span of time, 225n20
grumblers and gripers, desiring to halt therapy, 123
guidance, provided by God, 190–91
gulag, wilderness of a, 178

Hagar, 48, 251–53
Harris, Mark, 125
Hauerwas, Stanley, 211, 214, 215–16
heart(s)
    of [humanity] having no race, 96
    being "strengthened by grace," 155
    of God beating for the good of his children, 123
    healing through a wilderness, 72
    no way to bypass exposing in a wilderness, 36
    revealed by testing in a wilderness, 33
    setting the default mechanism of to God, 40
    turning back to Egypt, 38
    of wanderers versus sojourners, 113
heartless demand, on the part of the prodigal son, 221
heaven, as forever, 248
Hebrew children. *See* Israelites
Hebrews. *See also* Israelites
    blamed God or Moses for grief in the wilderness, 149
    cowered before the pursuing army of Egypt, 186
    long years of faithful suffering by, 89
    as a term of social or class description, 82n13
Hebrews 11, as the "faith chapter," 171–72
Heine, Dr., 213
The Help (Stockett), 73n12
"helper," of our brother and our sister, 218
Hendricks, Obery M., Jr., 82n13, 85, 96
King Herod, xiii
"hesed," 92, 93
Hitler, 188
holiness, 30, 171
holocaust, 32, 82
holocaust survivors, 207, 241n1
holy heart, wilderness ordeal forming within us, 73
Holy Spirit, 51n4, 138. *See also* Spirit
homecoming, of God's people, 246
hope, 241–50
    of God to gather into his arms the one he loves, 163
    as God-focused and eternal, 244
    not disappointing us, 155
    for perfect unbrokenness, 247
Mount Horeb, 3

Hosea, 158, 160
hospital chaplain, contracted the HIV virus, 5
The Hound of Heaven (Thomson), 166
"hounding," of God to be welcomed, 167
human experience, Jesus assuming the existential burden of, 147n2
human eyes, stereoscope working like, 13
humbling, of Moses, 29
humility, experiencing in a wilderness, 25–30
hurricane of hurt, far safer with God in, 203
hurt, as not forever, 249

"I am who I am," 181
idols, turning away from, 28
If God Kept a Diary (Morris), 76n21
illusions, not in accord with the facts, 183–84
impact, of a wilderness pilgrim, 134
imprisonment, God using to get Joseph to Pharaoh, 64
impurities, burning away, 50, 51
incongruity, in the ways of an infinite God, 6
Indian Pacific train ride, across Australia, 9
individualism, as a myth of modern American Christianity, 44–45
individuals, walking wildernesses as isolated, 212n8
"ineluctable" quality, of God, 5n7
innocent people, suffering due to the sins of others, 62
institutional sin, becoming victim of, 82
insubordination, as a chain reaction waiting to happen, 83
intentional choice, to step into a wilderness, 90
intentional will, of God, 63n12
iron chariots, of the people of the plains, 6
Isaac
    Abraham's call from God to sacrifice, 117
    attempting to thwart God's plan, 108n57
    Beersheba and, 10n1, 98n8
    Lord telling him not to go down to Egypt, 99–100
    uniqueness of, 31
Isaiah
    on Egypt and Pharaoh, 100–101
    on the faithfulness of God, 172–73
    on God knowing and feeling the distress of a desert, 147
    on God sharing in suffering, 227
    on God walking with us, 180
    on hope never disappointing, 244
    on Jesus' life of so much grace, 152
    on passing through waters, rivers, and fire, 184
    on the passion of Jesus, 150–51
Israel
    burying an entire generation in the desert, 32
    coming into their greatest good through a wilderness, 123
    found trouble when eating all they wanted, 20
    learning to close their hearts to sin, 224
    learning to sing praises in a wilderness, 232
    learning to trust God for all they needed, 41
    not knowing the end of their desert days, 11n5
    not trusting God's grace to be present and active, 154
    paralleled to Hosea's wife Gomer, 159
    paying forty years' worth of interest on a moment's worth of rebellion, 70
    as the people of God, 215
    postponing praise until the crisis had passed, 231
    praising God, 230, 236
    scarcely knew Yahweh at the time of the Exodus, 164
    struggling to trust God out of Egypt, 38
    suffering for a generation, 62

268 SUBJECT INDEX

Israel (continued)
    taking its focus from God, 186
    unable to discern the hand of God, 130
    as unfaithful, 159
Israelites. *See also* Hebrews
    firing a final verbal salvo at Moses, 129
    fruitful and multiplied greatly in Egypt, 103n32
    measuring the march of in terms of books and chapters, 11
    systemically dehumanized by the Egyptians, 79
    terrified as Pharaoh approached, 185–86

Jabbock, place of divine encounter for Jacob, 136
Jacob (Israel)
    adopting his grandchildren, 105
    alert regarding both Egypt and Joseph, 104n36
    arranging to lead the people out of Egypt, 110
    blessing Joseph's sons, 105n44
    claimed Ephraim and Manasseh as his own, 104
    demanding solemn oaths, 107
    engaged in extraordinary acts, 104
    experienced God picking a fight with him, 7n9
    at Jabbock, 136
    journeying to Egypt to see Joseph, 98
    learned that there was grain in Egypt, 102
    saw Joseph as completely Egyptianized, 105–6
James, Carolyn Custis
    on the barren women of Scripture, 11n3
    on God harnessing suffering to serve his good purposes, 47n23
    on God inviting us to participate, 93
    on "God is mysteriously at work in the mess," 156
    on God working from a divine balance sheet, 241
    on knowing Jesus, 53
    on Naomi and Job losing everything, 125–26
    on ordinary people moving the gospel with power, 92
    on small everyday battles turning the tide for the kingdom, 176
    on suffering as sacred, 152
    on wilderness perspective, 66
Jamieson, Philip D., 249
Jehoshaphat, 207–8, 232
Jenkins, Maria, 175
Jeremiah
    finding close kinship with, 233–34
    on going to Egypt to die, 100
    song of praise at the lowest moment of his life, 232
    stretches in prison, 45
    understood a wilderness in terms of love, 160
Jesus. *See also* Son of God
    answers to Satan, 239
    assaulted by Satan, 32
    awash in agony, 149n22
    bearing extreme hurt of a severe wilderness, 203
    called a rich man to walk away from his wealth, 190
    called fishermen and a tax collector, 189–90
    casting out demons, 47
    cried out in pain and wept in sorrow, 125
    death of as a matter of experience, 147n2
    demonstrating clarity of purpose, 117
    depending totally on God, 26
    died as a participant, 96
    endured a wilderness for forty days, 176
    endured the cross, 18
    experience consistent with God's known character, 147n3
    followed the Spirit into a wilderness, 113n16, 116

as a full-blown and full-grown
    from the start, 124–25
God purposed a wilderness for, 64
going to Jerusalem to suffer many
    things and be killed, 41
held sway over sea and sky, 47
idea of a developing, 124
indiscriminate in his choice of
    company to keep, 163n19
interpreting all of life in terms of
    glorifying God, 138
kept to the path laid out by God's
    wisdom and will, 203
laid down his life for us, 96
led by the Spirit, 47, 64
lived for the glory of God, 141
as a man for others, 96
needing an angel to remind him,
    154n34
never lost sight of where he was
    headed, xv
not deserving wilderness
    discipline, 48
not Hitler as Lord, 87
obeyed God because of who God
    is, 238–39
oriented to his father's will, 64
Peter, James and John not
    supporting in Gethsemane, 216
prayed that he had brought his
    father glory, 140
redeeming his most excruciating
    wilderness for our good and
    God's glory, 132
saw the joy-set-before-us part, 54
as a sojourner, 112
spiritual testing in a wilderness, 45
stepping in alongside us in our
    sins, 91
stepping into the sin wilderness, 95
stilling the storm on Galilee, 226
suffering in the furnace of affliction
    with us, 227
suffering of, 89
"tasted" death, 147
on those who mourn, for they shall
    be comforted, 185

understanding of his Father
    seeking "until he finds," 162
volunteering to satisfy God's wrath,
    76
walked victoriously through his
    final wilderness, 216
as a wilderness sojourner, 116
wilderness testing strengthening
    his character, 52
"Jesus and me," as a true but one-sided
    statement, 215
Jesus shape, concept of, 51n4
Jesus-followers, living in and as
    community as God's intent, 215
Job
    able to see God "mysteriously at
        work in the mess," 230
    attacked by Satan, 112
    bore the extreme hurt of a severe
        wilderness, 203
    as dazed but steady, 113
    emerged from desert days "coming
        forth as gold," 18
    emerging from his wait, 228
    as an example, 125–26
    faithfulness of, 176
    felt that God had turned on him,
        7n9
    illustrating Israel as it was meant to
        be, 236–37
    losing everything, 32
    not departing from the commands
        of God's lips, 68
    obeying God because of who God
        is, 238
    praising God after a day of disaster,
        229
    praising God after losing his
        health, 229–30
    proved worthy of God's bragging,
        238
    question of why he served God, 237
    remaining true to the word and the
        will of God, 203
    Satan testing, 62–63
    saw the coming-forth-as-gold
        part, 54

Job (continued)
  stranding in a wilderness to see what happens, 237
  as a wilderness wanderer, 113n14
  words of revealing intense pain, 126–28
Jochebed, 83–84, 89
John the Baptist, 45, 183
Jones, E. Stanley, 131
Jordan river, opening a dry-as-bone path through, 149
Joseph
  assimilated into Egyptian culture, 104
  comfort level of the oasis as too high, 109
  exchanged his expectations of God for hope in God, 244
  holding to the faith of his father, 177
  as an imperfect individual, 177
  left Egypt when Jacob died, 107
  made sick by the blessing of his sons, 105
  not deserving to be sold into slavery, 48
  placed in a coffin in Egypt, 110
  recognized what his brothers did to him as God's grace, 243–44
  redeemed what others had meant for evil, 142n24
  returned to Egypt, 109, 177n28
  as the savior of Israel, 63
  sent word to Pharaoh when Jacob died, 108
  sitting in prison for two years, 183
Joshua, 62, 71, 174, 191
joy, awaiting after a wilderness, xv, 18
Jude, 149
judgment, as severe in a wilderness of sin, 71
"just around the corner," as scant comfort, 18
"just like us," as not "all right" with God, 32n6

Käsemann, Ernst, 213–14
katartidzein, uses of the word, 121–22

keeper, as our brother's and our sister's, 218
Kempton, Sally, 37
Kessler, Jay, 75
Kidd, Sue Monk, 74
Kierkegaard, Soren, 124
King, Martin Luther, Jr., 88, 89
Kirvan, John
  on God alone sufficing, 30
  on God being there, 242–43
  on hope in a promise heard and trusted, 177n31
  on our own expectations as a stumbling block, 244
  on some part of us must die if we are to live, 190
  on the spiritual journey as cluttered with a pantheon of gods, 27
kiss of Jesus, suffering, pain, humiliation as, 161n16
knowledge, causing terrible things when forgotten, 79
Kornfeld, Boris, 178–79

Lamott, Anne, 7, 74, 228
land of bondage, leaving, 37
Land of Promise, Moses came up short of, 17
Lane, William L., 173, 182, 185, 205
Lassie, weekly heroics of, 77–78
Lazarus, 139
Leah Price, 149
leaning on the Lord, in death or deliverance, 175
Leitch, Elisabeth Elliot, 206–7
lesson, of a wilderness, 23
letting go, of all that keeps us from God alone, 27n7
leukemia, 139–40. *See also* cancer
Levison, Jack, 213
Levites, tendency to follow contentment into sin, 21
Lewis, C. S., 54, 160
liberation event, exodus as, 85
life
  Cheryl's definition of, 23–24
  Christian, 97, 213

SUBJECT INDEX   271

fully engaging without being entrapped by it, 248
God providing essentials in a wilderness, 193
threatened in a wilderness, 165
wasting of the prodigal's, 221
Life is a Gift (Claypool), 200
life-and-death situations, wilderness bringing us face-to-face with, 68
lineage, of Rahab, 133
live-free person, becoming, 40
lives, not viewing only through our personal perspective, 13
living
  for the glory of God, 138
  not on bread alone, 30
Livingstone, David, 187
Lord Have Mercy (Hahn), 61n4
loss of a child, no this-world compensation for, 242
lostness, 163, 166
Lot, 20n12
love
  cannot be separated from the one loved, 161
  of God, 158
  suffering for the sake of the one loved, 225
  wilderness as a place of, 160
lover, 159, 221
"love-your-neighbor-as-your-self" brand, of living, 92
Loving God (Colson), 178
Lucado, Max, 123
Luther, Martin, 204

Mack, Scottish collie, 206–7
"Made in a Wilderness," as God's finished product, 54
Magi, search for the infant king, xiv
males, Pharaoh declared death for all newborn, 83
man
  blind from birth, 138
  not living on bread alone, 25
Manasseh, 104
manna, 18, 34

map, equating mastering with traveling the territory, xiv
Mara, Naomi as, 126
marginal people, sought refuge in Egypt, 112
Mark, on preparation, 121
Mary and Martha, in mourning for three days, 183
material possessions, owned by Job, 237–38
material world, placing ahead of the spiritual, 27
Matthew, on preparation, 121
maturity, happening over prolonged time, 73n12
Mays, James Luther, 4n5, 36, 41, 159–60
meanwhile, as a long, hard stretch of time, 18–19
Meister Eckhart, 22
memories, of God rekindled in a wilderness, 165
mess, God of, 156
Messengers of God (Wiesel), 8n15
Metaxas, Eric, 87n37, 87n38
midwives, as Shiphra and Puah, 83
ministry, of other Christians as an invaluable resource, 217
miracles, making only fleeting impressions on God's Chosen People, 130
Miriam, 29, 89
misfortune, thrust Carretto upon new paths, 243
misplaced focus, of Israel on the banks of the Jordan, 186
missing, as not forever, 249
missteps, mattering in an oasis and a wilderness, 68
Moabite women, sexual immorality with, 20
Moltke, Count Helmuth von, 91–92
moral imperative, of a divine mission, 124n13
More, Thomas, 132, 216n30
Morris, Collin
  on a desire to domesticate God, 76n21

Morris, Collin (continued)
  on God writing in his diary entry, 194
  on God's relationship to his children as full of paradox, 5n7
  on learning to wait, 228n30
Moses
  answering God's call, 95
  assured Israel that the Lord God goes with them, 181
  bearing Midian's desert and Sinai's, 183
  called by God to lead Israel from Egypt, 113n16
  community grumbled against, 20
  on contentment in the Promised Land, 21
  demonstrating clarity of purpose, 117
  directed Israel's focus back to God, 186
  at the edge of the Promised Land, 33
  effect of the wilderness on, 124
  enduring a wilderness, 11, 17
  on God humbling the nation of Israel, 25
  images used by speaking to the Hebrew people, 19
  knew the ways and winding paths of the desert, 191
  learned the wilderness way, 35
  left Egypt in panic and fear, 94
  as Liberator of Israel, 89
  meeting with God, 181
  named by Pharaoh's daughter, 84
  needed wilderness humbling, 29
  never crossed the Jordan, 183
  pronouncing God's judgment on Egypt, 87
  as a prophet of God, 86
  reminding Israel on God's assaying of their hearts, 34–35
  request to Pharaoh, 198n2
  responding that the Lord will bring deliverance, 130
  as a sojourner, 112, 115–16
  speaking to the people of God as they emerged from the wilderness, 17–18
  spent the last two-thirds of his life in a wilderness, 176, 241
  stepped in alongside the sins and sufferings of others, 97
  stepping into the systemic wilderness, 94, 95
  stranded in a wilderness, 194
  suffered because of the sins of others, 62
  told up front that the trek would take forty years, 12
  trying to convince God that he was the wrong man for the job, 94
  understanding of a wilderness, 18
  urged the people of Israel to remember the faithfulness of God, 172
Mother Teresa, on suffering, 161n16
mystery, of God dwelling with his people, 152

name, of God, 181
Naomi, 66–67, 125–26, 241n2
natural instincts, not trusting God, 204
Nazi Germany, systemic evil of, 87
new beginning, wilderness as, 36
New Madrid Fault, running through St. Louis, 61
New Testament, definition of a wilderness, 50–51
Newton, John, 202
Nietzsche, Friedrich, 207
Night (Wiesel), 188
Noah, 103n32, 189
no-end-in-sight variety, of God's wildernesses, 12
nomad, Abraham lived as a, 115
non-gods, becoming attached to, 27
nothing-short-of-perfect oasis, of Job becoming an all-but-unbearable wilderness, 238
Nouwen, Henri J. M., 154, 212–13, 217n31
Nullarbor Plain, railroad track traversing, 9
numbness, 165, 182

oasis
  defined, 10
  guidance through, 191–92
  inclining our hearts more toward
    gifts, 26–27
  as the opposite of wilderness, 10n1
  as a place of contentment, 20
  subtle but lethal danger of, 111
  as a wilderness, 98–111
obedience
  being tested in, 36
  as better than sacrifice, 33
  to commands of God, 235–40
  coolie understanding only, 206–7
  as essential in a severe wilderness, 68
  flowing from trust in the
    shepherd's wisdom, 207
  honoring God, 205–6
  of Job, 237
  no one zapped with instant
    trusting, 125
  as preferable to disobedience, 77, 78
  sustaining in a wilderness, 240
  testing in the wilderness, 31–36
observers, 129, 131
Octopus, riding at Six Flags over
  Missouri, 192–93
original sin, fault of, 61n4
ourselves, trusting in a wilderness, 19
outback, towns in, 9

pain
  as the mystery of God's presence,
    152
  of the prodigal intensifying, 225
  as real, 231n17
  siphoning praise from, 233
  as temporary, 248
painfulness, of therapy, 122
panic, ensuing from misplaced focus,
  186
The Parables of Grace (Capon), 221
paraclete, 90, 96
parents
  of the author living through World
    War II, 12
  blaming God for the tragic loss of
    their son, 235

  knowing that children are not
    interchangeable, 242
  remaining faithful after the tragic
    loss of a child, 235–36
Paris, Kent, 182n7
"partakers," of Jesus's suffering, 147n3
participants, with God, 93–94
participation, as God's promise, 183
passion, of God becoming visible,
  159–60
passivity, of God, 222
past act of God, grace as, 149
"pastors," to Israel, 217
patience, from the same root as
  "passion," 225
Paton, Alan, 132
pattern, of God as seldom seen, 66
Patterson, Ben, 204, 223, 224, 288
Paul
  calling God's people to enter the
    fray, 85–86
  on the church as the new Israel,
    215
  on comforting those in any
    trouble, 91
  content in a wilderness or an oasis,
    247–48
  on dying, 141
  effect of the wilderness on, 124
  on the faithfulness of God, 173
  on God "comforting us in all our
    troubles," 184
  on God working for the good of
    those who love him, 123
  on God's glory, 138
  on grace, 194
  on group-discipline as meant for
    all, 45
  holding the cloaks of the
    executioners of Stephen, 133
  on Israel being "broken off because
    of unbelief," 154
  on Israel's desert days as examples, 8
  on Israel's wilderness journey as
    warning, 70
  in jail with Silas overnight, 183
  on keeping us from setting our
    hearts on evil things, 35

Paul (continued)
    on knowing whom he has believed, 207
    on the law of sowing and reaping, 62
    lifted songs of praise to God with Silas from the cell of a prison, 232
    on living in the visible but seeing the invisible, 248
    on maturity, 73n12
    on a "new creature," 75
    on the praise of God's glory, 142–43
    on preparing God's people, 121
    on present sufferings, 245
    on promises of God, 188
    on rejoicing in our sufferings, 155
    on restoration, 121
    on Scripture's narratives as essential, 70
    as a sojourner, 247
    on the story of Jesus' incarnation, 95
    on a thorn in his flesh tormenting him, 195
    on the unbelief of the Children of Israel, 153
    wilderness forced on him, 196
people, refining, 51
people of God, as pilgrim people, 214
people of Israel, wilderness journey of, 3
perfect will, God orchestrating, 66
permitting, a wilderness, 59, 64, 65
perpetual motion, BC equivalent of, 81–82
Perrin, Nicholas, 49–50, 103n32, 111
persistence, of God's love, 160
personal exercise in discipline, wilderness as, 44
personal expectations, distinguishing from biblical hope, 244
perspective
    of God, 13–14
    of a story, 33n10
Peter
    advice for weary wilderness travelers, 250
    on genuine faith put through suffering, 68
    on "glory just around the corner," 18
    on grace, 194
    on painful trials, 33–34
    on the people of God, 215
    rebuking Jesus, 41
    on restoration, 121
    "We have left everything to follow you," 190
Peter, James and John, sound asleep instead of supporting each other, 216
Peter and James, imprisoned but one freed and the other executed, 175–76
Peterson, Eugene, 4, 53, 199
Pharaoh
    asking God to soften his heart, 198
    cursing God's people, 103n32
    feigning repentance, 72
    having Joseph's family settle-in to the best, 106
    initial decision to treat Israel differently, 79–80
    as the mind behind systemic evil, 81
    Moses confronting, 86
    not knowing the Lord, 165
    political savvy out-flimflammed Jacob, 108–9
    trying to keep the slaves on the plantation, 37–38
Pharisees, 163n19
Phil, lost his wife Donna to cancer, 155
physical hungers, feeding while starving the spiritual, 27
physically disorienting experience, 192–93
Pilgrim at Tinker Creek (Dillard), 74
pilgrimages, xv, 64
The Pilgrim's Progress (Bunyan), 4
pillars, of cloud and fire, 191, 193
plagues, as a "judgment on all the gods of Egypt," 164
Poisonwood Bible (Kingsolver), 27n9, 32n6
political terms, God speaking in, 84–85

SUBJECT INDEX 275

Polyphemus moth cocoon, emerging from, 74–75
Potiphar's wife, sin of, 63
power, of God made perfect in weakness, 195
"The Power of a Promise" (Smedes), 187
practical care, of God for his people, 193
praise, 229–34, 231n17
praising, replacing asking, 202–3
prayer(s)
    asking God for desperately needed things, 202
    of the enslaved Hebrew people, 198
    of Hagar, 251–53
    of Jesus in the garden, 141
    reshaping heavy-on-asking into pure praise, 233
prayer-and-accountability group, keeping the author sane, 202
prayer-and-accountability relationships, maintaining as safe places, 233
"Precious Lord, Take My Hand" (song), 180
preparation, of God's people, 121
presence
    fitting into the same space, 154
    of God sometimes as perplexing as his absence, 152
    trusting God's, 180–88
present gift of God, grace as, 149
pride, 28, 30, 63
Princess of Egypt, laid claim to the child Moses, 84
printed page, decided advantage over wilderness-bound Israel, 11
problems, wilderness time getting to the root of, 227
prodigal son, Jesus' story of, 19, 220–27
prodigals, wandering with their hearts before their feet, 114
promiscuous nature, of both God's grace and love, 163n19
promise(s)
    of God, 173, 184, 185, 244–45
    of God's presence, 182, 188

prophetic voices, emerged after a disciplining period in the wilderness, 45
provision, trusting God's, 189–97
Psalm 95, quoted in Hebrews, 153
Puah, 83, 89
purpose
    of the Bible, xiv
    of a wilderness, 142
purposed wildernesses, 65
purposeful pattern, of a wilderness, 19
purposing, a wilderness, 59, 64

questioner, God never turning away a sincere, 200
questions, taking to God, 201
questions-and-answers, temporary end of for a child, 202

Rahab, 133
ravens, sent to Elijah, 193
reading perspective, 33n10
reality, of fallenness and brokenness, 60
reasons, for obeying God, 236
Rebekah, 108n57
rebellion
    God refusing to honor, 163
    of Israel, 3, 153
    slipping into quickly and easily, 72
    wandering as a result of, 113
reconciliation, wilderness as a form of, 160
Red Sea, parting for Israel, 149
refining, silver or lives, 52
refining process, as a test by fire, 34
rejection, God rejecting our, 163
relationship, with God-in Jesus, 245
release, Jesus's cry for, 141
repentance, God dealing with feigned, 72
resistance, boldly confessing by, 87–88
rest, as a legitimate danger to God's people, 21
restlessness, not dependent on physical, geographical wandering, 114
restoration, Paul and Peter on, 121

The Return of the Prodigal Son
(Nouwen), 217n31
righteousness and sin, war waged
almost daily between, 165
rock, affording water for Israel, 193
Romans, of the New Testament era, 82
rooftops, highwire act between, 67–68
route, God more than capable of
reconfiguring, 61
Rubik's Cube, living on a single face of,
65–66
Ruth, 126
Ruth (book of), 66

Sadat, Anwar, 92
salvation, of the lost tied to the
sanctification of the saved,
50n2
Samuel, 35, 199
San Andreas Fault, 61n4
sanctification, making effective witness
possible, 50n2
Sarah, 99, 183
Sarai, becoming Sarah in her wait, 228
Satan
attempting to alter Jesus' course, 47
direct attacks on God's people
permitting a wilderness, 62–63
on Job obeying God because of
what God did or did not do, 238
misjudged Jesus' reason for
obeying God, 239
tempting Jesus, 116
testing of Jesus as similar to his
testing of Job, 64
on why Job fears God, 237
King Saul, 35, 112, 199
Saul (Paul), 89
saving grace, not always arriving, 194
scapegoat, dumped in a wilderness to
die, 165
Schaeffer, Edith, 232–33
scouts, sent to explore Canaan, 130
Screwtape, to Wormwood, 51–52, 206
The Screwtape Letters (Lewis), 51, 206
scribes, Magi as an elite class of, xiv
Scripture
allowing a reader to jump ahead, 11

on remaining faithful, 176
in terms of the Kentucky plural,
"y'all," 213
testifying to the truth of, 7
training us to live God's way, 70–71
tying ancient stories to our own
stories, 8n15
wilderness stories in, 4n5, 8
security, for Joseph's return, 109
senses, prodigal son came to his, 19
Serpent, attacking Eve first, 218
set-free person, as not always a live-
free person, 40
settlements (cities), Abraham
experienced problems in,
20n12
settlers, 112, 114
Shalom, as the eye of the storm, 134
shared becoming, wilderness as about,
219
sharing, wildernesses with others, 92
sheep, finding a lost, 224
shepherd, God trusting as the good, 42
Shiphra, 83, 89
shoulder, therapy for a painful left, 122
Sibbes, Richard, 204
Silas, 183, 232
silence, of God, 204, 222
silver, refining, 51
"Simon," meaning "listening,"
"obedient," 217n30
sin
causing a fault line, 61–62
consequences of, 4
damaging our relationship with
God, 160, 162
enslaving us, 40
freeing ourselves from the shackles
of, 52
God allowing consequences of, 5n6
God removing, 76
God's people growing restless for, 20
as an old slave master, 40
of the prodigal son, 226
rarely overcome without a
wilderness, 40
routinely resulting in a prolonged
wilderness, 71

in settlements and at an oasis, 20
straying because of, 114n20
turning loose of, 224
wandering tied to, 114
wilderness resulting from, 59, 69
Sin (Sinai), wilderness of, 17
sin and rebellion, wilderness necessary for, 164
sin wilderness, 69–78
sinners, all of us are, 59
slave mentality, 37, 40
sleeping, mutual ministry of community and, 217n30
slow work of God, trusting in, 228
Smedes, Lewis B., 187–88
Snyder, Howard, 215
social security, family as, 220n2
sojourners
　clarity of purpose among, 113
　estrangement with this world, 248n31
　living life fully, 248
　Paul describing, 247
　on this earth as God's people, 247
　turning into settlers speeding up assimilation, 106
　walking a wilderness as, 117–18
　in a wilderness, 112
sojourning, 115, 115n30, 118
solitary traveler, wilderness trek deadly for, 216
Solomon, 34
Son of God, 54, 148n7. *See also* Jesus
song of victory, of Moses, 50
songs, beginning in pain but rising above it to praise, 231n17
sorrow, intertwined with grace, 154
sorrow and suffering, of Jesus, 125
sorrows and wounds, of this world cannot be compensated, 241n1
soul-making, as the endgame of a wilderness, 53
soul-making power, of desert days, xvi
soul-making side, of a wilderness and its discipline, 47
sovereign wilderness, 59–68
　being led into, 59

discerning facets and features of as difficult, 67
finding its source in God, 69
God waiting for us to become the person he desires us to be, 224
sovereignty, 5n6, 60–61
spies, sent to Canaan, 38
Spirit. *See also* Holy Spirit
　being people led by, 91
　Jesus following into a wilderness, 113n16, 116
　Jesus led by, 47, 64
　stepping in alongside us in our struggles, 91
　threw Jesus out into the desert, 125
　trusting in, 156
spiritual character, developing, 46, 48
spiritual formation, nothing quick or easy about, 73n12
spiritual growth, forming over long stretches of time, 73–74
spiritual ministry, wilderness essential to Jesus's, 124
spiritual progress, making occasional day trips into, 44
spiritual refining process, testing as, 34
spiritual substance and strength, developing, 45
spiritual vision, wilderness severely restricting, 150
spiritual wilderness, 35
St. Louis, Missouri, as home for the author, 246
Stephen, 38, 39, 89, 133
stepping in
　alongside those who are in distress, 91
　as the Christian thing to do, 92, 94, 95
stereoscope, viewing a double postcard, 13
Stevenson, J. W., 65, 150, 152, 160–61, 162
Storey, Peter
　on the cross as raised by God, 96
　on faithful suffering as never wasted, 89

Storey, Peter (continued)
  on God living where the fire of testing burns, 227
  on God speaking through us, 97
  on intervening, 92
  on learning to let institutions, 82
  on never underestimating the importance of ordinary people, 89
  on peace (*Shalom* in the Old Testament), 134
  on power in faithful suffering, 88
  on presence of Jesus, 187
  on suffering coming as a free choice, 97
storm
  as God's vehicle to get us to the other side, 47
  Jesus quieting into its teeth, 226
"stranger," "sojourner" often translated as, 115n30
straying sheep, Hebrews' wandering as that of, 115n28
street musician, walking with the old minister trying to find his son, 161
strip-and-shape aspect, to every wilderness, 190
strong-arm sovereignty, people preferring, 60
struggling, shaping us for kingdom purposes, 47
stubborn parts of us, not paying attention in an oasis, 22
sudden death, as sudden glory for daughters and sons of Yahweh, 142
Suenens, Leon Joseph Cardinal, 249
suffering
  because of someone else's sin, 62
  of the father of the prodigal son, 227
  as a gift of grace, 152
  God using Naomi's, 67
  how to approach, 132n19
  making us nearer to Christ, 53
  not precluding grace at Calvary, 152
  in order to become and possess everything, 97
  remaining faithful in, 88
  singing songs in the midst of, 231
  teaching us how to bear, 132
  waiting involving, 225
  way to approach, 132
  in the wilderness as always purposeful, 52–53
  wilderness of fulfilling life's purpose, 141
suicide, failed attempt, 139
surgery, effects of a wilderness comparable to, 76
survival, God teaching lessons essential for, 25
sustaining grace, of God, 194–95, 196
Sydney, Australia, author's first view of, 245–46
system, obscuring the role of the individual, 81
systemic evil, 79, 88
systemic wilderness
  all over the world, 82
  allowing evil to grow and spread, 80
  breaking the hold of on Israel, 87
  entering willingly, 90
  the father's intense pain and unending suffering regarding, 227
  killing Israel before God showed up in Moses, 81
  not resolving itself, 86, 89
  as a self-perpetuating system, 79–89
  of South African apartheid, 88

Taylor, Barbara Brown
  on experiencing encounters with the Divine, 77
  on the idea of divine dangerousness, 76
  on shutting the Bible to go outside, xiv
  on trust in the Spirit, 156
  on trusting God, 65n20
  on "the unscripted encounter with the undomesticated God," 136
temptation, of abandoning faithfulness, 68

SUBJECT INDEX

Teresa of Avila, 30
terrible things, not thwarting God's sovereign purpose, 61
testimony
    impact of Carol's, 140
    of those trekking through a wilderness, 131
testing
    of Abraham, 31
    in a wilderness, 32
theater soldier, as no soldier at all, 96
theologians, xiii
theology, moving us to being travelers, xiv
therapy, 122, 123, 128
Thielicke, Helmut, 28–29, 96, 221
things
    clinging to us, 22
    many kinds of not needed, 27n9
Thomas à Kempis, 29n11, 36n26, 156–57, 203
Thomas the Tank Engine, exploits of, 19
Thomson, Francis, imagery of, 166–67
"thorn," meant by Paul as a stake or peg, 195
Thornton, Brother, 52
thousand years, as a day in God's time, 18
"Thy will be done," praying, 220
Timothy, Paul's confidence to, 207
Torah, on a wilderness being Yahweh's blessing, 189
the tough, clinging in trust to God, 203
tough love, as the hallmark of a wilderness, 166
Tozer, A. W., xiii
train car, viewing a wilderness from, 10
training, through discipline in a wilderness, 44
trash, feeling like thrown-out in a wilderness, 128
trials, as the rule of all life, 4
Trophimus, 183
trouble, converting into a testimony, 131
trust
    beginning where knowing ends, 208
    versus certainty in a wilderness, 65
    crucial in a wilderness, 172
    as invaluable in a wilderness, 173
    of King Jehoshaphat, 208
    not resting on faith, 171
    as a problem for once-enslaved Israel, 39–40
    as taught in the wilderness, 37–42
trusting
    even in a wilderness, 197
    God, always demanding dying, 41–42
    God's character, 171–79
    God's presence, 180–88
    God's provision, 189–97
    God's wisdom, 198–208
truth, 27, 131
turning back, as costly to Israel, 71

ultimate will, of God, 63n12
unbelief, of Israel, 153, 154
unfaithfulness, 158, 159
unscripted encounter, with God, 136
"until he finds," persistent seeking of us, 166
Uriah, 35
usefulness, returning to intended, 122

views, of God, 119
vulnerability, to God's sovereignty, 61

wages, of a wilderness as death, 166
Waite, Terry, 132
waiting, 220–28
walk of faith, facing, 68
wanderers, 112, 114
wandering, 113, 115
wandering community, 217
wars, as similar to wildernesses, 12
ways and thoughts, of God as not like ours, 6
weakness, of Paul, 195, 196
wealth, 21
Weatherhead, Leslie, 63n12
A Week in the Life of God: If God Kept a Diary (Morris), 194
Wegemer, Gerard, 225
Weil, Simone, 222

"well-watered place," in God's
    endgame, 55
"Where is God?" driving ourselves
    mad with, 149n22
White Rabbit, on "How long is
    forever?" 225n20
Wiederkehr, Macrina, 22, 36, 134
Wiesel, Elie, 114, 127–28
wife of Job, 230, 236
Wilburforce, William, 142n24
wilderness
    as call and choice, 90–97
    defined, 4n5, 10, 18, 50–51
    of sin, 223
wilderness pilgrims, learning from by
    watching, 134
wilderness trekkers, as never left alone,
    191
"wilderness wandering," 113–14
Wilkerson, David, 201
will, of God, 204, 205
Will of God (Weatherhead), 63n12
Willimon, William H., 211, 214, 216
wind and waves, frightening
    wilderness of, 46
wisdom, trusting God's, 198–208

witnesses, God never leaving himself
    without, 131
Wolterstorff, Nicholas, 7, 53
woman, lost her husband, son and
    infant grandson in less than a
    twelve-month span, 134
Woolman, John, 142n24
word of love, wilderness as, 163, 165
world
    as fallen, 59–60
    pursuing, 27
worshiper, lifting his own life to God, 32

Yahweh. *See also* God
    as the God of gods, 164
    as the good shepherd to his people,
        42n24
    keeps all his promises, 188
    "making love" to Israel in the
        wilderness, 159
    using a wilderness as means of
        wooing back into friendship,
        7n9
Yancey, Philip, 176

Scripture Index

OLD TESTAMENT

Genesis

1:28	103n32
2:1–7	200n16
2:18	218n36
2:19–24	218n36
3:5	7n9
4:9	218n35
4:9a	218n35
4:12	114n18
4:12b	115n25
4:13–14	114n19
4:17b	114n21
4:17c	114n22
6:5—7:5	189n2
8:17	103n32
8:21–22	173n15
9:1	103n32
9:7	103n32
9:50	109
12:1	12n8, 65n19, 115n31, 115n32, 189n3
12:1–3	173n15
12:1–4	99n10
12:1–4a	113n16
12:1–9	112n7
12:1—21:5	183n13
12:2–3	115n33
12:3	103n32
12:4	115n31
12:10	99n12
12:11	99n13
12:12–16	99n14
12:17	99n15
12:18–20	99n16
15:1–20	99n11
15:1–21	173n15
16	251–53
16:1–16	48n28, 65n17
16:11–12	173n15
17:6	103n32
18:1–10a	173n15
20:13	115n26
21:8–21	48n29, 65n17
21:14	115n29
21:22–34	10n1, 98n8
22	31
22:1	31n2
22:1–2	117n38
22:1–18	183n11
22:1–19	90n1
22:2	12n7, 239n26
22:2a	31n3
22:2b	31n5
22:12	33n8
22:19	98n8
23:4	248n29
24:23	173n15
25:23	108n57
26:1	99n17
26:2–5	99n18
26:6	100n19
26:22	103n32
26:23–24	98n8
26:23–33	10n1

Genesis (continued)

26:25	98n8
26:26–33	98n8
26:32	98n8
27:1–40	108n57
28:1–4	103n32
28:10–22	98n8
32:22–25	7n9
32:22–31	136n3
32:24–31	136n4
34:3	159
37:2–11	63n11
37:12–30	48n26, 65n18
39:1–23	48n27
39:1—41:41	183n12
41:40–44	98n2
41:41–44	104n39
41:45	104n37
41:50	104n37
41:50–52	104n38
41:51	104n41
41:52	104n42
41:53—42:2	112n1
41:53–57	102n28
42:1	102n29
42:1–2	98n6
42:2	102n31
42:4	102n30
42:5	102n28
42–50	102
44:8	104n40
45:26a	98n1
45:26b	98n2
45:28	98n4
46:1	98n5, 98n7
46:3–4	99n9
46:4	107n56
46:31—47:12	103n34
47:3–4a	112n1
47:4	106n51
47:5–6a	106n52
47:27	103n32
47:28	109n64
47:28–31	109n65
47:28—50:26	176n28
47:29–31	107n53
47:30a	107n54
47:30b	107n55
48:5–6	104n43
48:10	106n50
48:12–16	105n46
48:15	105n45
48:17	105n47
48:18	105n48
48:19	105n49
50:5	109n63
50:5a	108n58
50:5b	108n59
50:6	108n60
50:7–8a	108n61
50:14	109n62
50:20	244n7
50:24–25	176n29
50:26	110n69

Exodus

	82n13
1:1–21	230n10
1:6–10	103n32
1:6–22	104n35
1:8	79n1
1:9	80n8
1:9–10	79n2
1:11a	79n3
1:11b	79n4
1:12	80n9
1:12b	80n5
1:12b–14	80n6
1:14	80n9
1:15	83n16
1:16	83n15
1:17	83n17
1:18–19	83nn18–19
1:22	80n8, 83n20
2:2	83n22
2:3	84n23
2:4	84n24
2:5–10	84n25
2:11–15	94n15
2:11—Deut 34:8	183n14
2:15–22	94n16
2:22	94n18
2:23	94n17
3:1—4:20	113n16

SCRIPTURE INDEX

3:1–10	94n19	8:31	80n7, 80n8
3:1–14	173n15	8:32	198n3
3:7–8a	50	9:6	80n9
3:7–10	85n26, 94n14	9:7	198n3
3:9	80n9	9:9	80n11
3:10–12	94n20	9:11	80n9
3:13—4:9	94n21	9:12	198n3
3:16–17a	85n27	9:14	80n7, 80n8
3:18b	198n2	9:15	80n8
3:19	198n5	9:22–25	80n11
3:20–22	80n9	9:27	80n8
4:10–12	38n4	9:27–28	72n11
4:10–17	94n20	9:30	80n7
4:18–20	94n22	9:34	80n7
4:21	198n3	9:34–35	198n3
5:1	86n32, 165n21, 198n1	10:1	80n7, 198n3
		10:2	80n9
5:2	86n33, 165n22	10:6	80n7
5:4–18	86n34	10:7	80n7
5:19–21	86n35	10:15	80n11
5:22–23	87n36	10:16–17	72n11
6:5–7	80n9	10:19	80n11
6:6–7	214n14	10:20	198n3
6:6–8	173n15, 215n17	10:27	198n3
6:20	83n21	11:1	80n10
7:3	198n3	11:3	80n7, 80n9, 80n10
7:4	198n3	11:8	80n7
7:5	80n9	11:9–10	198n3
7:11	80n7	12:12	164n20
7:13	198n3	12:13	80n10
7:14	198n3	12:23	80n9
7:18	80n9	12:27	80n9
7:21	80n9	12:30	80n7
7:22	198n3	12:33	80n9
7:23	198n3	12:35–36	80n9
7:24	80n9	13:9	148n11
8:4	80n7, 80n8	13:17–18	3n1, 43n2
8:7	80n11	13:21–22	191n14
8:8	72n11	14:4	198n3
8:9	80n7, 80n8	14:5	80n7, 80n10
8:15	198n3	14:8	198n3
8:16–17	80n11	14:9–10	80n9
8:19	198n3	14:10–12	186n31, 231n15
8:21	80n9	14:12	32n6, 129n3
8:24	80n7, 80n11	14:12–13	80n9
8:25	38n2	14:13–14	130n4, 186n32
8:28	38n3	14:17	198n4
8:29	72n11, 80n7, 80n8	14:18	80n9, 129n1

Exodus (continued)

14:19–31	149n20
14:23	80n9
14:24–25	131n11
14:25–27	80n9
14:30–31	80n9
14:31	230nn11–12
15:12–13	50
15:25b–26	173n14
15:27	20n10
16:1–3	38n4
16:2b–4	20n11
16:3a	39:n8
16:4	34n17
16:11	44n3
16:13	44
16:32	148n11
17:1–3	38n4
18:1	148n11
19:1–6	215n17
20:2	148n10
22:16	159
23:20	191n17
23:20–21	191n13
23:20—24:8	173n14
29:46	148n10
34:10–28	173n14
34:15–16	158n2

Leviticus

11:45	148n10
19:2	171n2
19:36	148n10
22:32–33	148n10
25:38	148n10
25:42	148n10
25:55	148n10
26:1–46	173n14
26:9–12	215n17
26:12	215n15
26:13	148n10
26:45	148n10

Numbers

9:15–23	191n15, 191n16
9:17a	191n15
9:17b	191n16
12:1–16	29n14
12:3	29n12
13:1–33	62n6
13:17	38n6
13:27	130n5
13:30	38n7, 130n7
13:30–33	130n6
13:31	186n33
13:31–33	130n9
14:1–3	39:n10
14:1–4	38n4
14:1–23	69n1
14:1–38	62n7
14:8	130n8
14:11	39:n10
14:20–35	71n7
14:25	71n8
14:29–34	71n9
14:34	11n6, 90n2
14:39–40	72n10
15:41	148n10
16:1–35	165n23
16:1–50	71n6
20:1–12	29n13
20:16	148n11
21:4–9	165n24
23:19	171n2
25:1b–3	20n13
26:63–65	166n25
32:10–13	113n12
32:13	114, 115n29

Deuteronomy

1:2	3
2:1	3n2
2:1—3:20	112n8
4:1–40	173n14
4:12–14	215n17
5:6	148n10
6:1–25	173n14
6:12	148n11
6:21	148n11
7:7–9	172n4, 173n15
8:1–20	173n14
8:2	25n2, 33n8, 35n18
8:2–9	18n2

8:3	23n20, 25n2, 25n3, 26:23–33, 44n4	13:5–8	199n9
		13:5–14	199n7
8:10–20	21n15	13:7b–9	199n8
8:14	148n11	13:8–10	199n10
8:16	25n2	13:11–12	199n11
11:1–32	173n14	13:13	199n12
13:3	35n19	13:13–14	199n13
13:5	148n11	15:22	33n7
13:10	148n11	16:7	35n25
16:1	148n11	23:7—27:3	35n21, 65n17
20:1	148n11		
21:17	220		
26:8	148n11		

2 Samuel

11:1–27	35n23
15	113n13
15:1—18:33	112n3
15:1—19:8	35n22, 65n17
15:20	113n13
23:7—24:22	112n2

26:16–19	173n14
27:18	114n20
28:1—30:20	173n14
29:5	173n13
29:15	148n11
31:6	181n3, 185n27
32:1–43	232n22

1 Kings

8:16	148n13
8:21	148n13
8:51	148n13
8:53	148n13
9:9	148n10
9b–21	46n11
18:16—19:21	65n17
19:1–18	112n5, 113n15
19:9a	45n10
19:15	216n24
19:15–21	216n25
19:18	216n26

Joshua

2:9–11	133n24
3:4	191n12
3:14–17	149n21
7:1–26	62n8
14:10	114n17, 115n26, 115n29
24:6	148n10
24:17	148n16

Judges

1:19	5, 6
2:1	149n18
6:8	148n17
19:3	159

2 Kings

	76
21:8	114n17, 115n28

1 Chronicles

12:8—21:29	65n17
17:21	148n12
29:15	247n18
29:17	33n11, 35n24

Ruth

1:20–21	126n17
1:21	126
2:13	159

1 Samuel

10:18	148n14
12:6	148n14

2 Chronicles

6:5	148n10

2 Chronicles (continued)

20:1–3	232n19
20:1–4	207n39
20:5	232n20
20:5–10	232n20
20:6	232n20
20:10	232n20
20:12	208n40
32:24–31	65n17
32:31	33n11, 182n6

Ezra

7:10	xivn7

Nehemiah

9:28	21n14

Job

	113n14, 176
1:1—2:10	113n14
1:2, 4–5	238n12
1:3	238n11
1:3a	238n9
1:3b	238n10
1:4–5	238n12
1:6—2:5	62n9
1:6—2:10	112n4
1:8	237n5
1:9	237n6
1:10	237n7
1:11	237n8
1:13—2:10	113n9
1:13–17	229n1
1:18–19	229n2
1:20	229n3
1:21	229n4, 237n4
2:1–3	65n17
2:6	63n10
2:7–8	230n5
2:9	230n6
2:9a	236n1
2:9b	236n2
2:10	230n7, 237n3
2:11–13	238n13
3:12–13	113n14, 126n19
3:16–17	113n14, 127n20
3:26	113n14, 127n21
6:1–4	113n14
6:2–3a	127n22
6:4	7n9, 127n22
7:17–18	33n11
9:25	127n23
10:1	127n24
12:24	115n29
23:10	18n4, 33n11, 212n7
23:11–12	203n21
23:12	68n24
23:20	xvn9
35:10	231n18
42:1–6	113n10

Psalms

	231n17, 232
22	231n17
22:31	182n6
23:4	184n21
40:10	172n6
46:1	10n2
51:10	40n15
66:10	33n11
66:10–12	55n14
78:19b–20	39:n9
78:22	130n10
78:52–53	181n2
81:10	148n10
89:1–8	172n6
89:33	172n6, 173n11
95	153
95:7b–11	71n7
102:18	134n29
106:8–11	230n13
106:12	231n14
107:4	115n29
107:40	115n29
118:6–7	185n28
119:10	115n28
119:19	247n18
119:21	115n28
119:75	172n6
119:86	172n6
119:118	115n28
119:138	172n6
119:176	115n28

135	215n17	42:1–3	100n22
137:4	231n16	42:4	100n23
		42:7	100n24
		42:11a	100n20
		42:11b–12	100n21
		42:12b–19a	100n25

Proverbs

3:11	48n29
17:3	33n11, 34n14

Isaiah

Lamentations

13:14	115n28	3:19–20	233n25
25:1	172n5, 173n9	3:19–24	231n17, 232n23
28:7–8	114n20	3:21–24	234n26
30:1–11	101n26	3:22–23	172n5
40:11	180n1		
43:2	184n22		

Ezekiel

43:19	78n24	6:9	158n2
43:20–21	215n17	16:1–63	158n3
48:10–11a	54n13	24:15	240n27
49:23	244n9	24:18	240n28
53:3	150n25	36:22–38	76n20
53:4a	151n26	37:1–10	156n41
53:4b	150n25		
53:5–6	151n26		

Daniel

53:6	115n28	6:1–28	183n16
53:7a	150n25	8:27	204n25, 205n26
53:7c	150n25	9:15	148n15
53:8–10a	150n25	12:8	205nn27–28
53:9	52n7	12:9	205n29
53:10b–12	151n26	12:13	205n29
55:8–9	6n8, 199n6, 201n19		
63:9	147n1, 227n27		

Hosea

Jeremiah

		2:2	158n1
2:6	148n16	2:2–23	158n3
2:13	162n18	2:5b	159n5
3:6—4:4	158n3	2:14–16	159n6
3:9	158n1	2:21–23	215n17
9:2	158n1	3:1–3	158n4
9:7	33n11	9:17	115n26
11:20	33n11	11:1	148n10
14:10	115n28		
17:10	34n15		

Amos

20:7	159	2:10	148n10
29:11	123n8		
29:23	158n1		

Zechariah

31:2	78n23, 148n8	10:2	115n27, 115n28
31:23–34	76n20		

Zechariah (continued)

13:9	33n11

NEW TESTAMENT

Matthew

	47n18, 47n19
1:5–6	133n25
1:16	133n25
1:21	133n25
1:23	96n26
2	xiv
2:1–3	xiiin2
2:2	xivn6
2:4a	xiiin3
2:4b	xiiin4
2:5–6	xiiin5
3:1–6	45n7
3:13—4:1	116n34
4:1	64nn14–15, 116n35, 124n13
4:1–4	239n19
4:1–11	45n9, 64n13, 112n6, 113n16, 116n36, 176n25
4:2–11	116n37
4:3–10	47n24
4:4	239n22
4:5–7	239n20
4:7	239n23
4:8–11	239n21
4:10	239n24
4:11	239n25
4:18–22	189n4
4:21	121n4
5:4	185n25
6:11	25n4
8:18–22	190n7
8:18–23	46n16
8:23–27	46n12, 226n22
8:24	46n13
8:25	46n15, 47n22
8:27	47n17
9:9	190n5
10:37–39	190n8
14:1–10	45n8
16:21	40n20
16:22	40n21
16:24–25	42n23
17:21	40n14
19:16–26	190n6
23:38	216n27
26:36—27:50	113n16
26:38	154
26:39	141n17, 203n21, 239n18
26:40	216n28
26:40–41	216n30
26:42	141n18, 239n18
26:44	239n18
27:46	128n26, 149n22, 239n17
27:50	238n16
28:29	185n26

Mark

	47n18, 47n19
1:12–13	45n9, 112n6
1:14–20	189n4
1:19	121n4
2:14	190n5
4:35–36a	46n16
4:35–41	46n12, 226n22, 226n23
4:37	46n13, 46n14
4:38	46n15
4:41	47n17
6:14–27	45n8
6:14–28	183n20
9:29	40n14
10:17–27	190n6
10:28	190n10
14:36	238n15, 239n18
14:37–38	216n30
14:39	239n18
14:50	216n29
15:34	128n26

Luke

	47n18, 47n19, 51n4, 64
1:5–25	183n17

1:57–66	183n17	15:24	166n28, 223n13, 227n26
1:80	45n6	15:32	166n29
3:1–3	45n7	17:11–21	183n18
3:20	45n8	18:18–25	190n6
4:1–4	239n19	18:25–43	183n18
4:1–13	45n9	21:12	131n12
4:1–14	xvn10	21:13	131n13
4:5–8	239n21	22:42	154n34, 239n18
4:9–13	239n20	22:43	154n34
4:13	112n6	24:26	142n25
4:14	64n16		
4:38–44	183n18		

John

5:1–11	189n4	1:1, 14	96n27
5:12–26	183n18	1:14	96n27, 96nn28–29
5:19	47n20	1:14–18	163n19
5:20	47n21	3:14	124n13
5:27–28	190n5	4:4	124n13
7:1–10	183n18	9:1	138n12
7:18–23	183n18	9:3	138n13
8:22	46n16	9:4	124n13
8:22–25	46n12, 226n22	10:16	124n13
8:23	46n14	11:1–44	183n10
8:24	46n15	11:4	139n14
8:25	47n17, 226n24	12:27–28a	132n18
8:26–48	183n18	12:28	141n20
9:23	190n8	12:34	124n13
9:57–62	190n7	14:16	90n3, 90n4
10:1–9	183n18	14:26	90n3, 90n4
13:10–17	183n18	15:26	90n3, 90n4
14:1–7	183n18	16:7	90n3, 90n4, 141n22
15	223	17:4	140n16
15:1–32	223n14	17:15–16	247n19
15:3–7	160n9	17:19	50n2
15:4	223n16	18:11	141n19
15:4, 8	160n12	20:9	124n13
15:8	160n12, 223n16	20:24–29	241n3
15:8–10	160n10	21:19	141n21
15:11–13	114n23		
15:11–24	160n11		

Acts

15:11–32	19n7, 220n1		51n4, 196
15:12	221n4	1:1	51n4
15:13	221n5, 222n9	1:6	205n30
15:13–16	225n19	1:7	205n31
15:17	19n8, 223n12	2:33	51n4
15:20	166n27, 223n13	3:1–10	183n18
15:20b	161n15		
15:20b–24	161n16		
15:22–24	223n13		

Acts (continued)

4:29–31	93n12
6:8—7:58	133n23
7:1–60	89n45
7:39	38n5
7:54–60	176n24
7:60	133n22
8:1	89n46
8:4–8	183n18
9:32–35	183n18
10:38	183n18
12:1–2	176n22
12:1–17	183n15
12:23–17	175n21
14:8–10	183n18
14:17	129n2, 131n14
14:19–20	176n23
16:16–40	183n9
16:24–25	232n21
19:1–20	183n18

Romans

3:3	153n31
3:4	131n15
3:23	59n2
4:20	137n5
4:20–21	154n32
5:3–5	155n37
6:1–23	40n11
6:15–23	40n13
6:23	166n26
8:5–17	40n12
8:18	245n12
8:28	13n9, 118n41, 123n9, 124n11, 132n17
8:28–29	50n3
8:29	219n40
8:35–39	161n14
8:37	184n23
9:1–33	215n16
11:20	154n33
11:36	137n5
12:1–2	40n16, 247n19, 247n20
15:4	70n3
16:27	137n5

1 Corinthians

1:9	172n7
1:18–25	199n15
1:25	199n14
6:19	213
10:6	8n13, 35n20, 45n5
10:11	8n14, 45n5
10:13	63n10, 172n7
10:31	137n6
12:12–27	215n22

2 Corinthians

1:3–7	91n6
1:4	184n24
1:10	194n19
1:20	137n5, 188n38
2:9	33n11
3:18	50n3, 219n40
4:4–12	137n7
4:17—5:5	248n32
4:18	248n30
5:6	247n24
5:8	247n25
5:9	247n27
5:17	75n19
10:11–12	70n4
11–13	196
11:29–30	196n23
12:5	196n23
12:7	196n24
12:7–10	195n21
12:8	196n25
12:9–10	196n23, 196n26
13:4, 8	196n23
13:8	196n23

Galatians

1:5	137n5
5:1	40n13
5:16–25	40n12
5:22–26	73n12
6:1	121n2
6:7	62n5
6:16	215n16

Ephesians

1:3–14	138n8, 143n26
1:12	138n10
1:13–14	138n9
4:11–12	121n5
4:11–16	50n3, 73n12, 215nn21–22, 219n40
6:12	85n30
6:13–18	86n31

Philippians

1:11	137n5
1:23	141n23
2:5–8	113n16
2:5–11	95n24
2:7–8	113n16
2:8	40n22
2:11	137n5
3:20	247n18, 247n20
4:11–13	248n28
4:12–14	113n11
4:20	137n5

Colossians

1:12–13	247n18, 247n20
1:13	148n9
1:28	219n40
3:1–10	40n13

1 Thessalonians

2:4	33n11
3:10	122n7
5:24	172n7

2 Thessalonians

3:3	172n7

1 Timothy

1:17	137n5

2 Timothy

1:12	207n37
2:13	172n7, 173n10
3:16–17	71n5

4:20	183n19

Hebrews

	47, 213
1:1–4	163n19
2:9	147n2, 147n3
2:11	148n6
2:11–12	147n2
2:14	147n3, 148n5
2:17	147n2, 148n4, 172n8
2:18	148n7
3:7–19	71n7
3:7b–19	153n30
4:14–16	156n40
4:15	52n7
4:16	8n16, 196n27
5:7	128n27
5:7–10	125n14
5:8–9	48n25
10:5–7	113n16
10:21–25	212n4
10:23	172n8
11	171, 205
11:8	205n32
11:10	118n40
11:11	172n3
11:13–16	113n11, 247n18
11:13b	247n22
11:16a	247n23
11:19	117n39
11:22	176n30
11:24–27	17n1
11:35b	175n17
11:35b–40	175n19
11:37–38	115n29
12:2	xvn10, 18n3
12:2–3	xvn11
12:5	48n30
12:11	43n1
13:5	185n27
13:6	185n28
13:9	155n35
13:20–21	122n6

James

1:3	33n11

James (continued)

1:12	243
1:17	171n1, 238n14
4:4b	7n9
4:5–10	7n9

1 Peter

1:7	33n11, 68n25, 212n7
1:18–19	52n7
2:1, 11	247n18
2:9	215n18
2:11	247n18
4:10	162n19
4:12	33n11, 33n12, 250n36
4:12–13	18n5
4:13	34n13, 147n3, 245n14, 250n36
5:10	121n3

2 Peter

2:9	194n20
3:8	18n6

1 John

1:9	172n7
2:1	90n3
2:15–17	247n19, 247n21

Jude

5	149n19

Revelation

14:8	82n13
16:19	82n12
17:5	82n12
18:2	82n12
18:10	82n12
18:11	82n12
21:4a	246n15
21:4b	246n16

EARLY CHRISTIAN WRITINGS

á Kempis, Thomas	29n11, 156, 203
Imitation of Christ	36n26, 157n43
Augustine	243
John of the Cross	44

www.ingramcontent.com/pod-product-compliance
Lightning Source LLC
Chambersburg PA
CBHW050624300426
44112CB00012B/1648